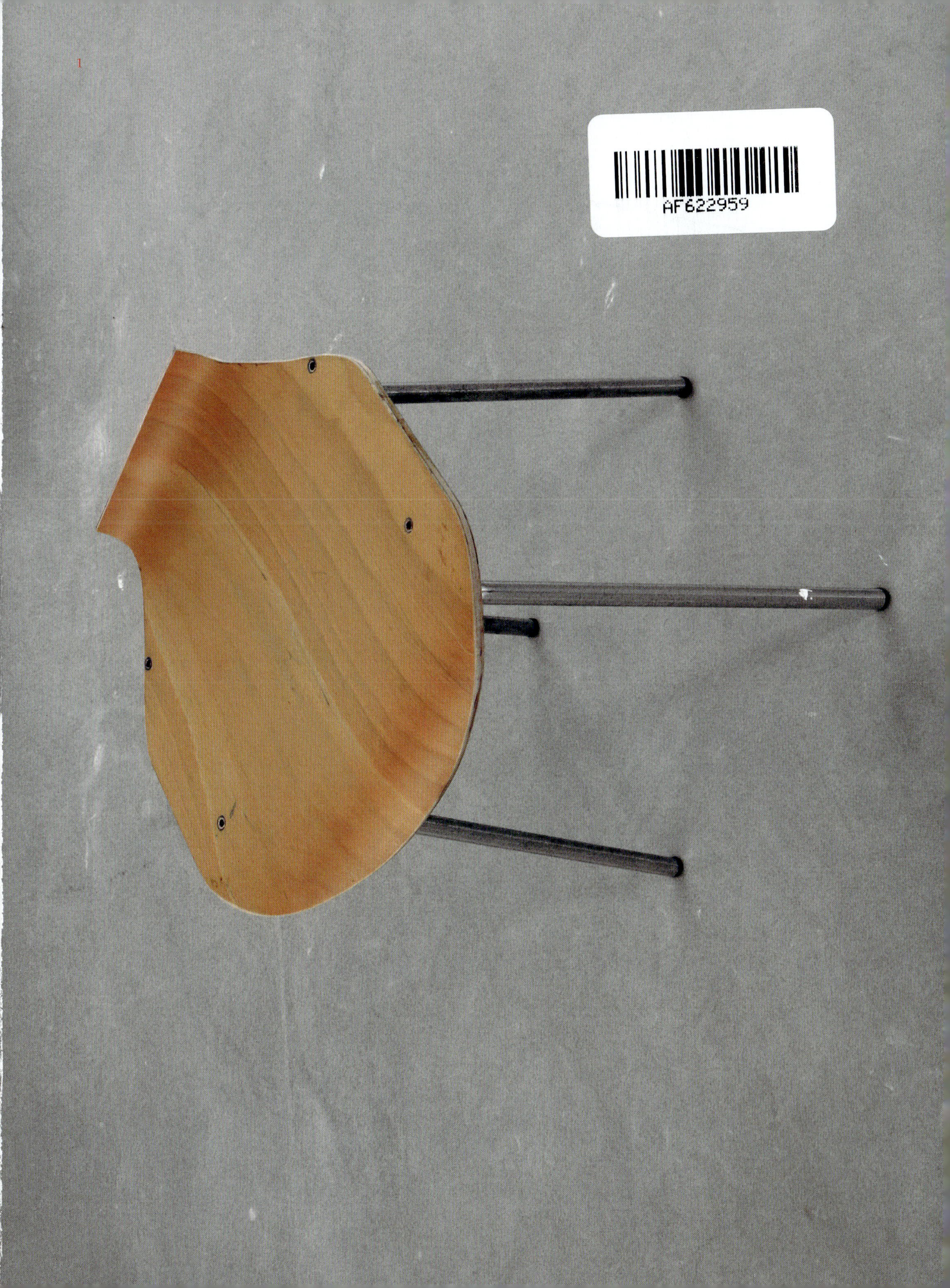

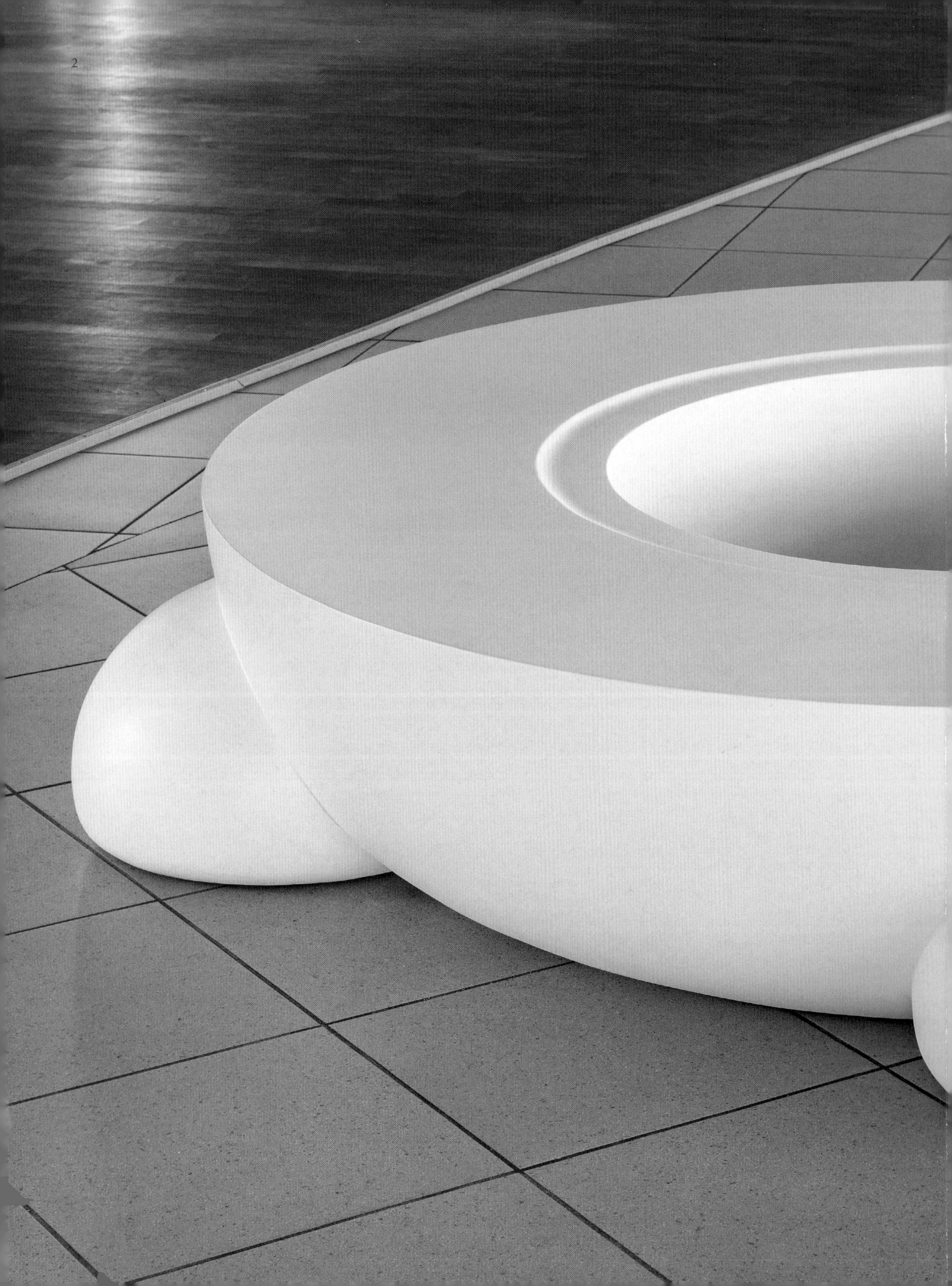

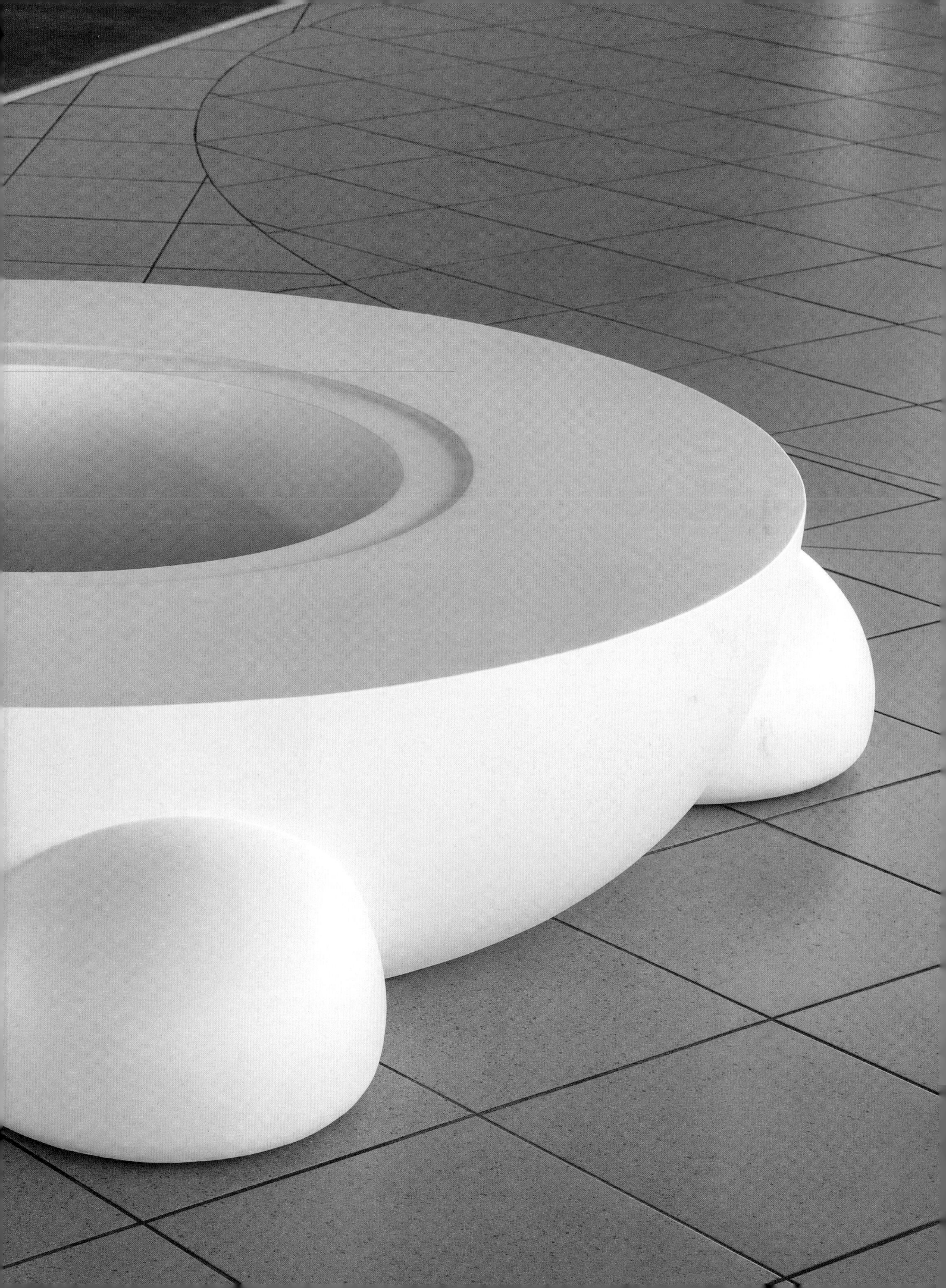

3

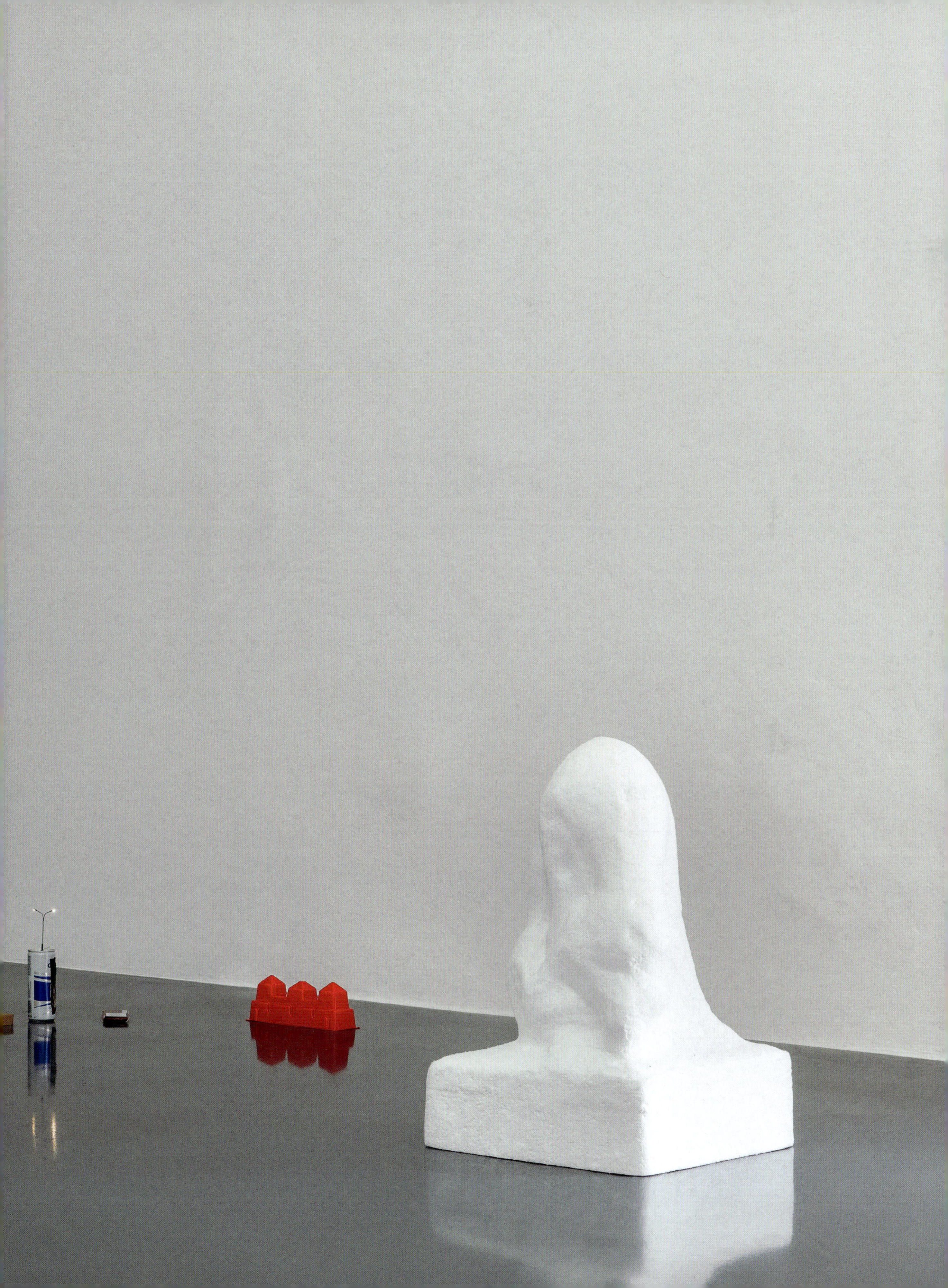

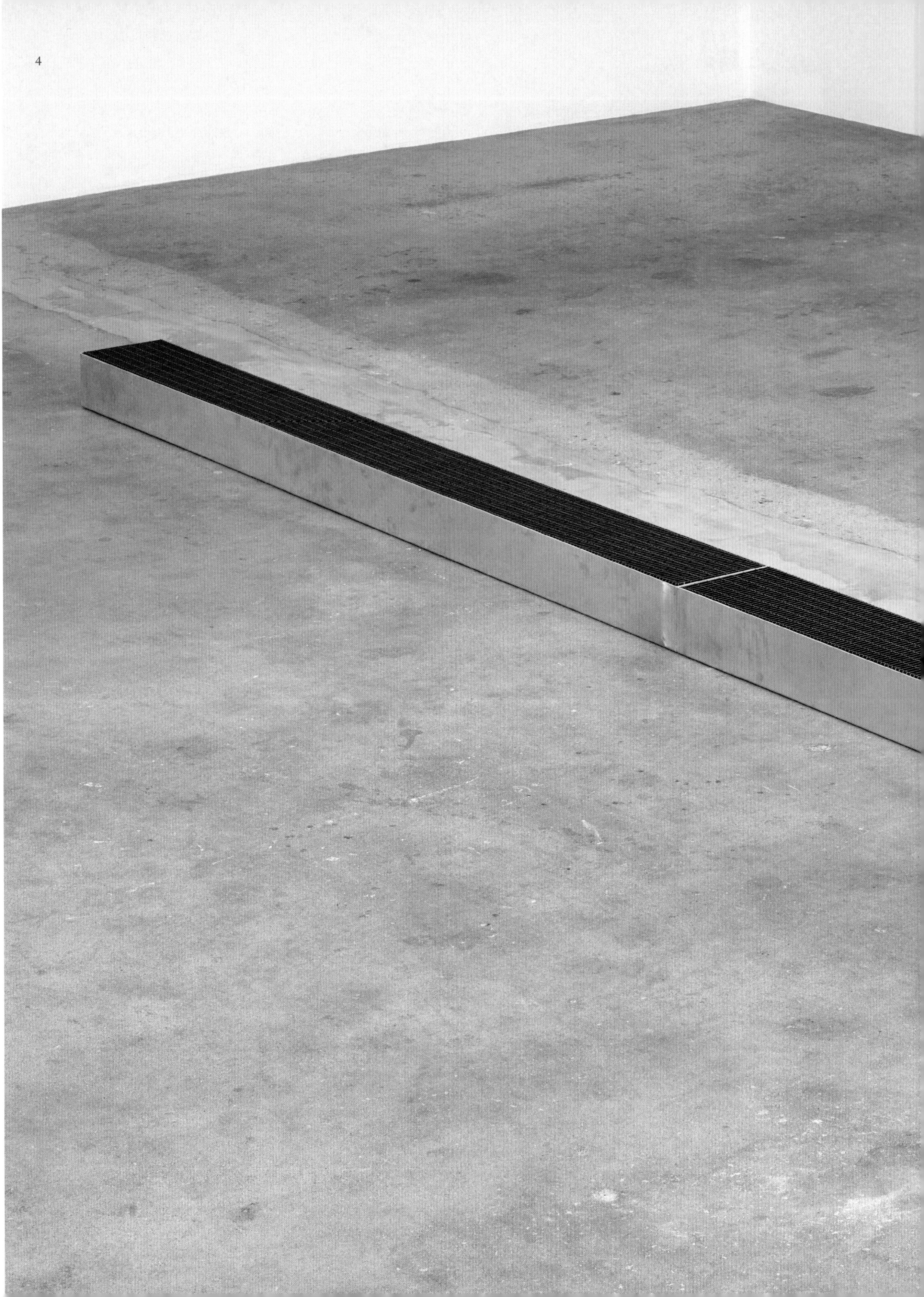

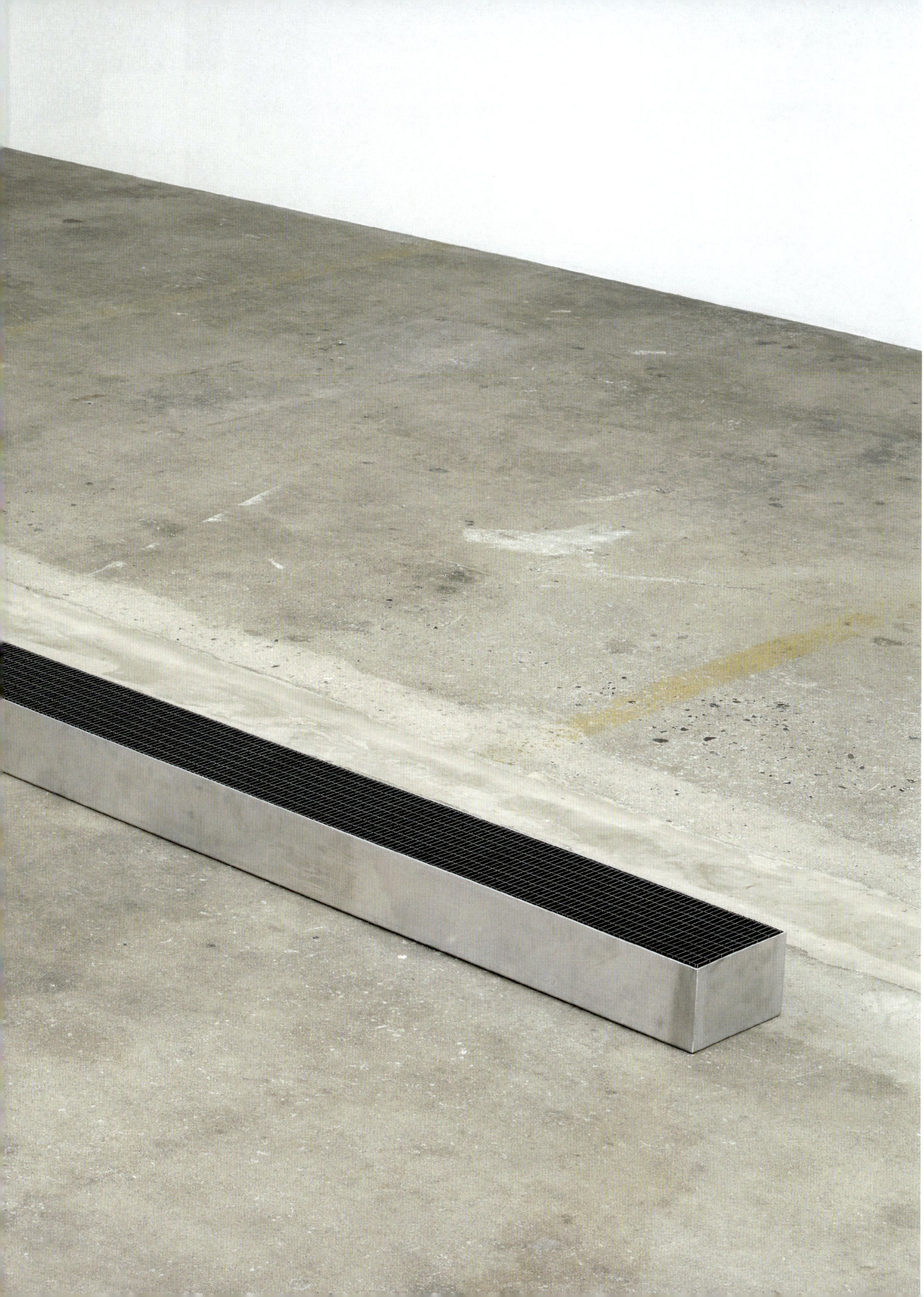

5

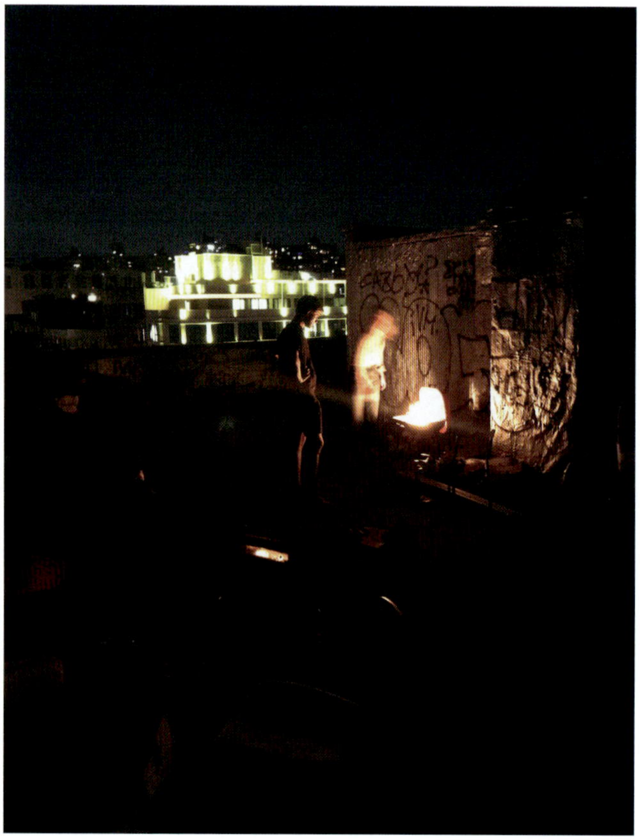

Benjamin Hirte
Modest Homes

Mousse Publishing

6

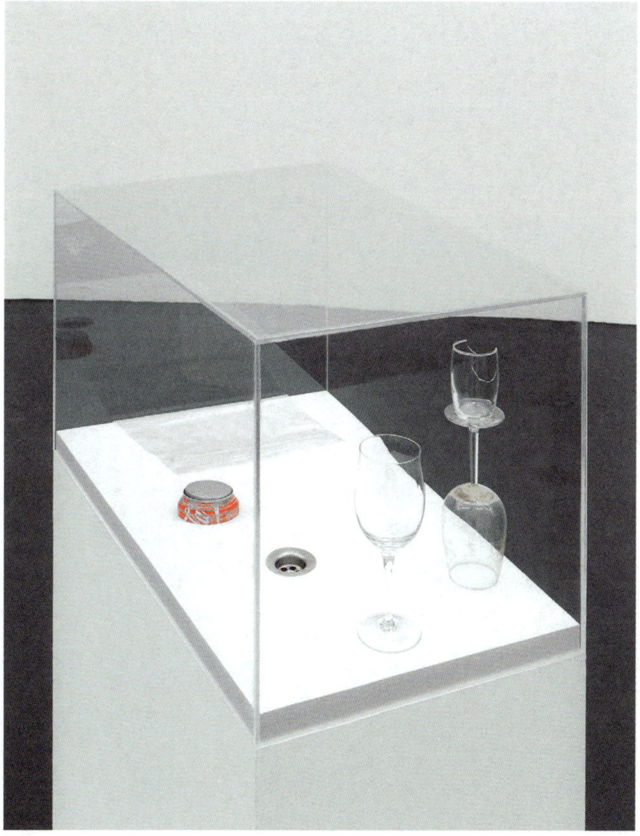

Alphabet and Drain: Teaching Things to Walk

Katharina Hausladen

7

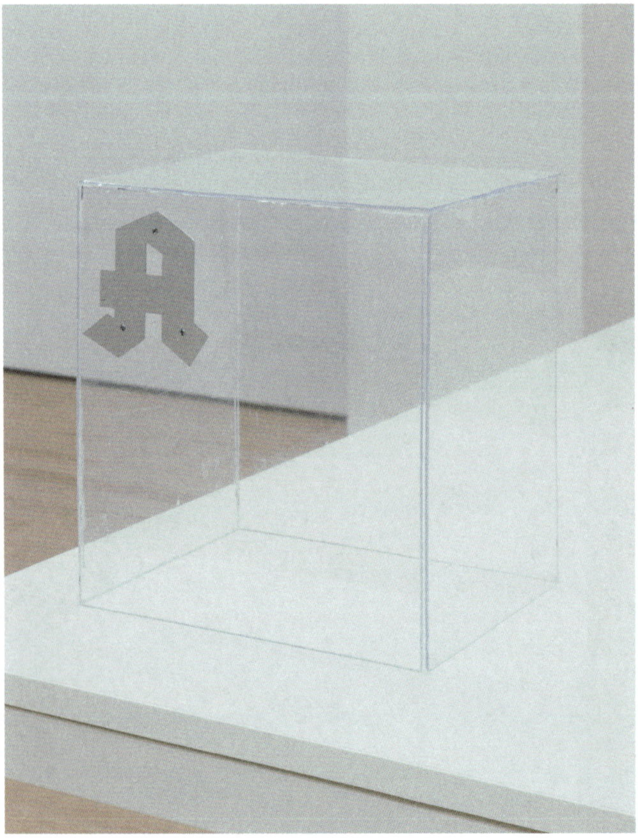

Infrastructures ensure a society's functional processes, including the supply of goods and services as well as the provision of symbolic acts of communication and distribution. The growing attention to so-called "critical" infrastructures—ones that our lives depend on—has alerted us to the "visible and invisible ways" in which they "characterise our present."[1] Be it the supply of energy or medical care, the production and processing of food, media reporting, transportation, or the processing of payment transactions—infrastructures keep a society functioning, both by enabling certain kinds of behavior and by checking, preventing, or penalizing certain others. Who benefits from which infrastructure and who remains excluded, directly or indirectly, from the infrastructural instantiations of being allowed, able, and expected to benefit from them, or who is regimented by them to a special degree, is always also a reflection of very specific social majorities and therefore an ideological construct.

1 – Exhibition text of *Conditions and Frameworks: Infrastructure as Form and Medium* curated by Martin Beck, Sabeth Buchmann, and Stephanie Damianitsch, Exhibit Galerie, Vienna, March 9–May 21, 2022, https://www.akbild.ac.at/en/museum-and-exhibitions/Exhibit/exhibitions-events/current-exhibitions/2022/einrichtung-und-gegebenheit-infrastruktur-als-form-und-handlung?set_language=en.

Second-Order Objects

The aspects of functionality and utility that attend infrastructures come to the fore in Benjamin Hirte's works primarily in the guise of the stuff of their making: as substance or material on the one hand, as instrument or method on the other. For his exhibition *Hamilton Beach* [7, 15, 40, 41], which was presented by Hirte's Vienna-based gallery Layr at JTT Gallery, New York, as part of the gallery festival CONDO New York, he produced an installation composed of the works *Factory*, *Barrel*, *Water tower*, and *Apotheke / Pharmacy* (all 2018) that reads at first glance as a hawker's tray of daily life. The four objects arranged on a white table [41] like utensils from the collection of a technical or local history museum recall models of objects that betoken various promises of usefulness: the pipes tied up with seaweed strings in *Factory* might be parts of a larger system of conduits; the black letter A—the symbol identifying pharmacies in Germany—cut out of aluminum that adorns a fiberglass box [7] in the format of a first-aid kit in *Apotheke / Pharmacy* signals health care; and *Water tower* looks like a miniature archetype of the titular structure knocked together out of elements from the building supplies store, like corrugated metal sheets and wood. The beholder's growing inkling that the functionality of the objects in the presentation is a mere projection is confirmed by the sight of the fourth object, *Barrel* [15], which consists of a crudely sanded-down beverage can filled with straw and studded with what look like projecting little flues: What does the little barrel represent? A wood-burning stove, a kind of heating system or incinerator? However intently the eye scrutinizes the object, its purpose remains a mystery. The effect is a gnawing suspicion that the other things, too, are not in fact minuscule replicas of existing devices, not representations of infrastructures familiar from daily life. The acrylic glass box *imitates* a first-aid kit, the pipes *suggest* a system of conduits, the canopied funnel in the wooden grill *mimics* a water tower. Yet these are not naturalistic renderings of functional ensembles but abstractions of them. Although Hirte quotes selected details from infrastructural environments, he assembles them in second-order objects. That is why it takes the beholder a moment to realize that the optical signifiers they recognize do not, in these specific combinations, match anything in reality.

This may read as postmodernist play—a combination and recombination of elements that suggest and in part possess functionality—in the tradition of Austrian post-war architects and artists such as Hans Hollein, Walter Pichler [14], and Franz West. But Hirte's conception does not evince the participatory dimension that was characteristic of their work. At the very least, sculptures like *Untitled (stool)* (2010) [1], one of his earliest pieces in this vein, exceed the use to which they can be put. For this work, he built a stool modeled on a wooden chair designed by Arne Jacobsen in the 1950s that is indeed usable—one can take a seat on it. But then Hirte displaced the visual markers of its functionality in a way that leaves the beholder uncertain of whether they are in fact encouraged to sit down. He cut away the Danish design classic's backrest such that the rear section of the seat still bends upward, hinting at the original's characteristic curvature. And he screwed the legs of another chair to the bottom of the seat—the screw holes of the original legs can still be seen on the surface but no longer align with the new legs. It takes a trained eye to recognize that Hirte's version of the Jacobsen chair consists of components from no fewer than three different chairs.

Realism and Readymade

8

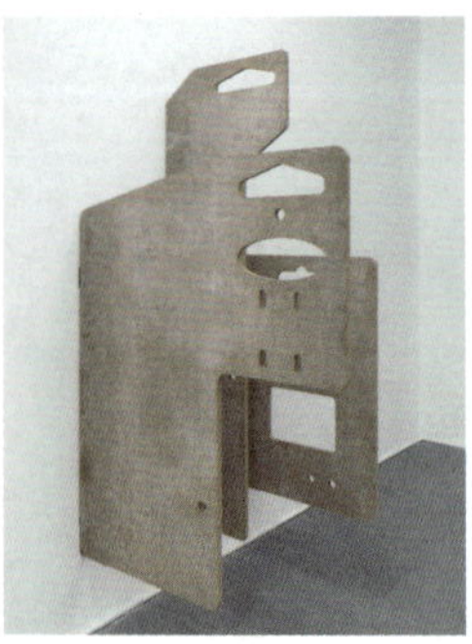

Such defamiliarizations of product forms and infrastructural signifiers of consumerism become legible in Hirte's work as reflexes of the construction of the normal. As such, they are not maquettes of a reality that awaits realization; in other words, Hirte is not interested in building alternative worlds that encourage interaction with the objects on display, be they functional or dysfunctional. Rather, he extends offers of communication that, by directing visual perception toward the formal quality of a thing, invoke codes that refer to something that exists in the world. The model or template quality through which Hirte lends objectivity to his representation of the perceptible world, then, serves the illusion of reality, as though a thing were speaking about itself. He achieves this realism mostly through basic subjects such as chairs, pipes, or sinks; through geometric clarity and rigor that suggest functionality; and often through cool and robust materials such as aluminum and stone. The oversized aluminum hooks (*1.1, 1.2,* and *1.3*; all 2014) [17], for instance, which recall enormous staples and are set out in the gallery like sculptures, seem to lead a life of their own, thanks to their figurative traces. Or consider what appears as monstrous product packaging that Hirte builds out of cement-bound panels of particleboard (*Untitled [tags]*, 2014) [8, 35], setting some against the wall and mounting others to project perpendicularly from it. Some of the holes cut into them are in a standardized shape known as the Euro slot hanger, which lets retailers present products for sale on hooks. The packaging giants exude a self-possession and authority that derive not just from their size but also from the figurative rhetoric that makes them look like excerpts from the real world of things.

In a certain sense, Hirte's play with figurative operations like these resembles the filmmaker John Wilson's technique in his HBO comedy docuseries *How To with John Wilson* (2020–22). Roaming the streets of New York, Wilson captures what feels like an unending stream of images showing instants of typically involuntary slapstick comedy in public settings, often precipitated by found objects. The fact that, and the way in which, the camera records these objects confers the status of public sculptures on them and casts them as readymades, which also adds a social-anthropology component to the situational humor. By revealing public life to be an aesthetic experience "to behold," as Kevin B. Lee has argued, Wilson "endows his images—a bag of bread dangling from a subway handrail, a woman coaxing a pigeon into a shopping bag—with the weight of a place and time."[2] Hirte's works, too, are sustained by the obfuscation of the artifacts' relation to their real context. And in Hirte, too, the fundamentally narrative quality both of the conjunction of irritating details in a thing (why is the bowling ball in *Gamebreaker*, 2013 [21], not round but cropped?) and of its wayward recontextualization (the screw threads and pipes in ~, 2013 [16], form the shape of a pistol) yields a comedic effect that marks a distance from the existing universe of physical as well as symbolic exchange values in Western societies. What is thus unsettled is not regularity, not the possibility of invoking some rule or other of meaning-making. Rather, it is the invocation of established rules governing the distinction between found object and creative manipulation that is destabilized in Hirte's art.

2 – Kevin B. Lee, "How to Make Internet Comedy (Without the Internet)," *Texte zur Kunst*, no. 121 (2021): 48–52.

Calculus of Cuteness

Two interrelated stratagems in Hirte's work that play a not insignificant role in this connection are his handling of proportions and an aesthetic of industrial manufacture that engenders distance. Both suggest a kinship between his works and the practices of (post)minimalist artists such as Cady Noland—minus Noland's signature brutality—on the one hand, and exponents of Pop art such as Claes Oldenburg, on the other. Noland's influence is most evident in Hirte's use of metallic surfaces, reduced formal vocabulary, and interest in the institutional and commercial manifestations of the public sphere, as when he stages Americana like the red Marlboro roof as a large-format PVC tarp (*Vector [Marlboro theme]*, 2016) [67]. Oldenburg's influence, by contrast, is first and foremost one of spatial dimension. The oversized marble replica of a spray nozzle (*Untitled*, 2012) [24] and the stool in the shape of a vertebra made out of synthetic leather, felt, and foamed plastic (*Backbone*, 2017) [25], for example, seem to have sprung straight from the Oldenburgian repertoire of monumental sculptures representing everyday objects. Closer inspection of Hirte's bone stool reveals that the vertebra's processes might just as well be the clapping hands of a cartoon character that were sewn on too close together; the egg-yolk yellow of the seat, too, encourages associations with Pikachu, emoji, the Simpsons, etc.

9

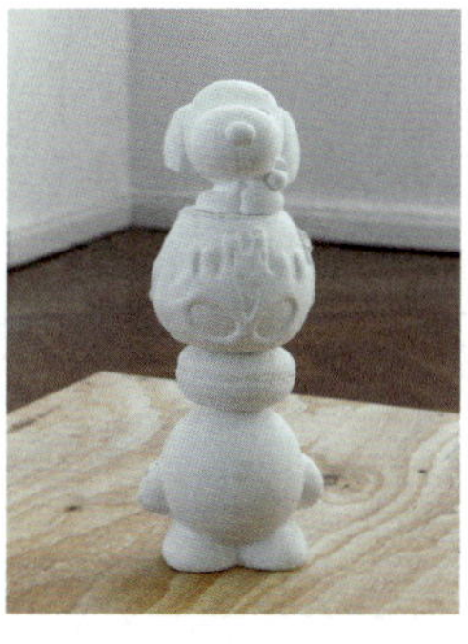

More generally, the aesthetic vocabulary of Hirte's oeuvre has increasingly integrated cute rounded shapes into the otherwise largely sober-minded visual language of his installations. Physical and symbolic materializations of popular figures and linguistic signifiers already feature in earlier works such as *wig* (2012) [22], a silk-screen print on linen showing the Disney version of a Baroque-style peruke. But more recent sculptures by Hirte such as *The Robbers* (2019) [9]—a kind of totem composed, in the manner of a fold-in picture puzzle, of elements as disparate as the torso of a round-bellied cartoon character, a macaroon, a comic-

10

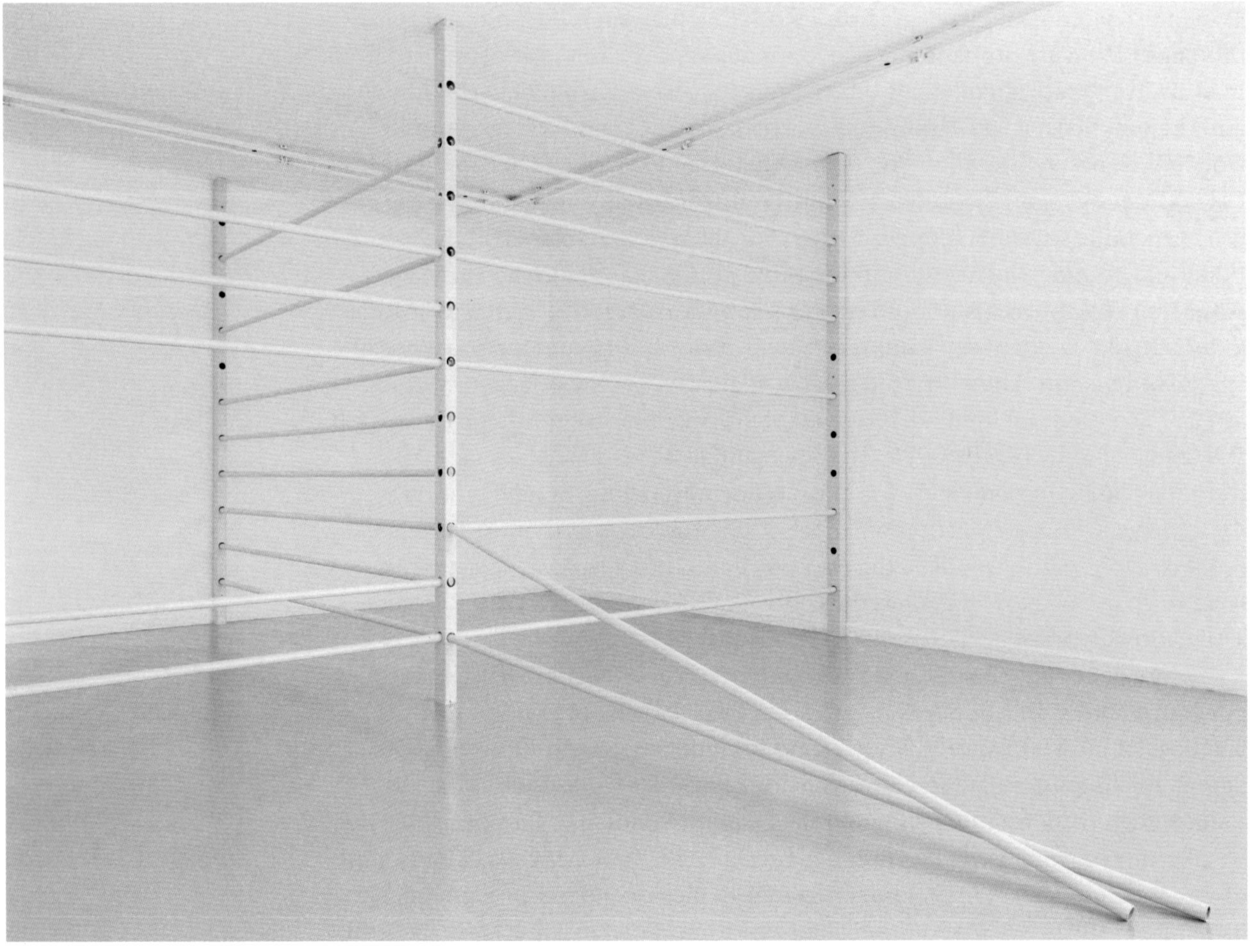

strip parody of a skull, and a compressed variant of Snoopy with a large childlike head—*explicitly* address the commodity character of the cute, which we may define with Sianne Ngai as the wish for a more intimate, more sensual relationship with the commodities we consume, and as the desire to take the things we perceive as cute in hand or to fondle them, overcoming the distance of cognitive engagement for an affective-tactile attachment to the desired object.[3]

3 – See Sianne Ngai, *Our Aesthetic Categories: Zany, Cute, Interesting* (Cambridge, MA: Harvard University Press, 2012), esp. 13, 27, and 54.

Signifier and Affect

It is precisely such moments of affective involvement and apparent elimination of the distance between beholder and work that now occur frequently in Hirte's art. They may be due in part to the fact that he has increasingly worked with "softer" and more amenable materials like plaster, polystyrene, and synthetics. A case in point is *Solace* (2021)[2], another variation on a piece of furniture that he created especially for Neuer Kunstverein Wien: a circular bench made of painted polystyrene and glass-fiber reinforced plastic with four bulbous feet on its periphery. Running around the hole at its center is an indentation, a screw thread or rabbet, as though—following the logic of *The Robbers*—one might slot further body parts or parts of objects into this base. The work is interesting also because it unites different elements that recur in Hirte's output. There is, for one, the "flange principle," or the method of slotting together and of modular, extendable screw joining, that Hirte has worked with since the early 2010s and that manifests itself in the repeated use of pipes, gutters, and drains as loci of passage, consumption, and expulsion. Another effect of the pipe or drain is that a turn into the third dimension always already looms behind the two-dimensional front view, a backward or downward deepening or expansion that, in the case of the drain, can even be thought of as infinite. As something that structures and models space, then, the flange principle is prototypically sculptural. Another motif that is central to Hirte's art and resolutely articulated in *Solace* is the applied dimension of seating furniture: unlike the earlier *Untitled (stool)*[1], this work decidedly invites the beholder to sit down and linger—and, if the promise extended by the title is to be believed, find solace—as though it were a bench in a park or in the lobby of a commercial building. The potential of usability, which has always played a prominent part in Hirte's art, takes on considerably greater significance in the piece; indeed, the work emphasizes the interaction between the domains of applied and fine art, whose influence, the one's as much as the other's, his practice has always acknowledged. In the final analysis, *Solace* also intertwines two further aspects: the conjunction of cuteness—evoked by the rounded shape and the little feet, which refer to mass-cultural figuration—with the functionality of a bench that might actually exist as such in a public setting is what allows the piece to be read as a public sculpture. One would not be surprised to see a work fueled by reflections both on its applied-art status and on the cuddly-mascot quality of an object of daily life in a city like Vienna be returned to where, conceptually speaking, it originated: the public sphere.

This lends the question of the specific mode of reference in Hirte's work to infrastructural signifiers in contemporary mass cultures a genuinely narrative or, more generally speaking, linguistic cast. In other words, the flange principle here recurs on the plane of the linguistic signifier. The semiotic constellation (in principle, extendable ad infinitum) of found and self-made objects, of the ready-made and the multiple, for which Hirte's artistic and design practice stands, uncovers the contexts of (aesthetic, political, social, etc.) utility and function that underlie the engagement with objects and form its "alphabet." This can be seen not only when he integrates letters from the *Plumbers Font* [20], a typeface of his own design for which he took inspiration from the formal structure of perforated metal tapes, into installations (such as *C* [46], 2017, and *untitled (A)*, 2015 [44]). A grate is a fountain is a stair tread is a soccer field. Hirte's sculptures are never integrally present, never identical to the semiotic material from which they are made. As materializations of social life, they always also direct our attention to the infrastructural conditions on which their own production is premised.

In the case of Hirte's work *We labour but not for ourselves* [27]—produced for the exhibition *Antwerp*, which he conceived together with Nancy Lupo at the Mackey Garage of the MAK Center, Los Angeles, in 2021—this means, above all, the economic logic of the authoritarian, or even internalized, exploitation of those who supply the labor. The sculpture milled from polyurethane represents a beehive, which is based on the emblem [26] of an Austrian housing cooperative that, following World War II, was financed by the Marshall Plan. Like the bee in the bee colony (we might conclude by analogy), labor in Austria's historical socialism entailed a form of social action aimed at a cooperative economy. In today's late capitalism, by contrast, labor, though still directed toward the social world, is highly individualized. Economic rationality, by consequence, prevails also and especially where offers of identification are asserted even as the subjects find themselves isolated, their very individuality valorized. It is the merit of Hirte's realism that his reference to the beehive as a symbol for socialism in economic and living arrangements becomes legible on the one hand as iconic—as politics cast into an image—and on the other hand as dialectical—as open contradiction to the social reality in which the reference originated. To act under the sign of language, in this perspective, means to teach things to walk.

11

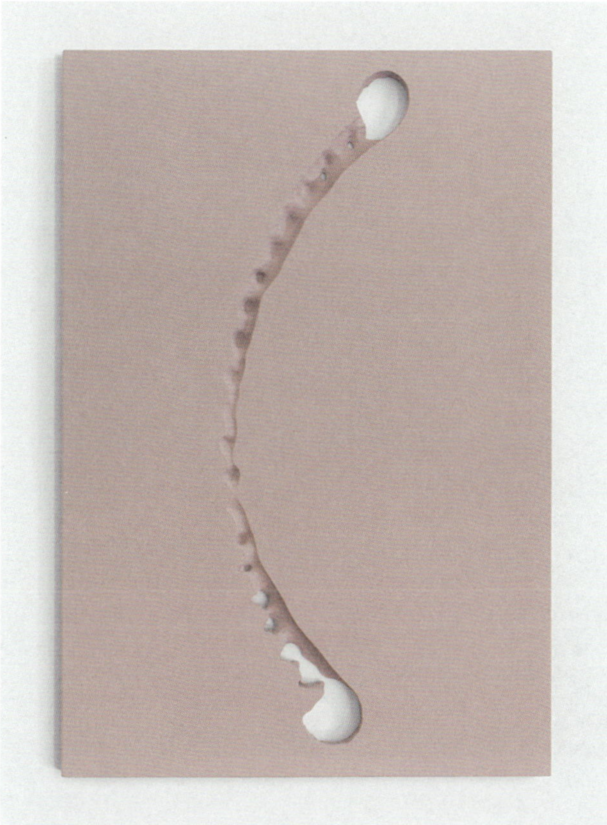

12

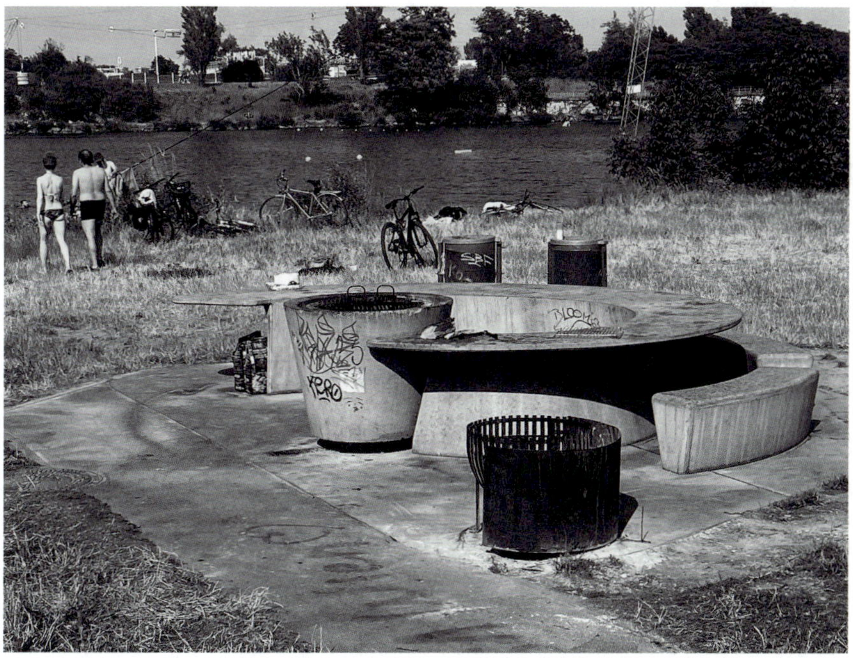

13

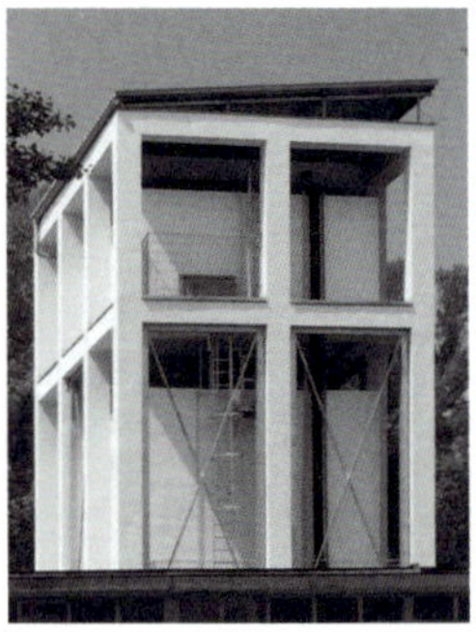

14

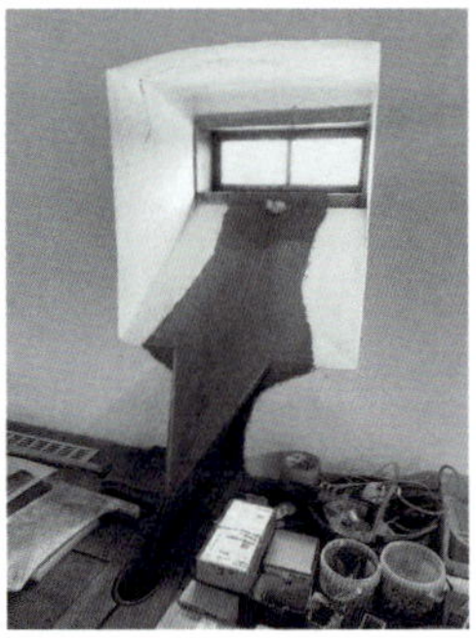

15

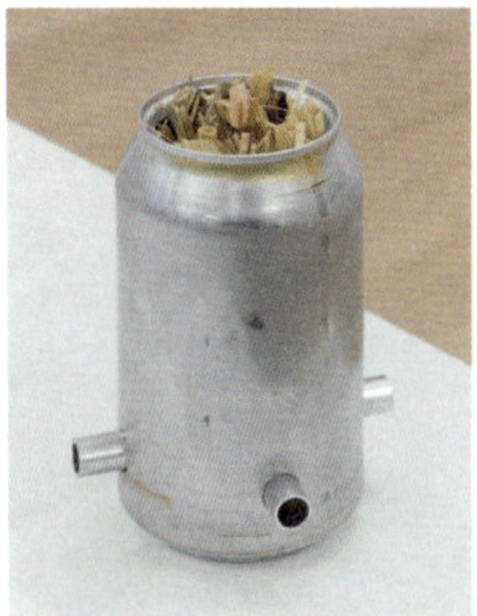

16

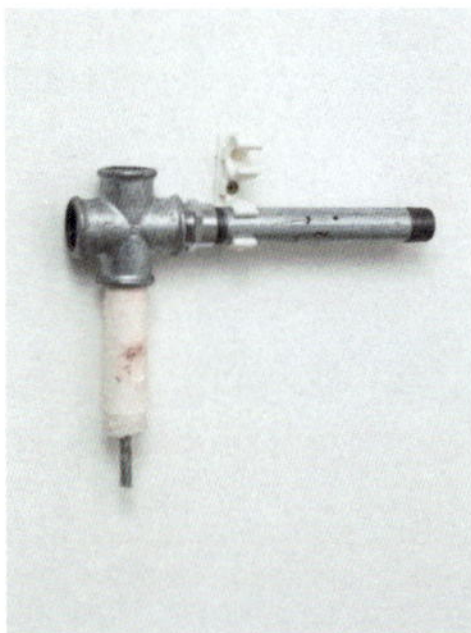

17

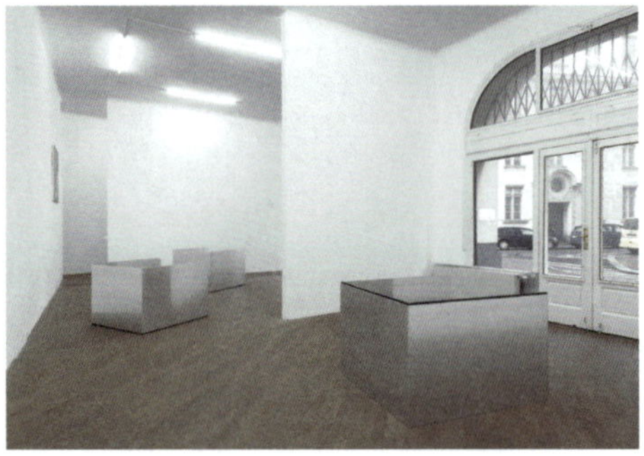

18

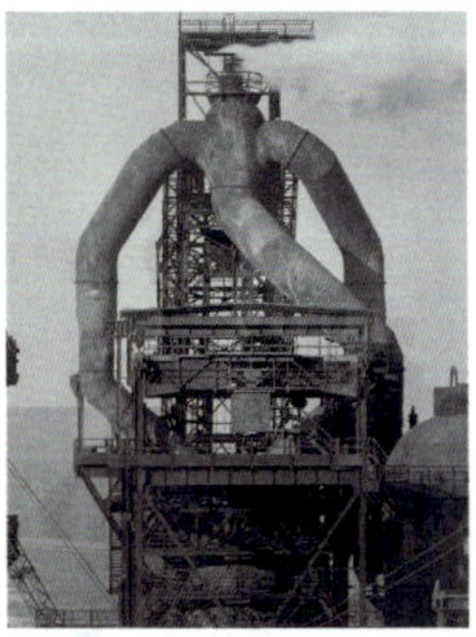

19

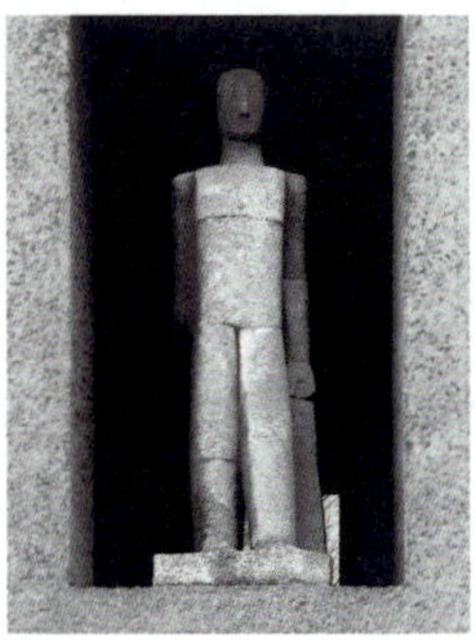

20

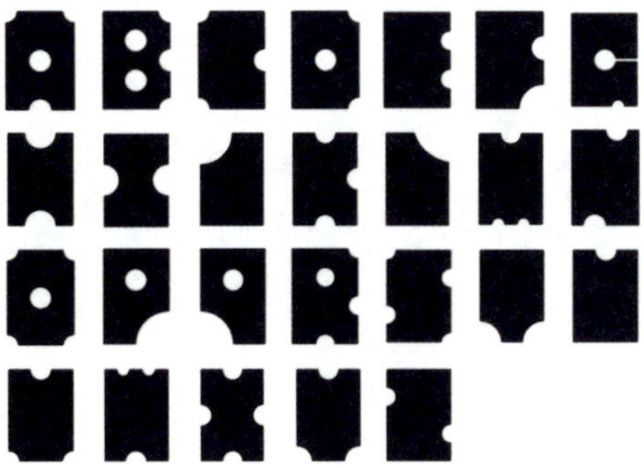

21

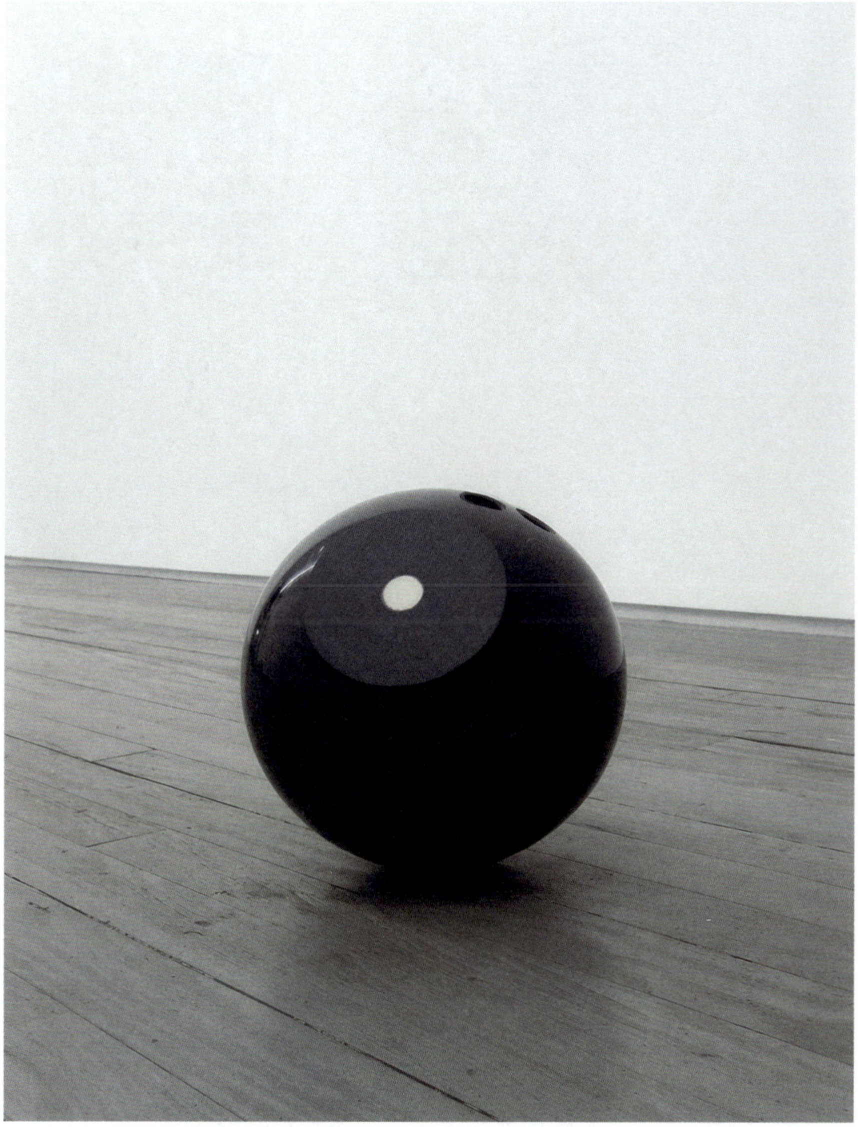

22

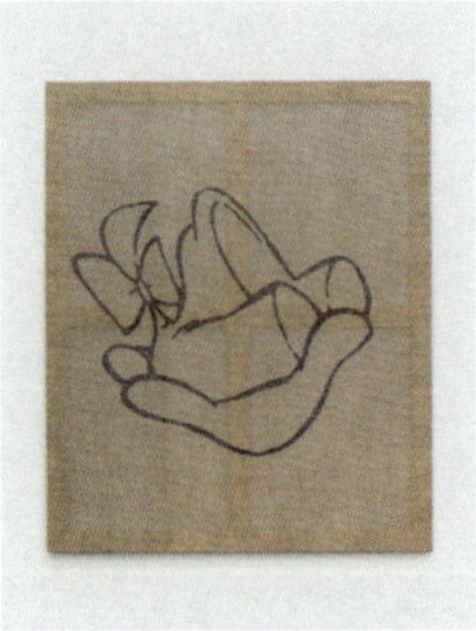

23

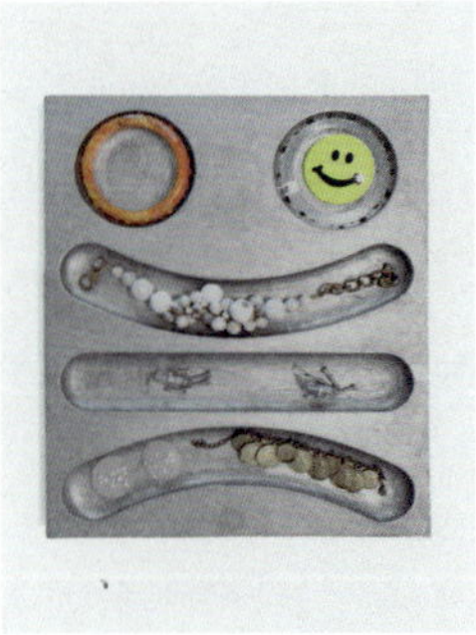

24

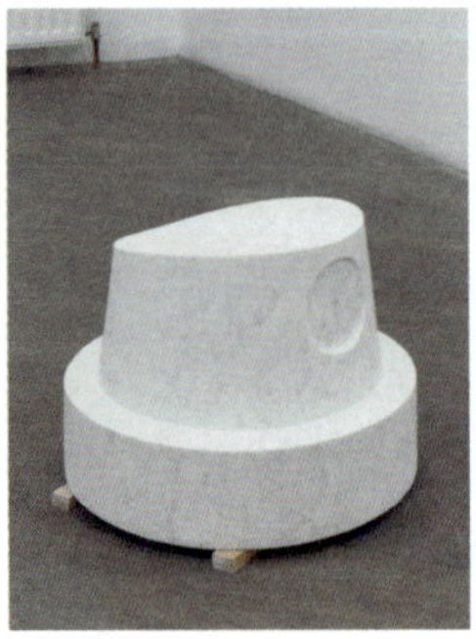

25

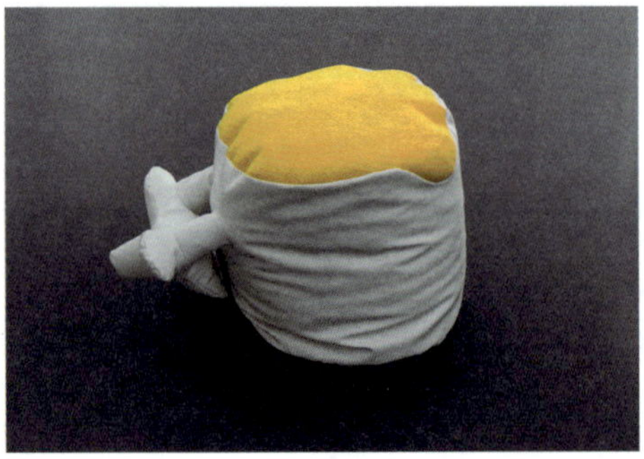

26

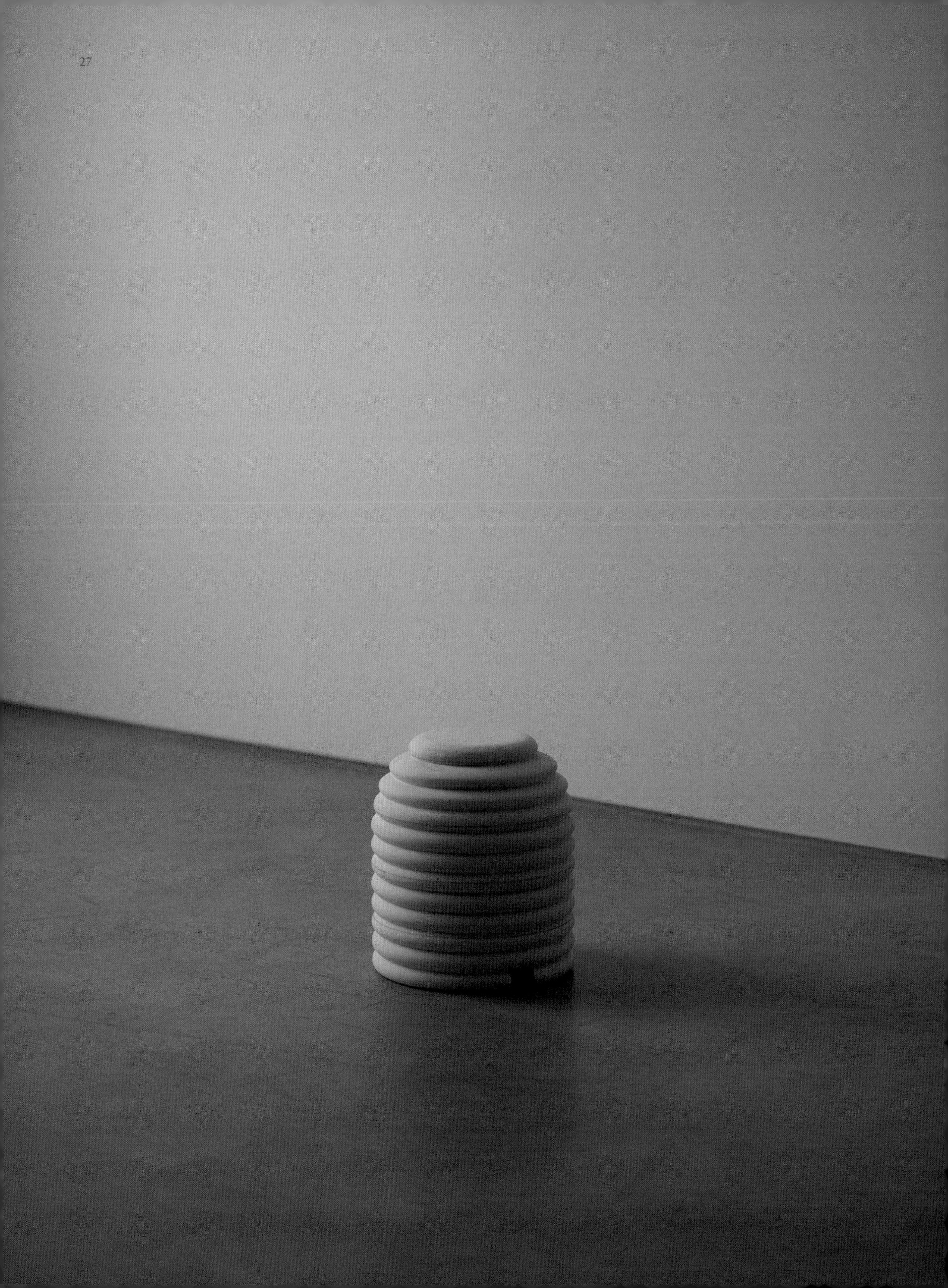

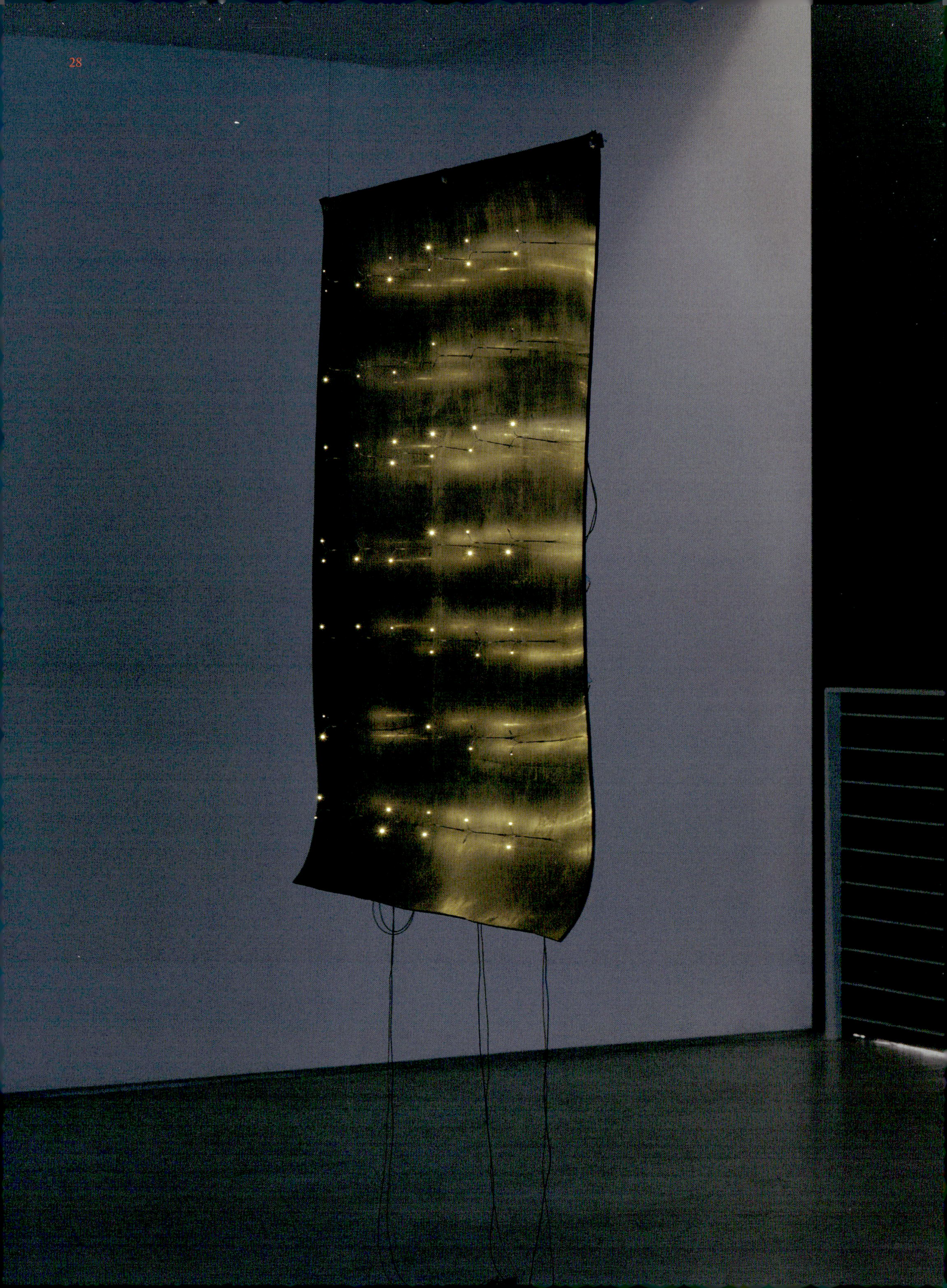

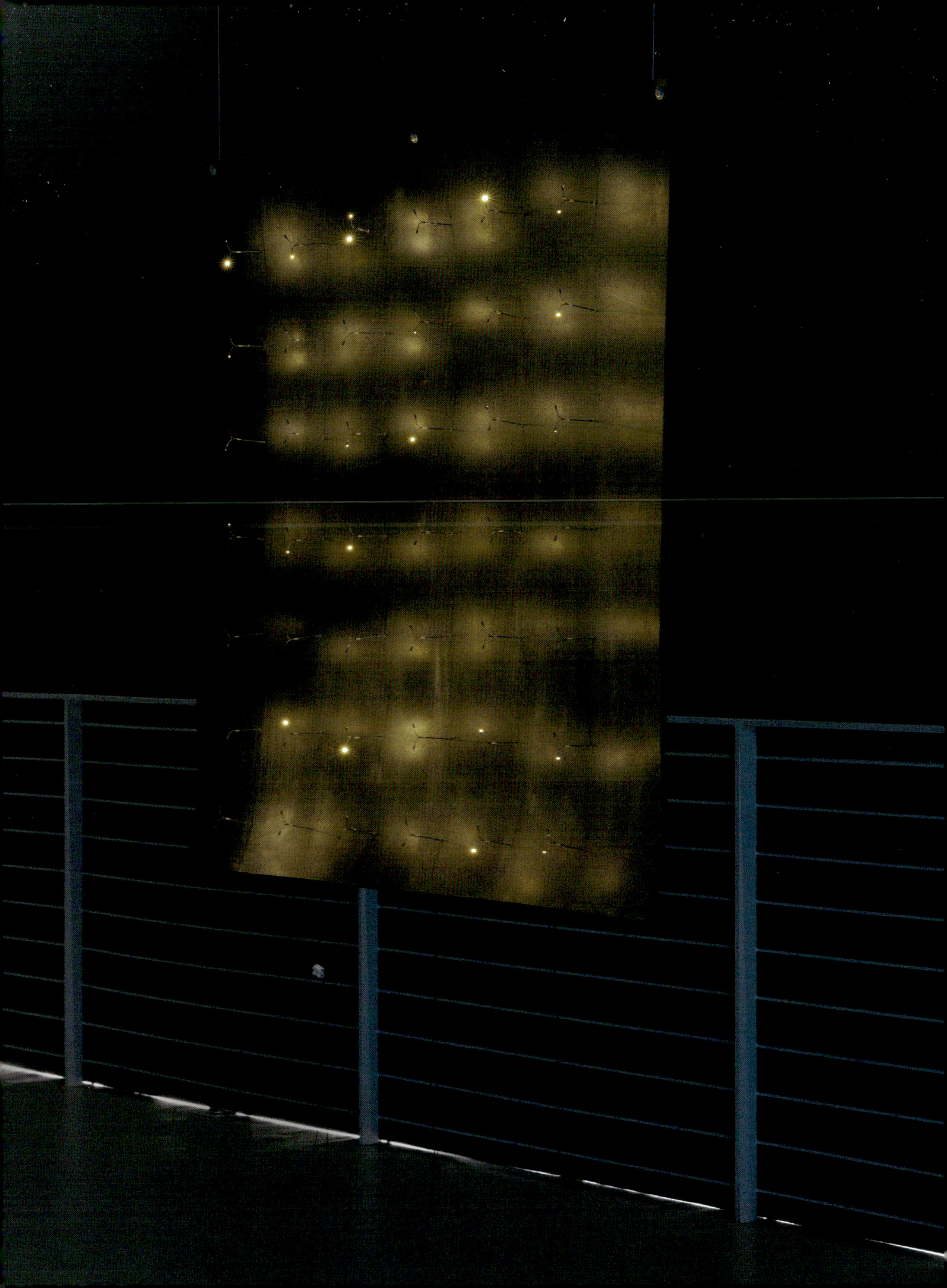

29

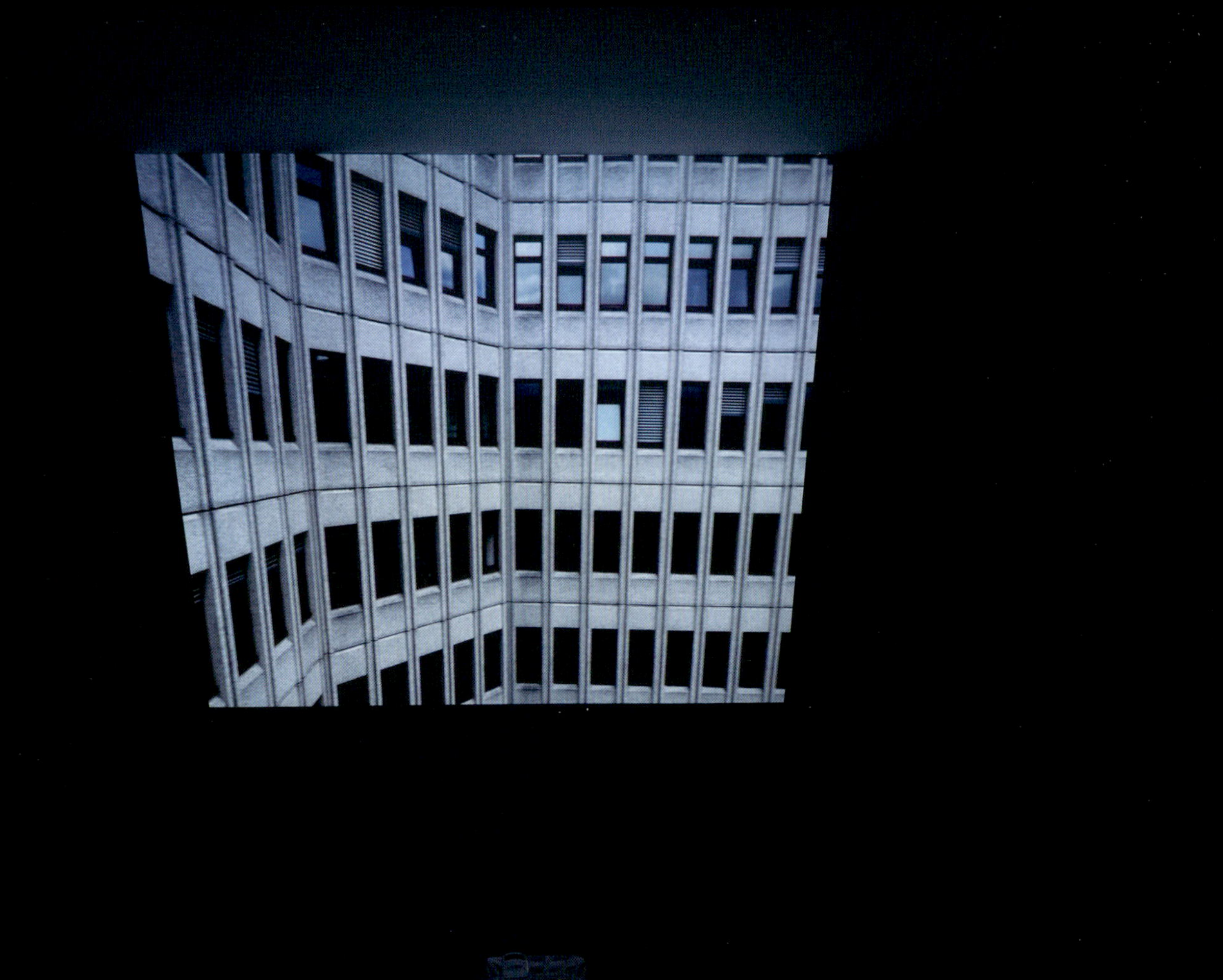

30

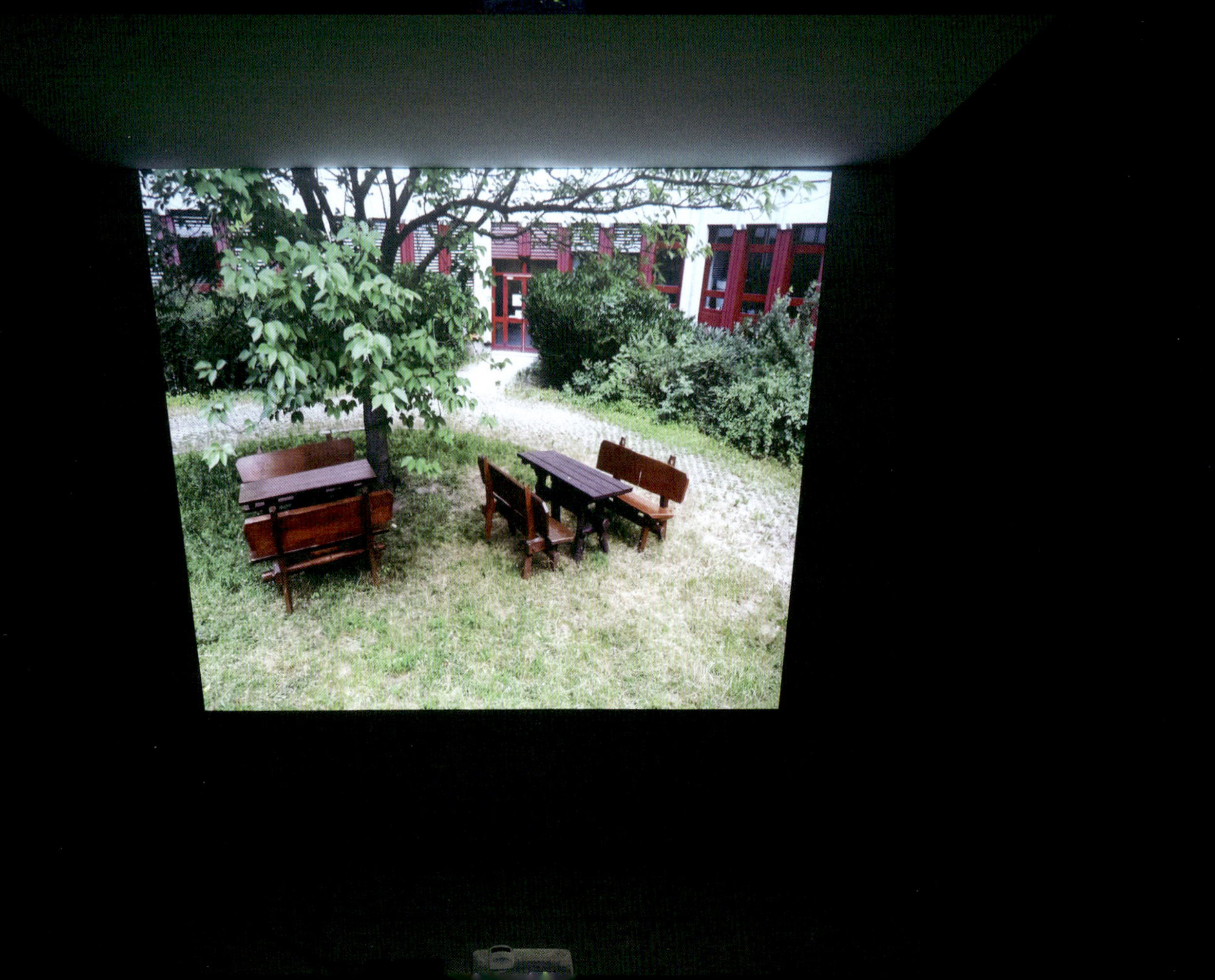

31

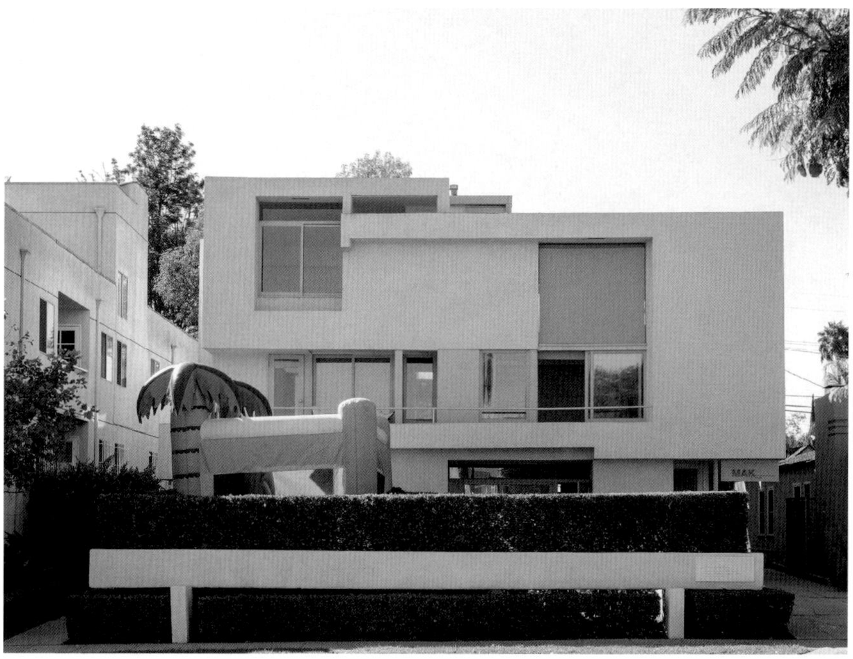

32

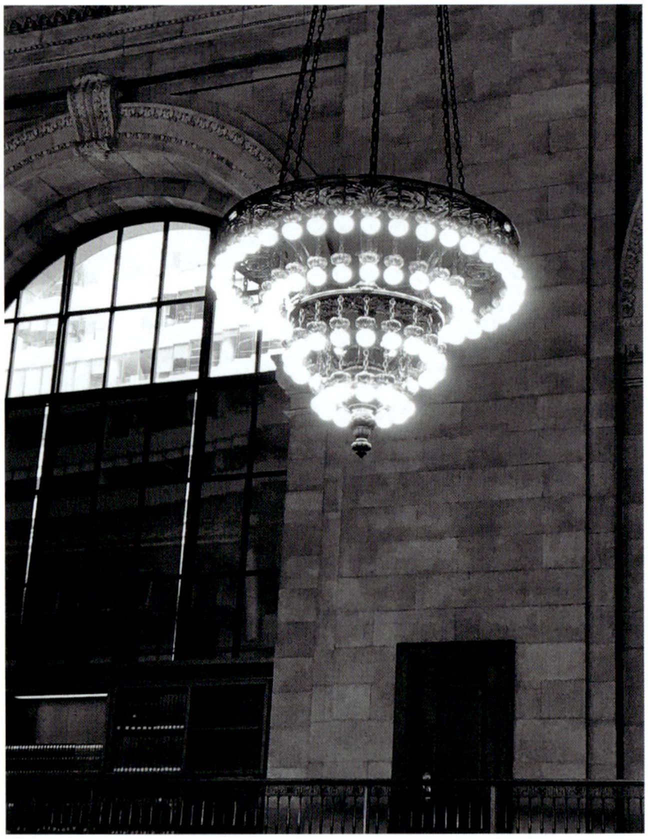

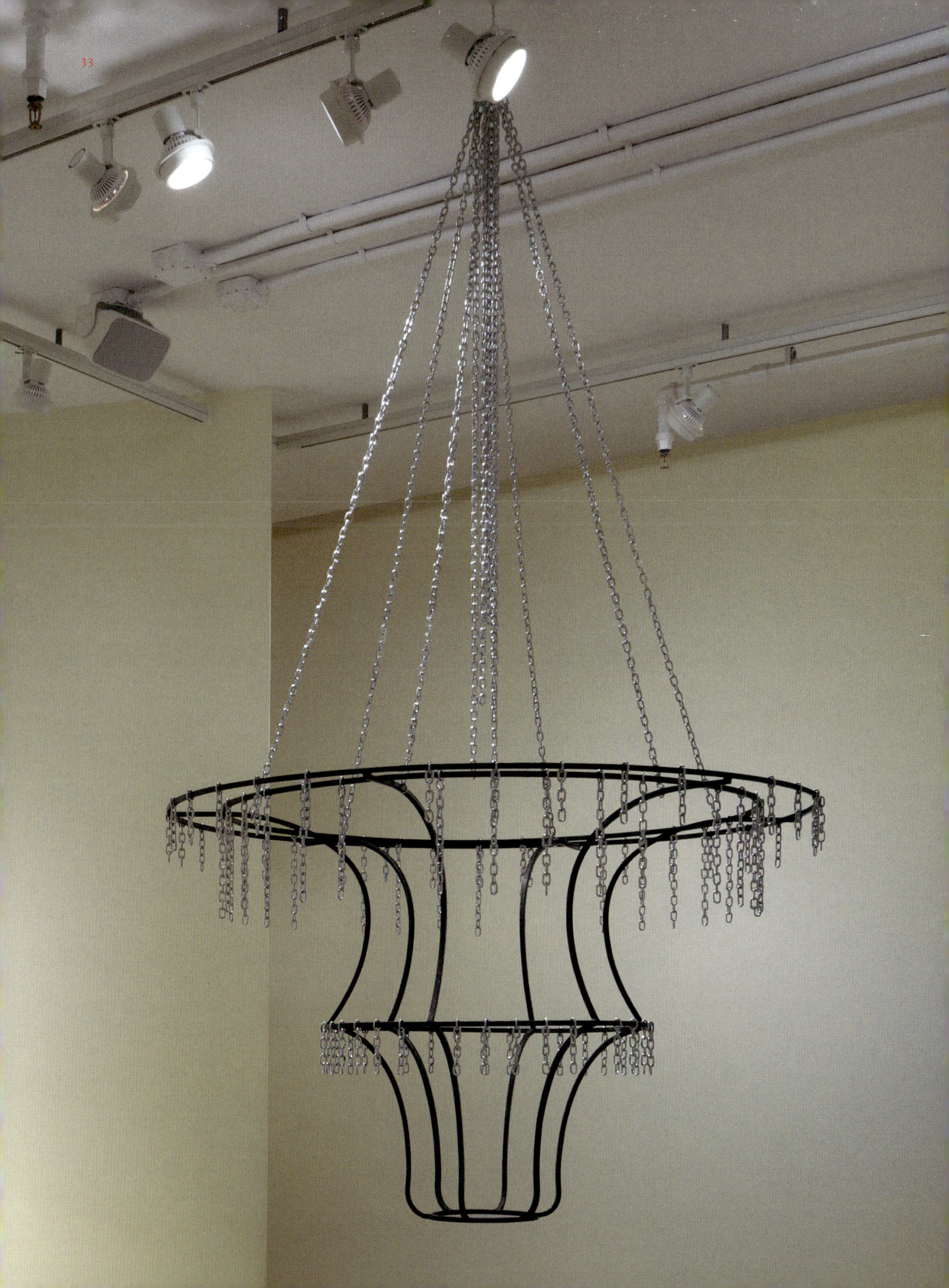

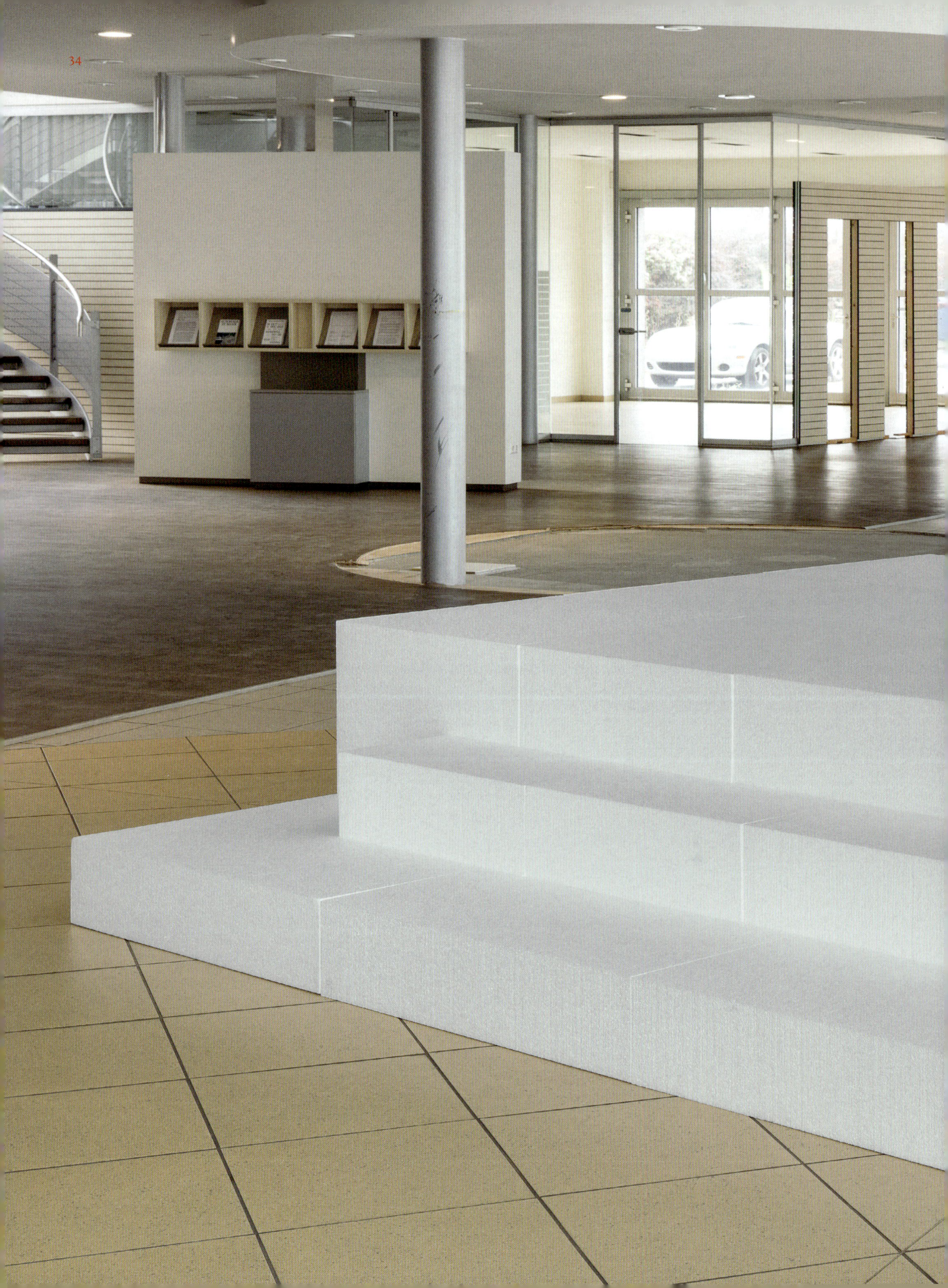

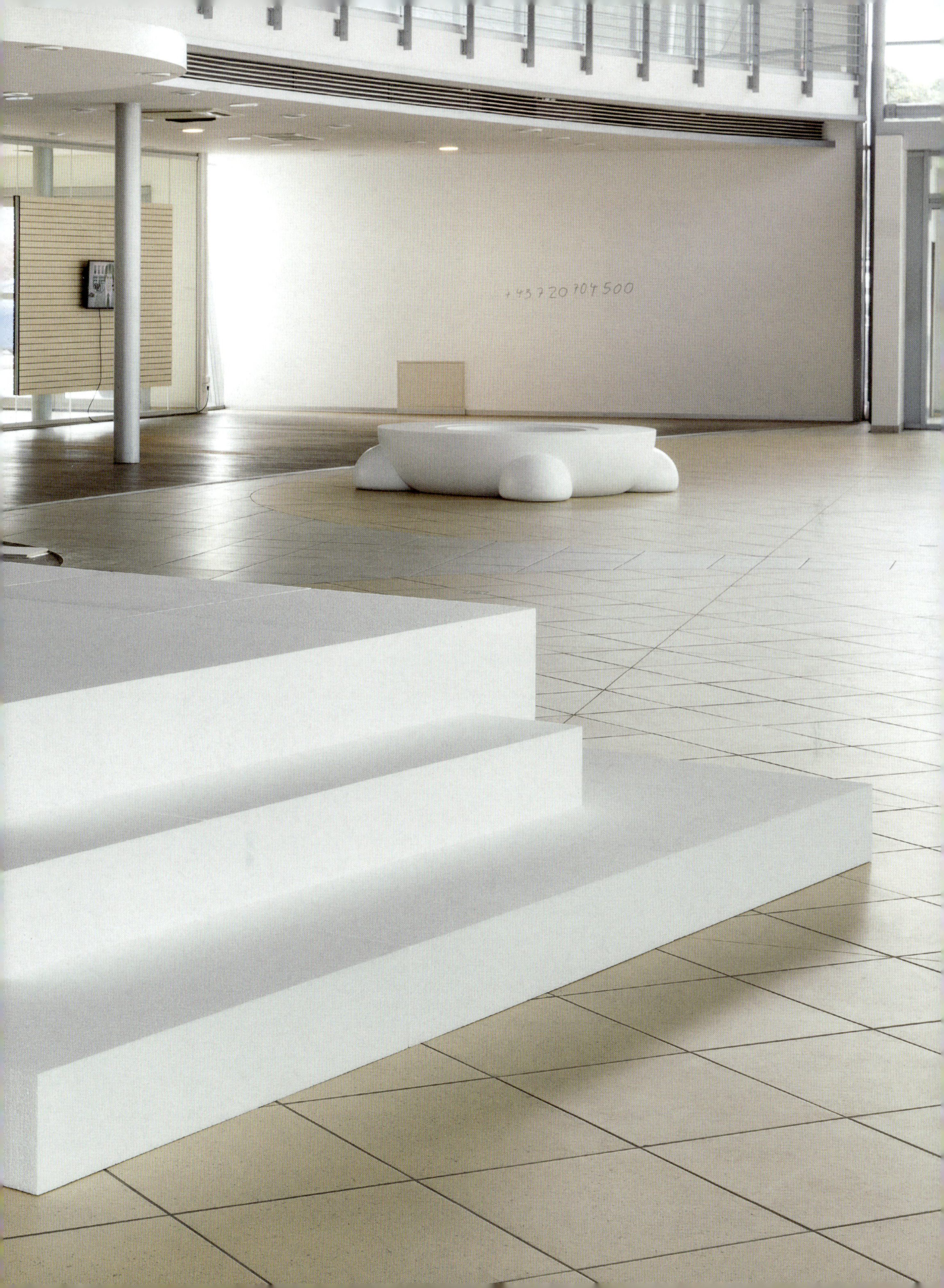
+43 720 704 500

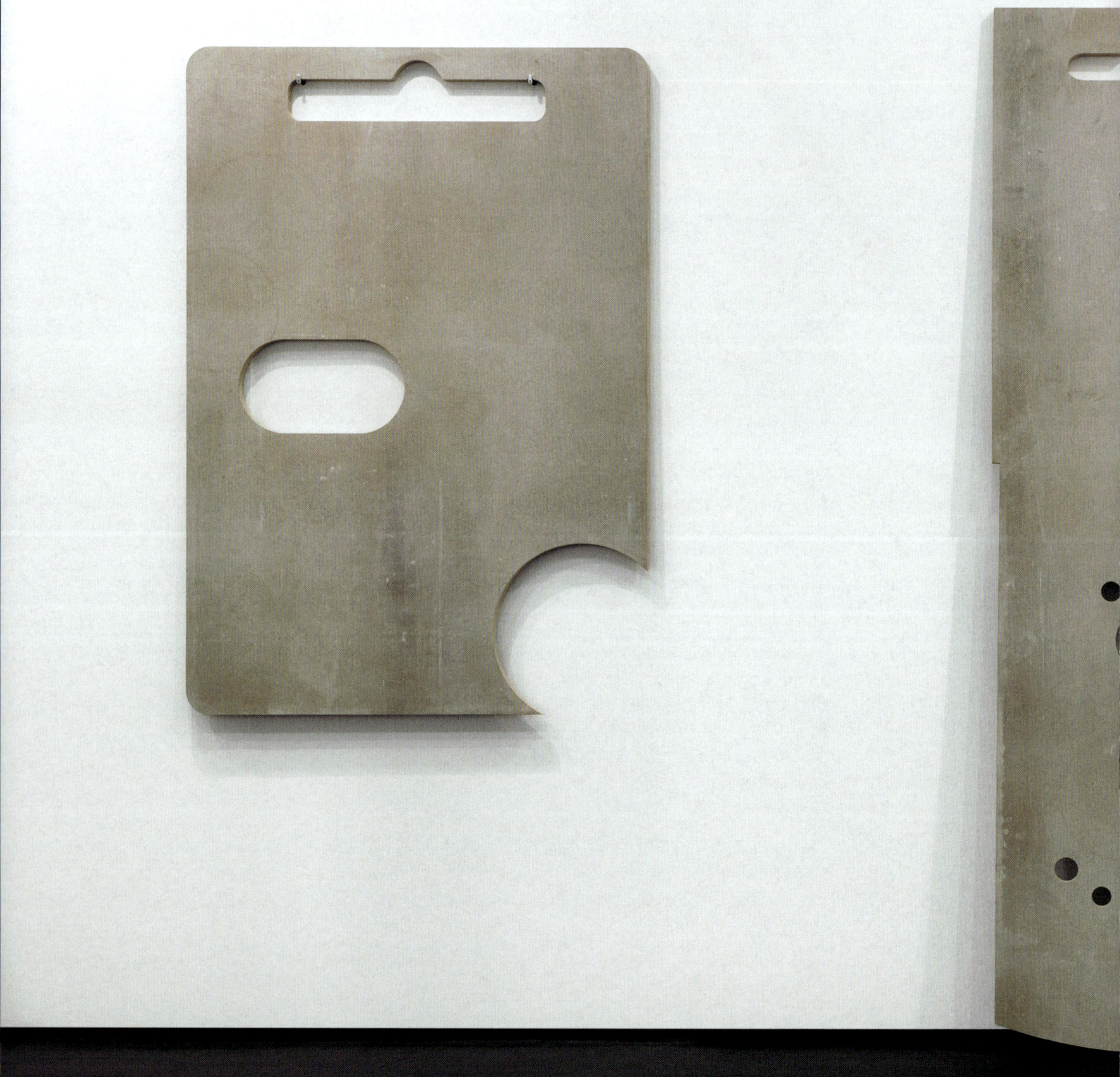

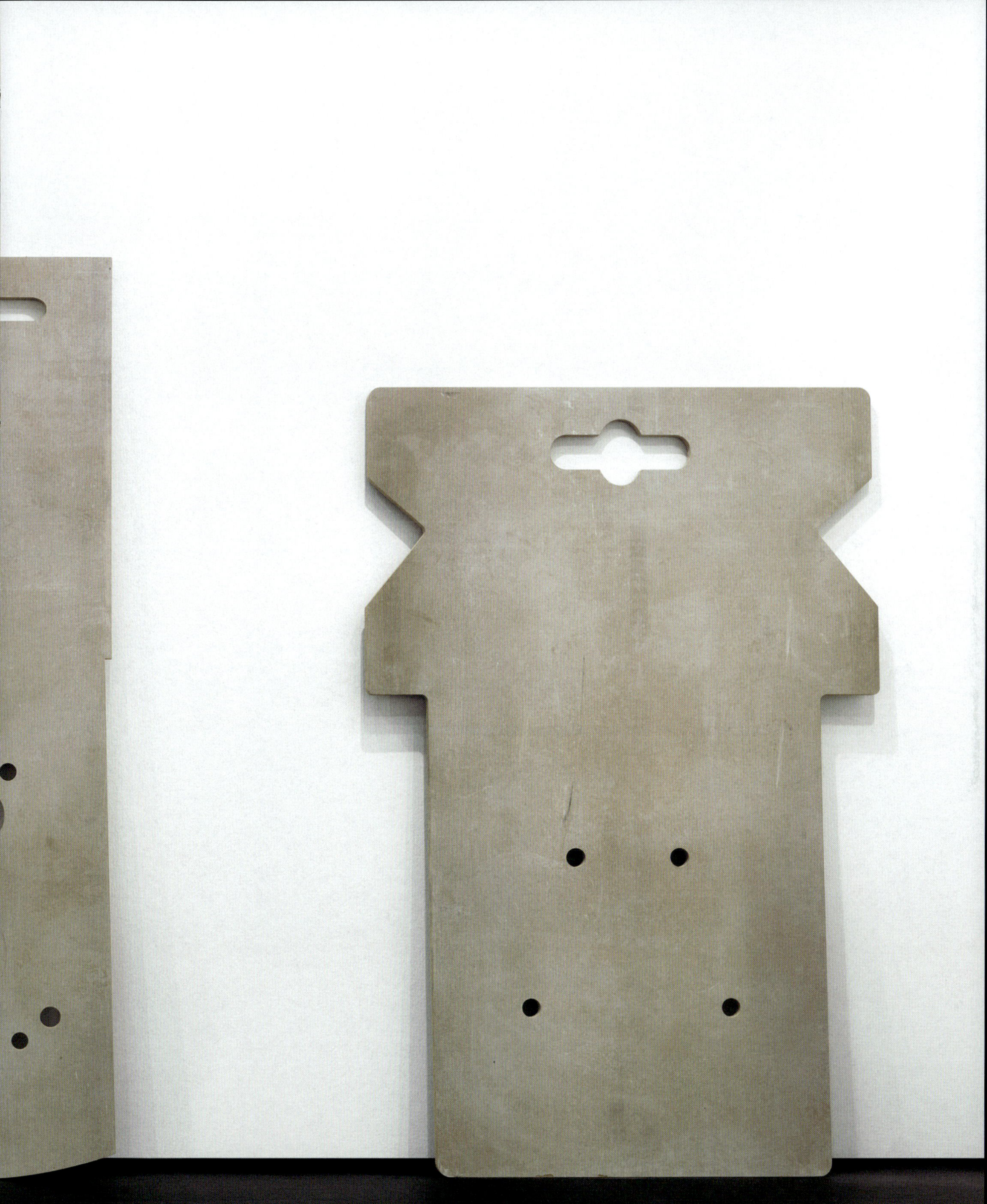

36

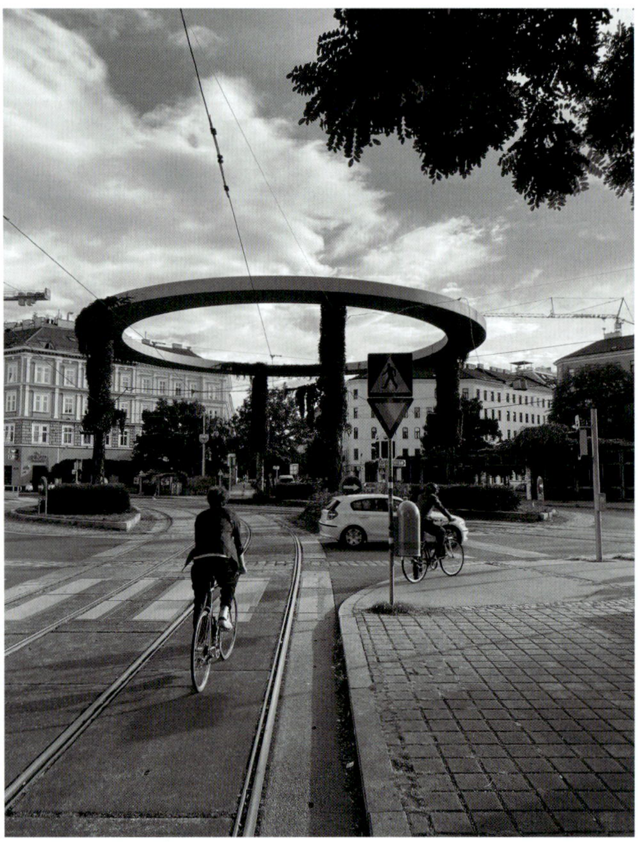

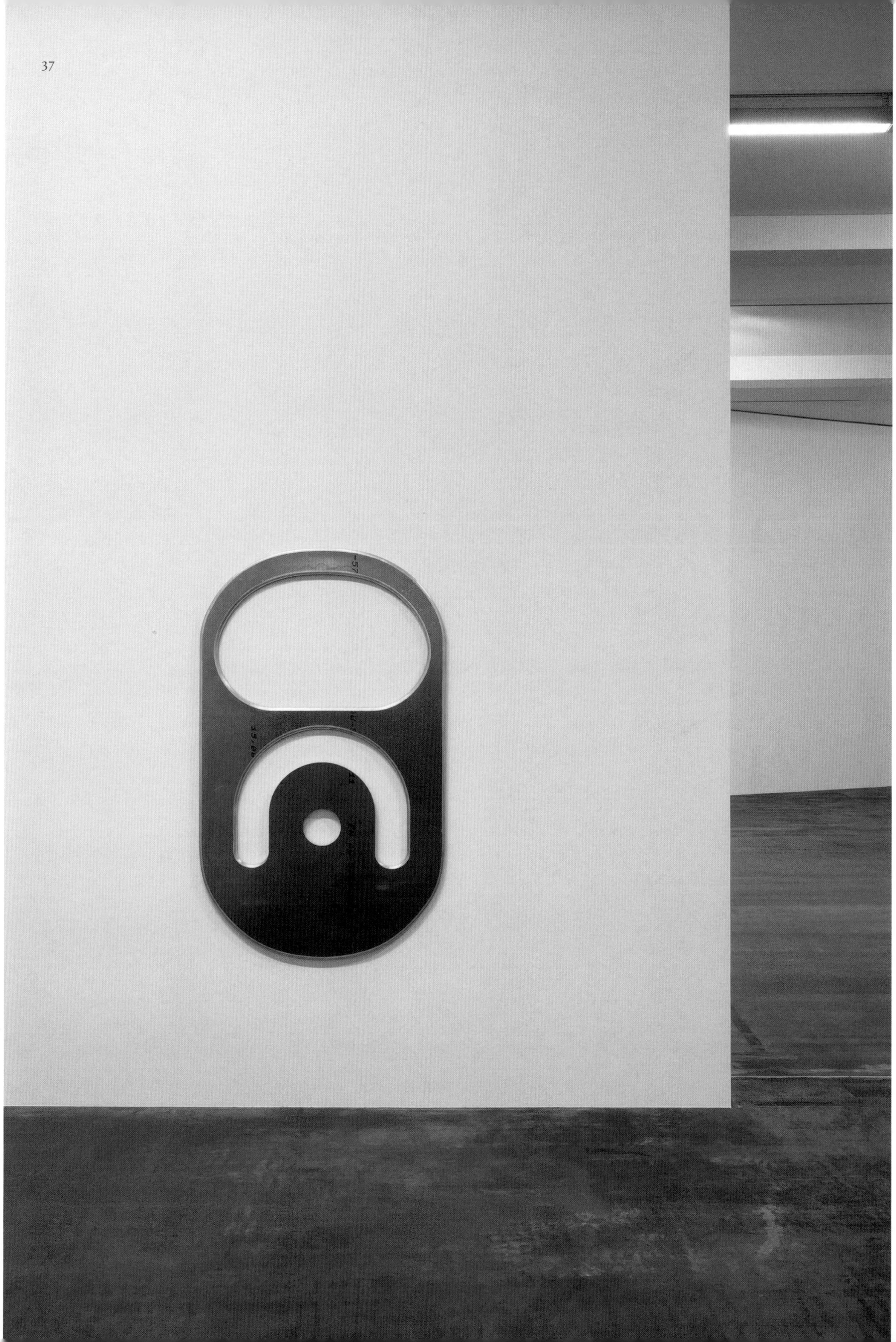

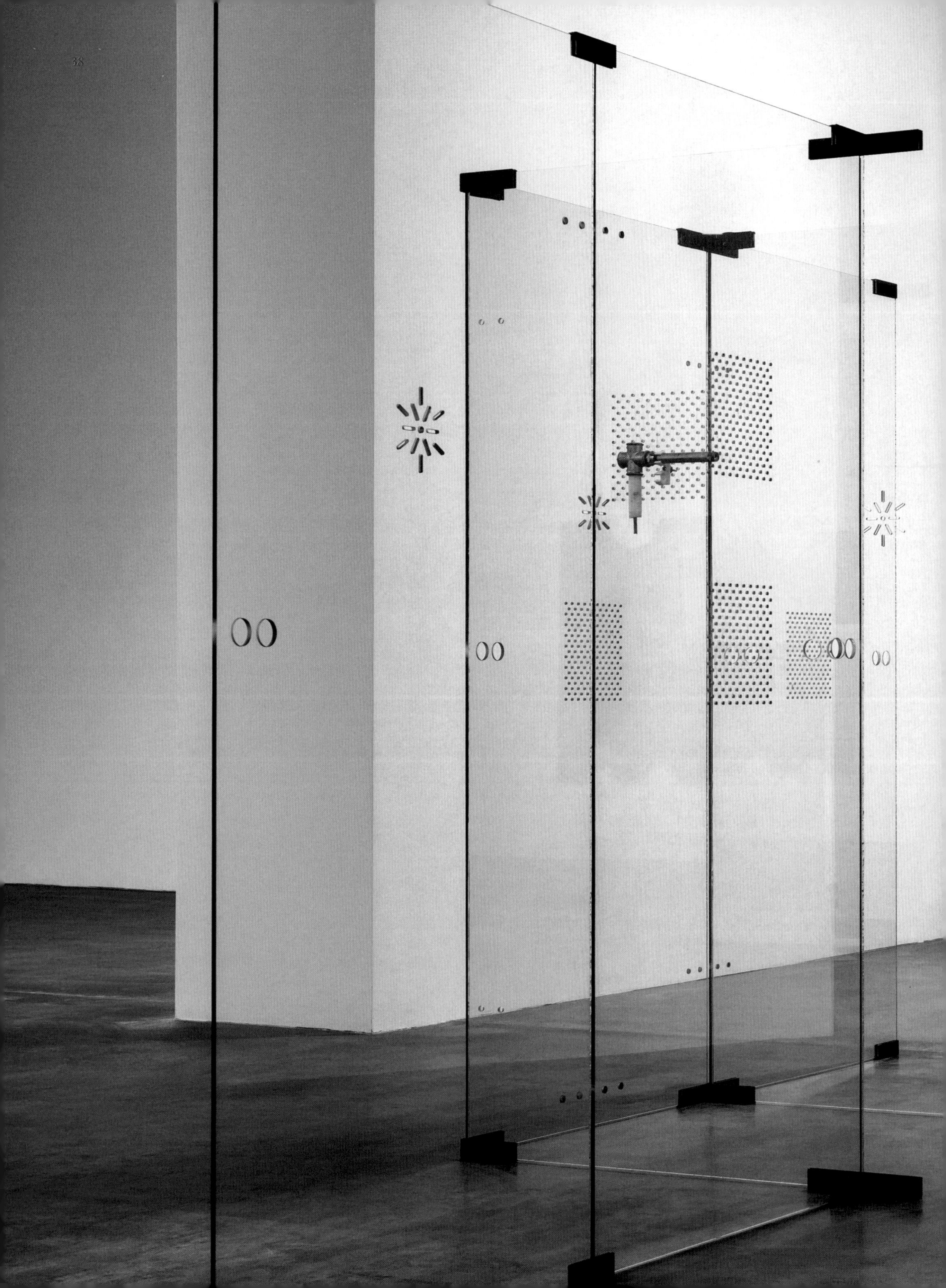

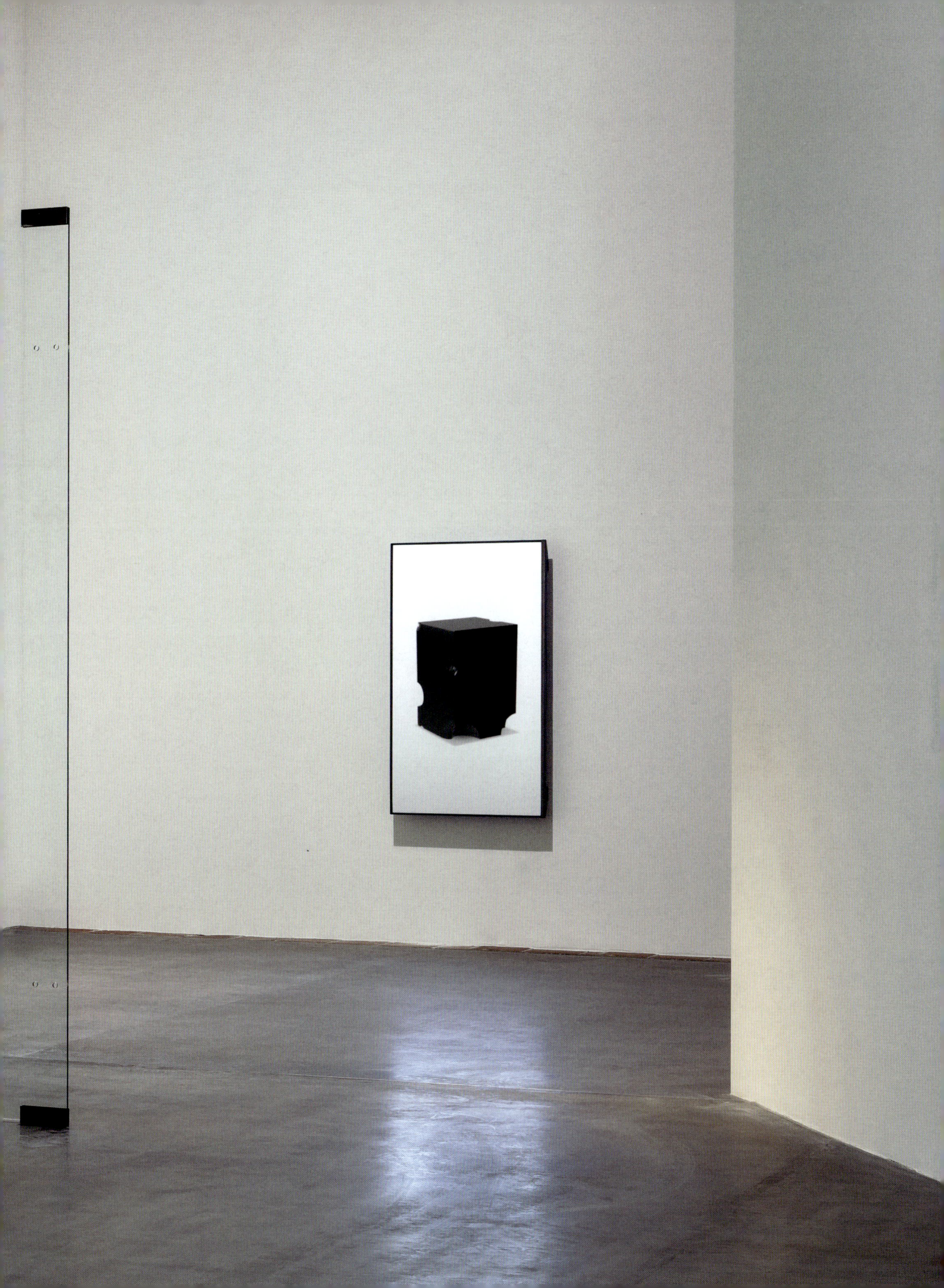

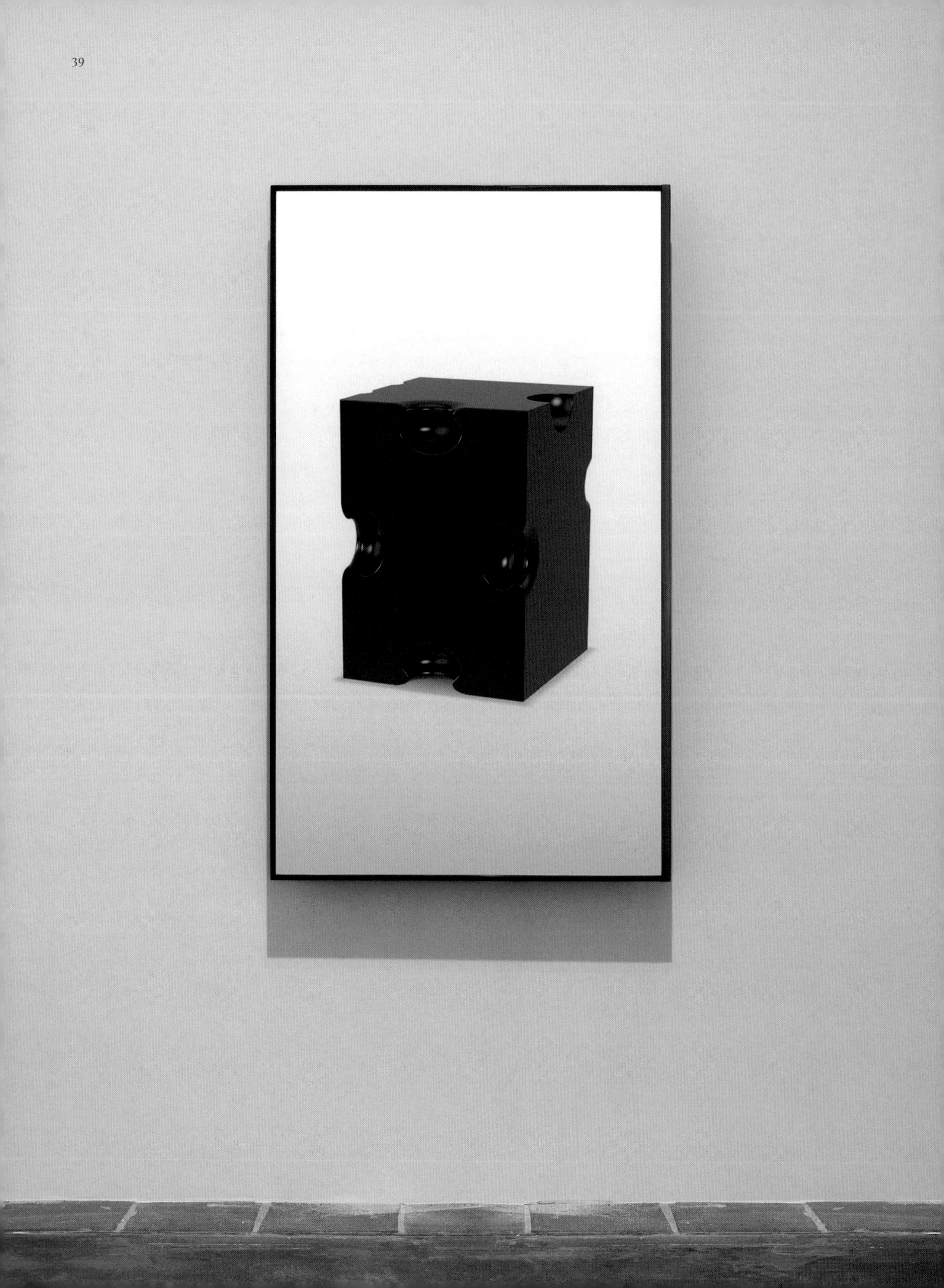

40

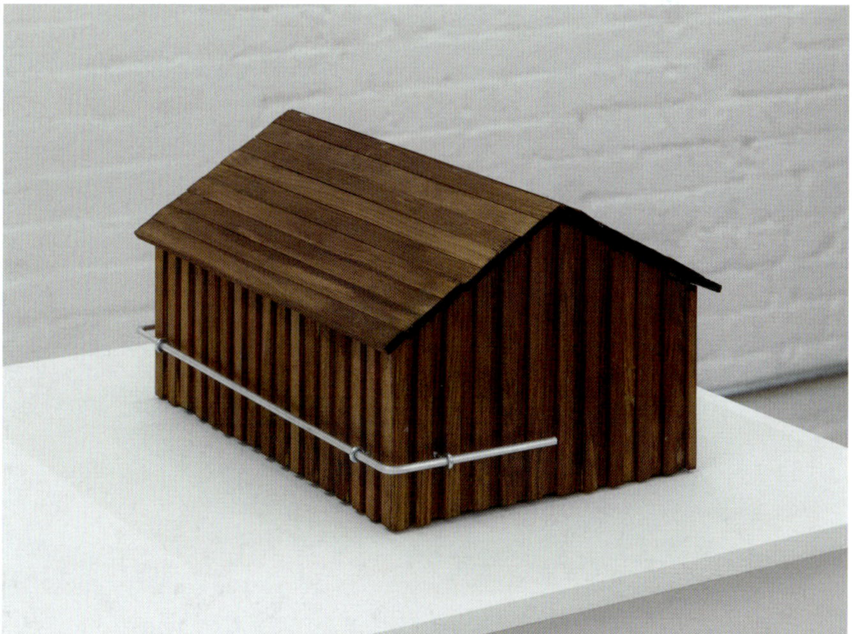

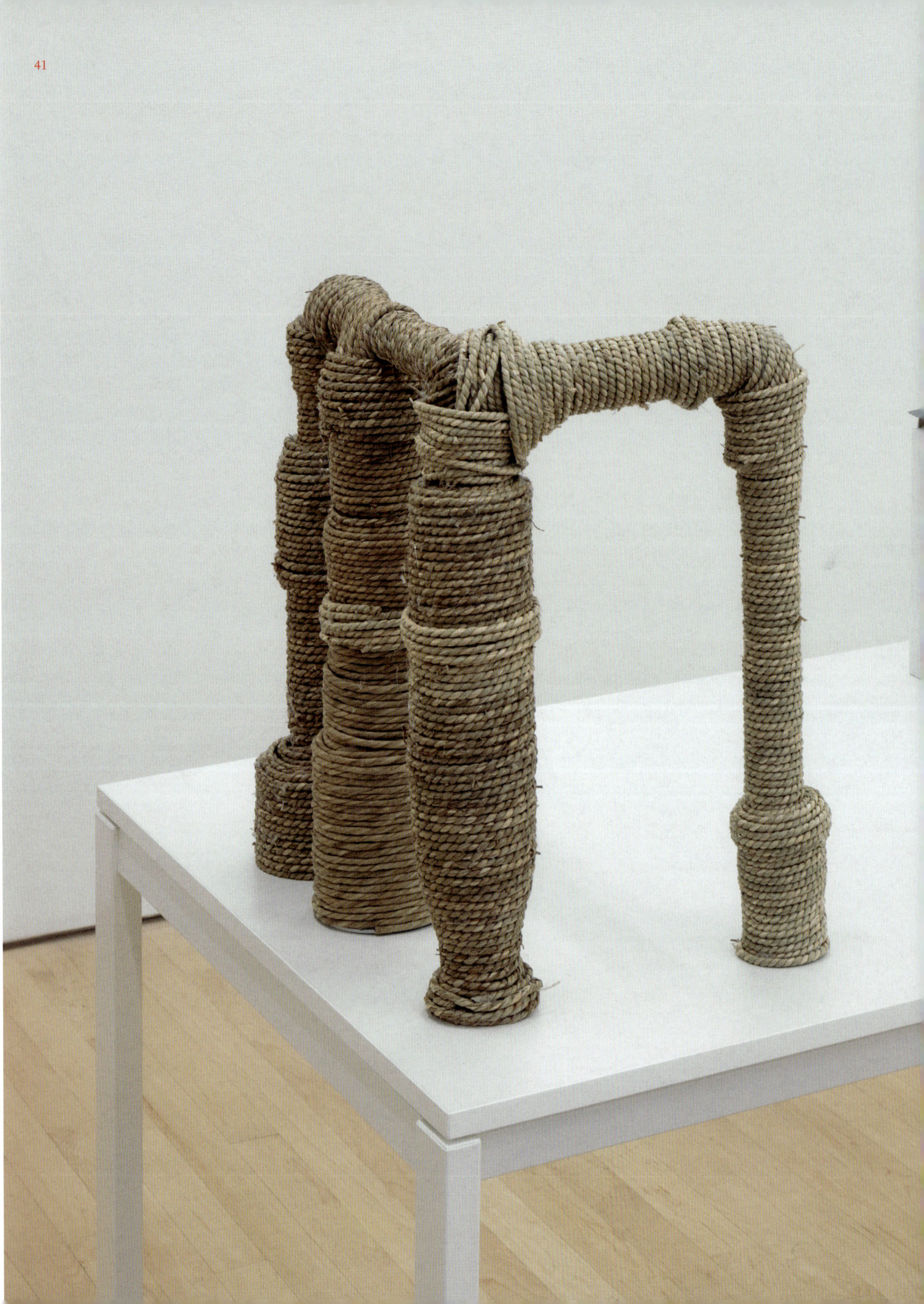

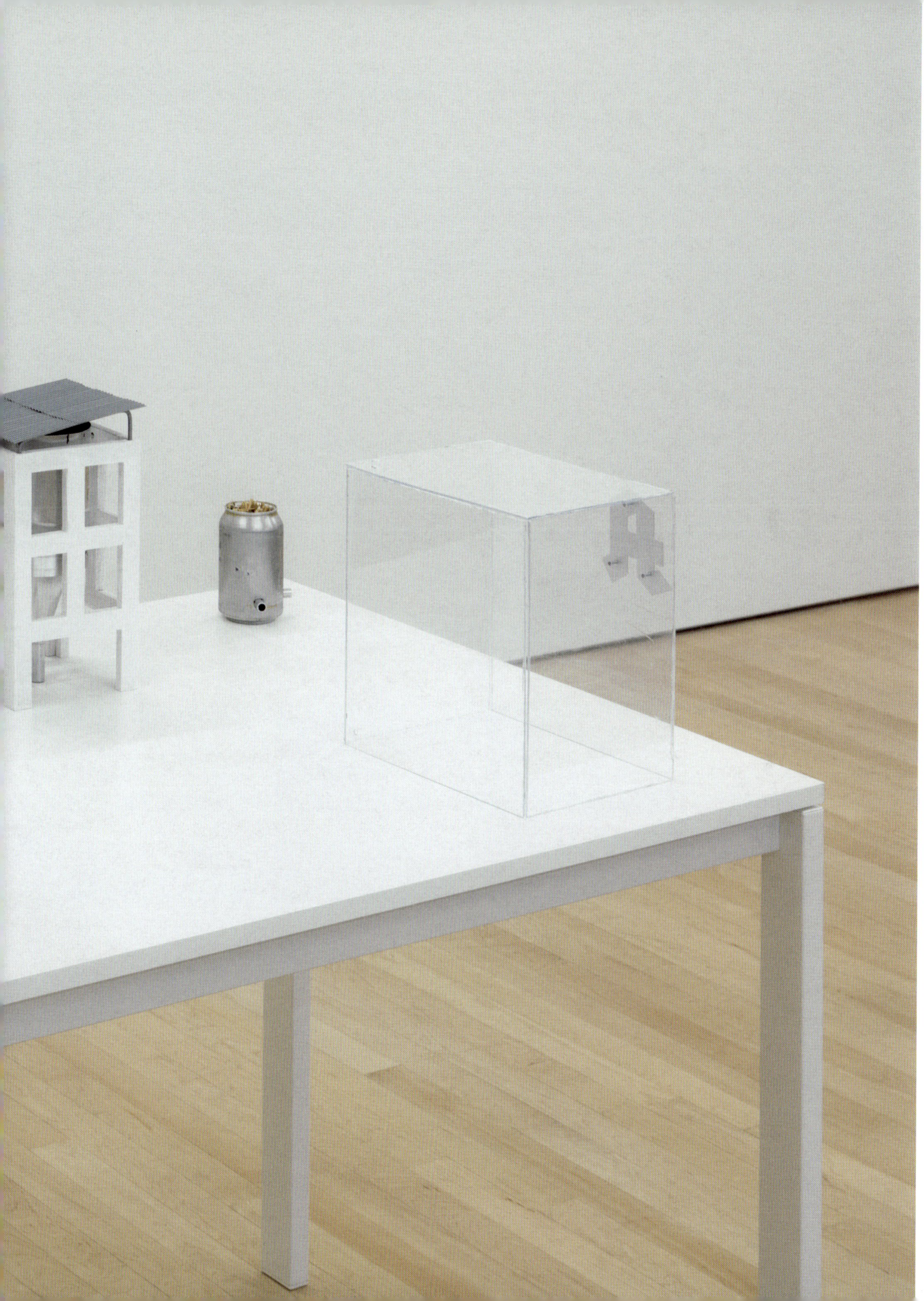

42

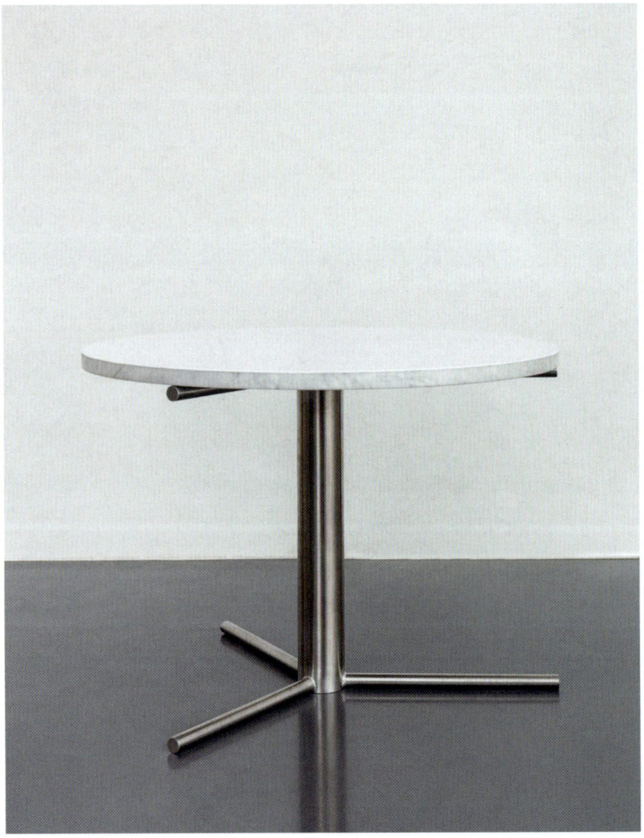

43

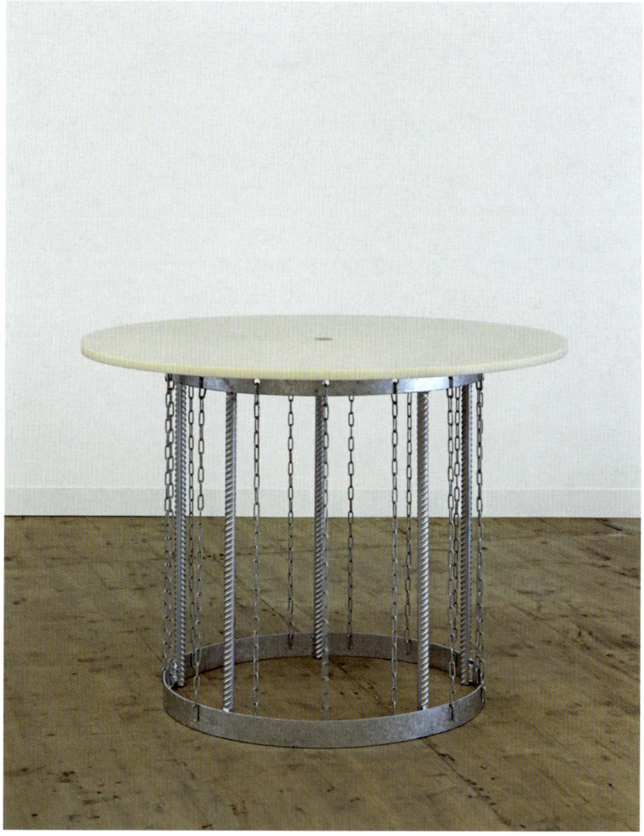

44

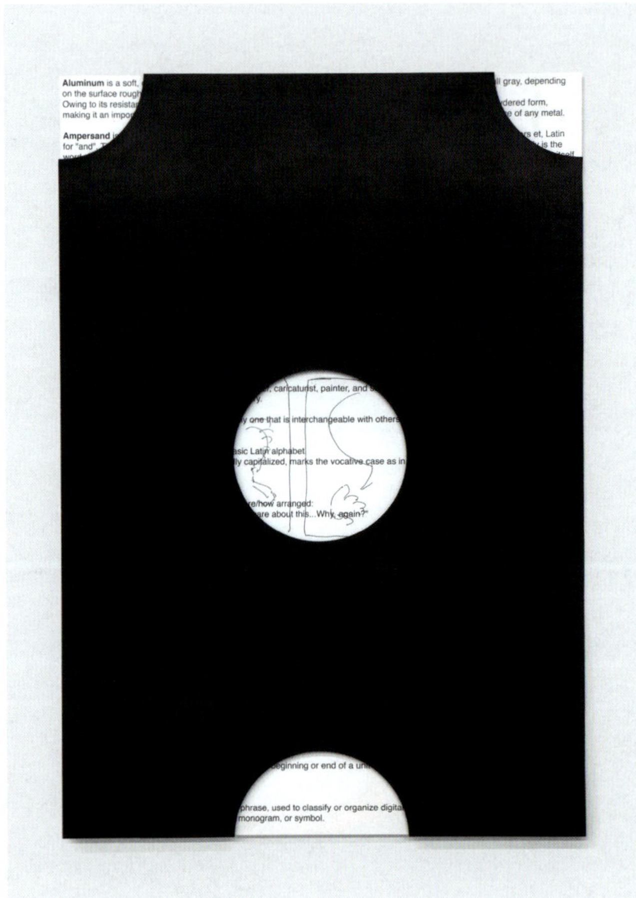

45

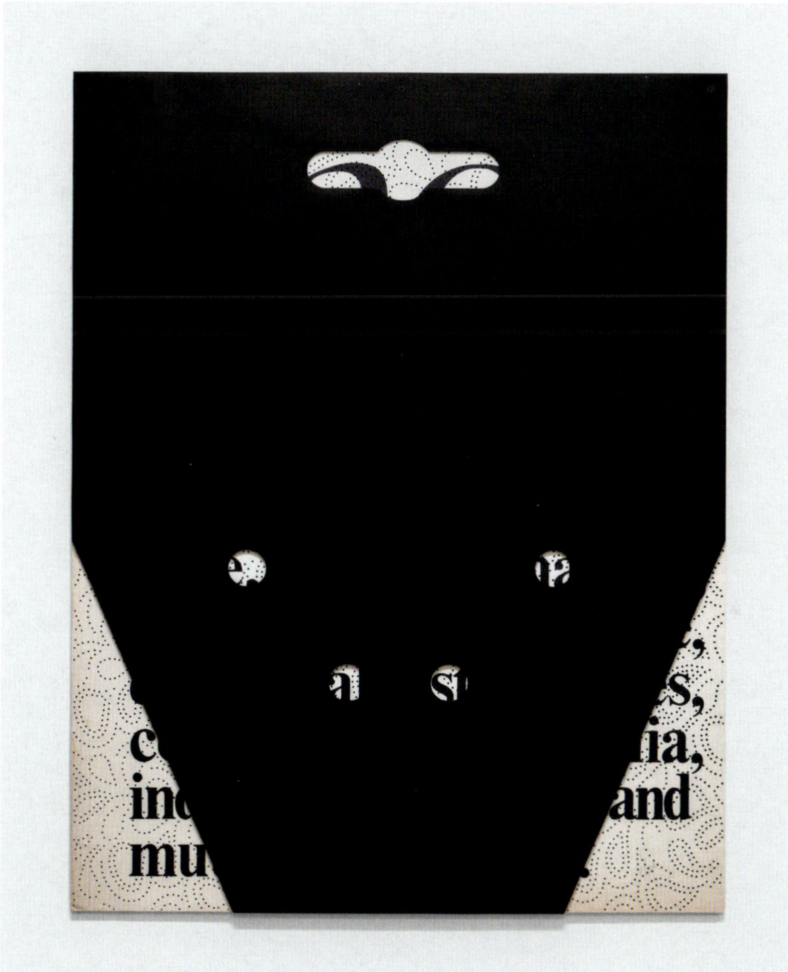

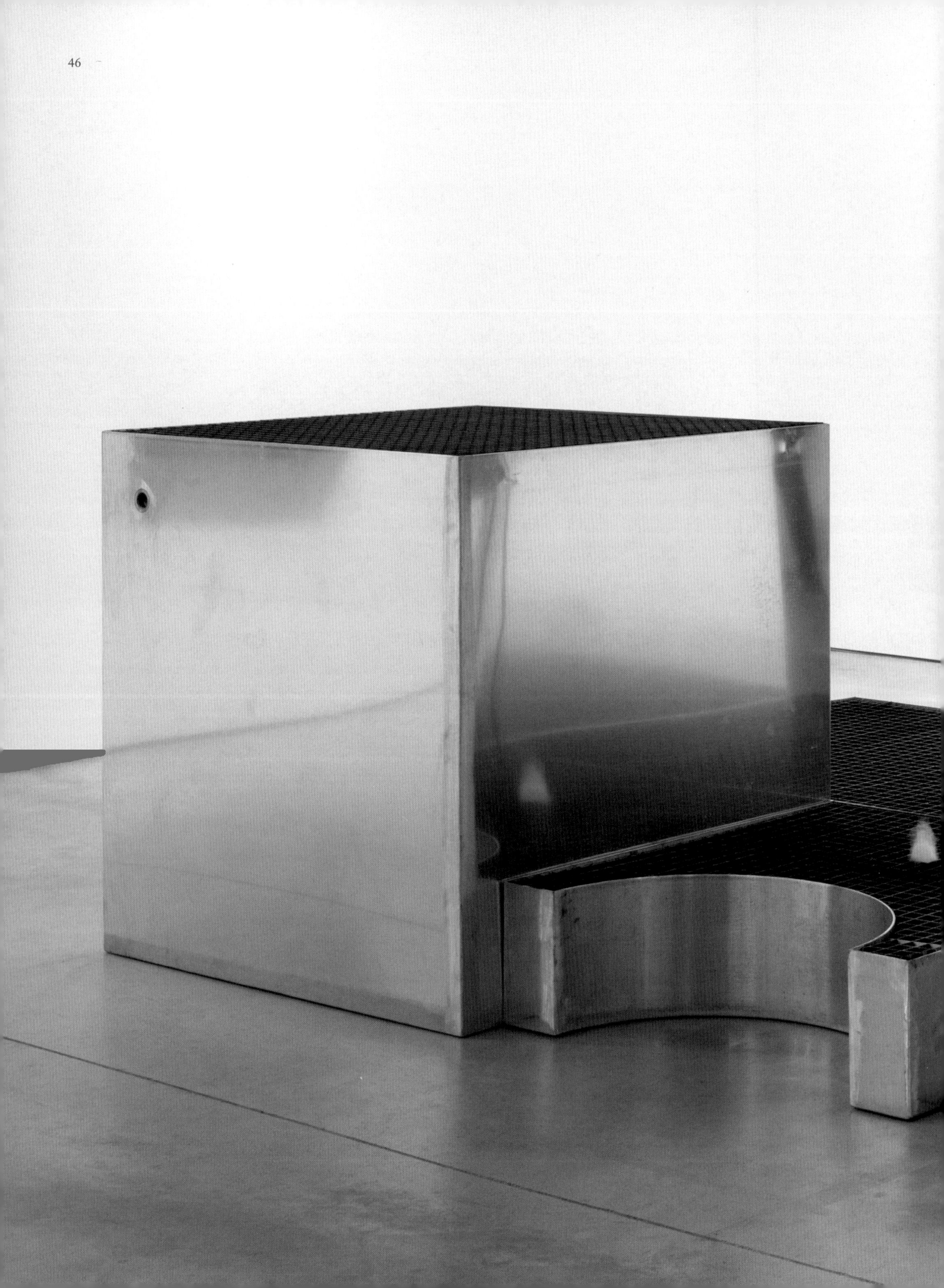

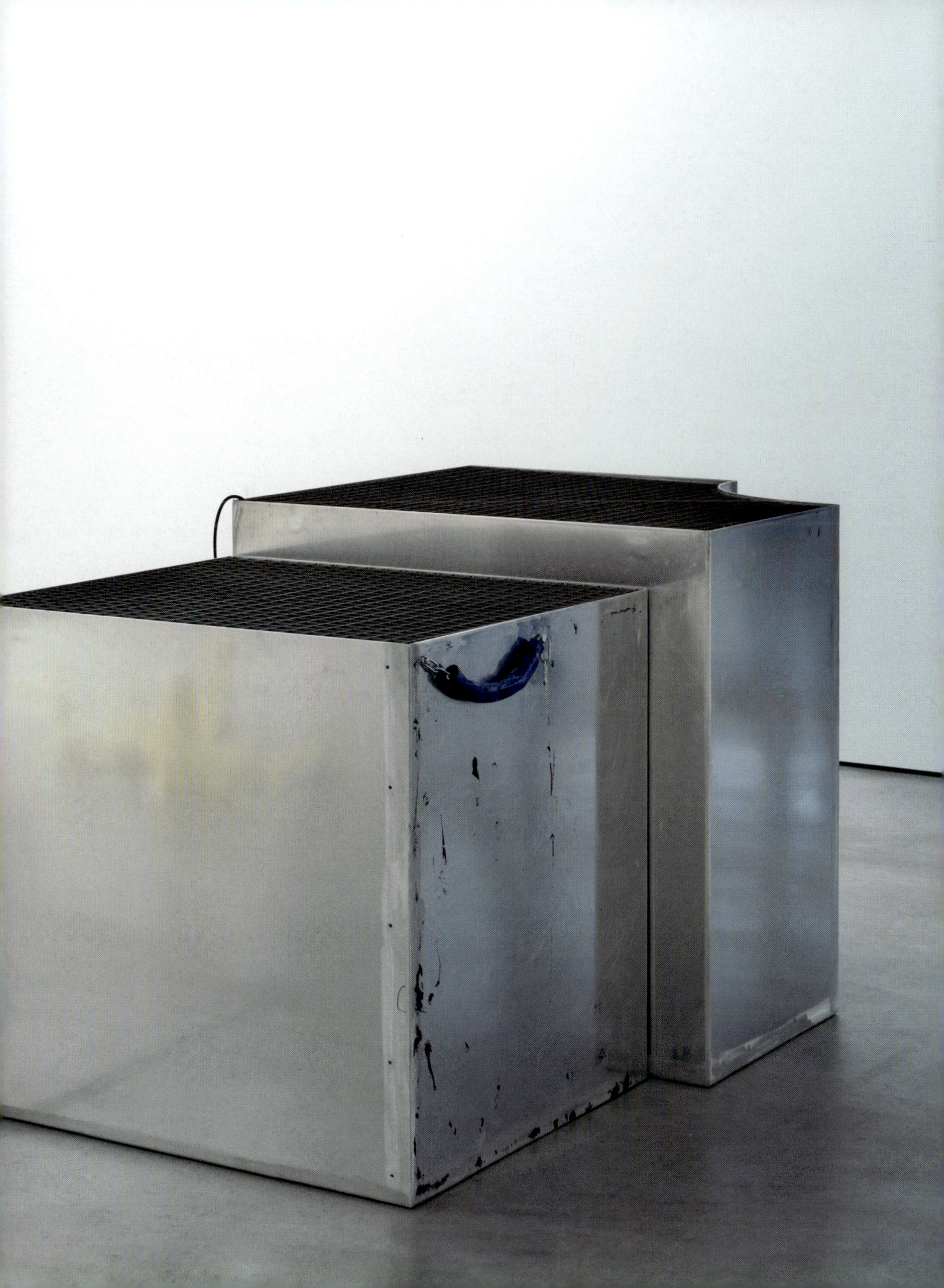

48

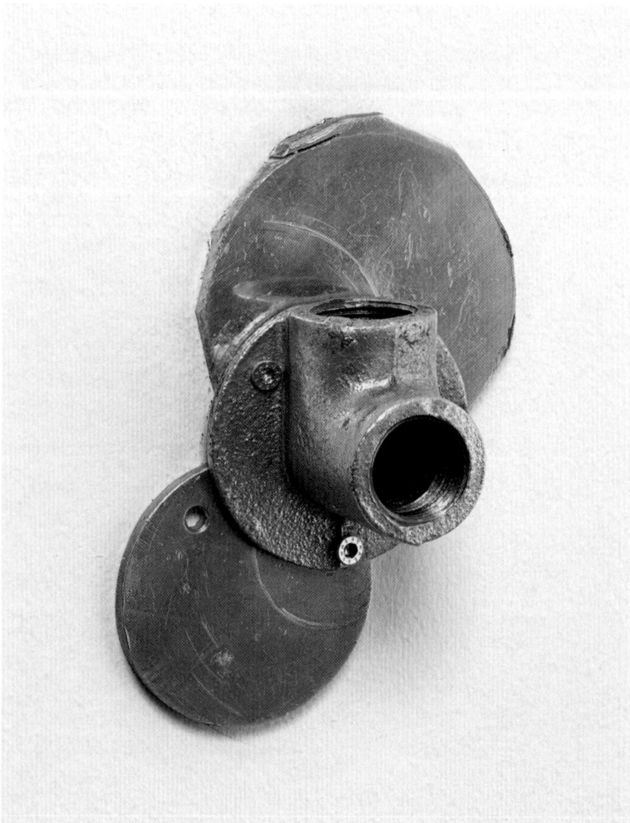

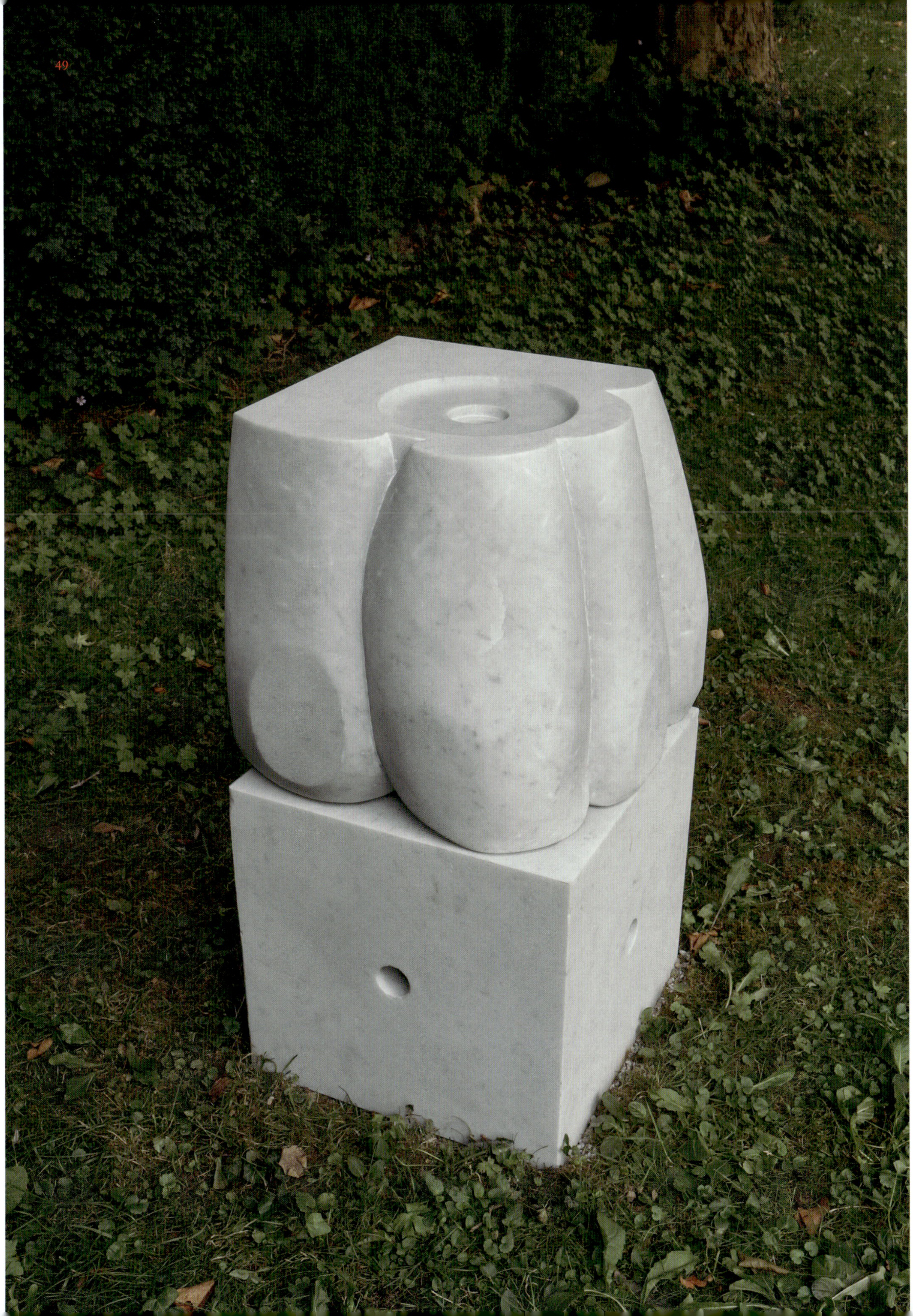

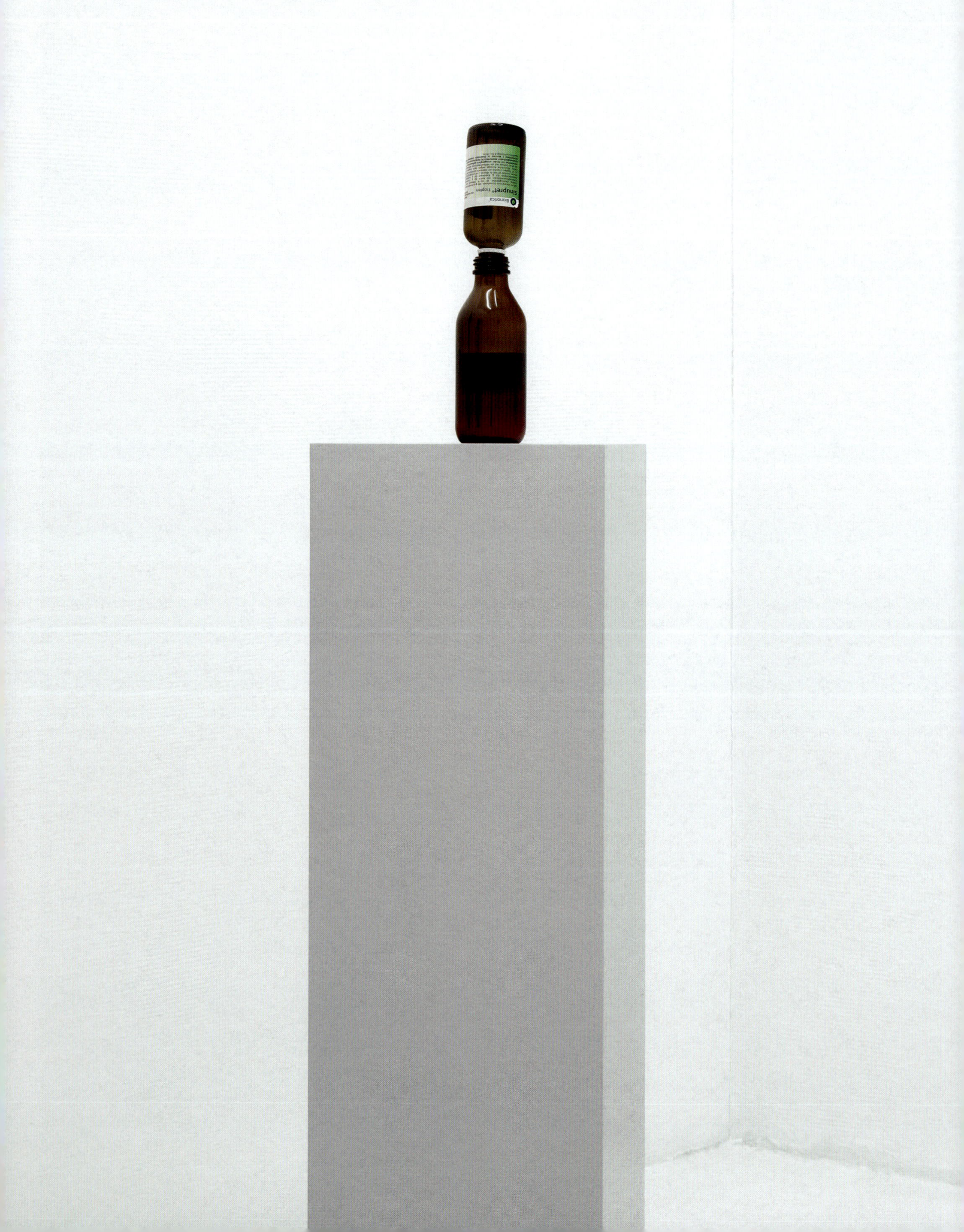

51

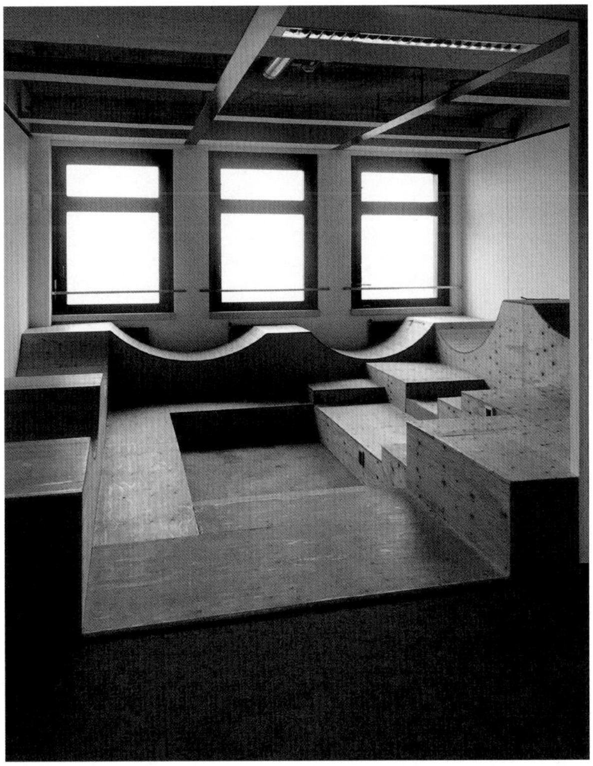

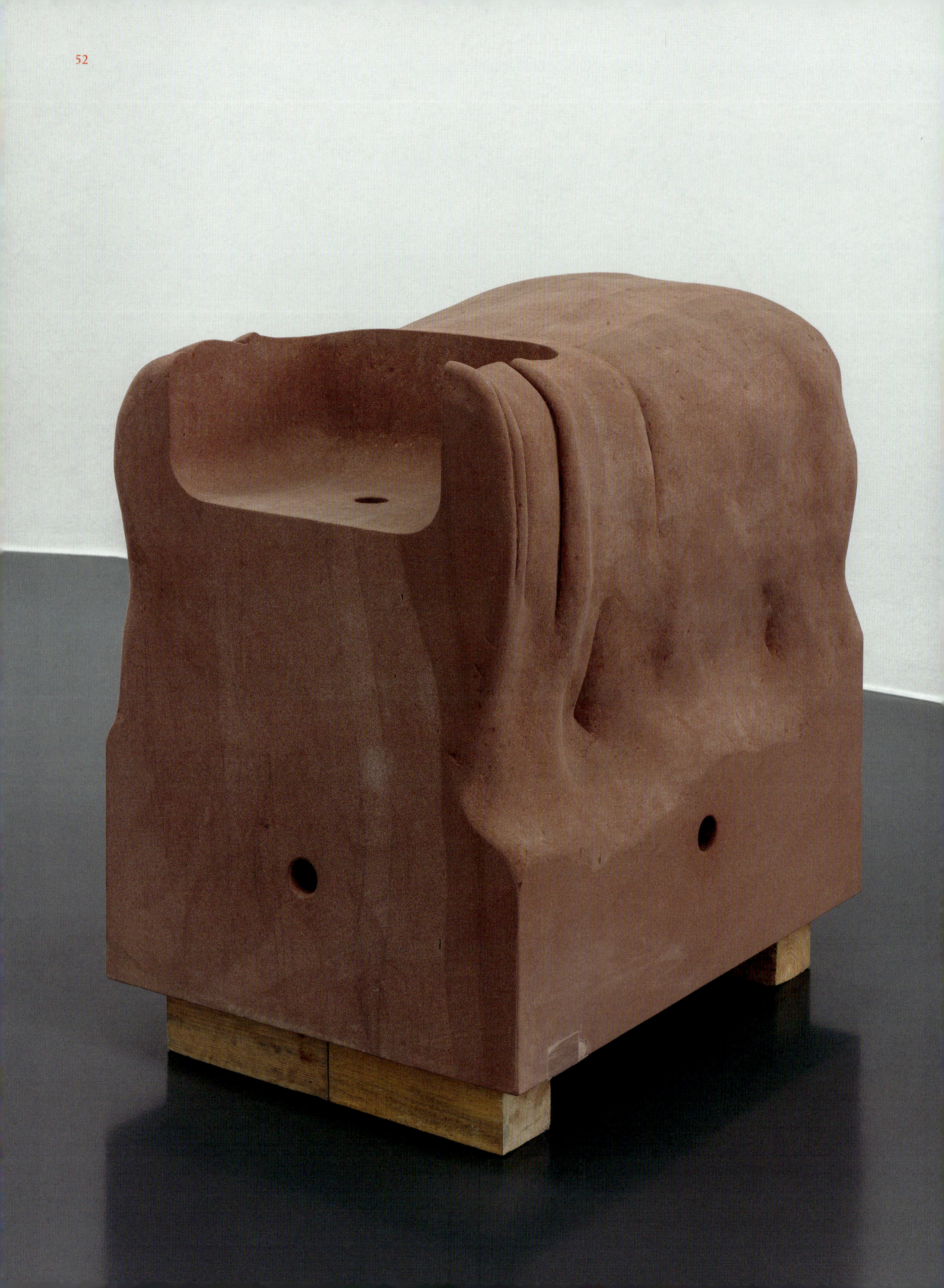

Style's Exhaustion and Forms of Class Conflict

Pujan Karambeigi

It was a big year for New York's Lower East Side. In 1935, not only did the neighborhood witness the construction of First Houses, the first public housing units ever built in the United States, but the very same New Deal policies that realized public housing also funded the building of Hamilton Fish Park Pool [54], a new public pool within walking distance from where the Black, Hispanic, and Asian communities were now supposed to take shelter. Amenities such as a high-tech filtering system, underwater lighting, blue glazed terra-cotta, scum gutters, a bathhouse with a capacity of 2,200 people, an Olympic-sized main pool, and two adjacent diving and wading tanks composed what was in 1936 a rather fancy recreational facility. In fact, in their initial form—arranged in a semicircle—the three pools created something like an air of inclusion, even if only halfway.

This was, however, only the third stage of government-implemented measures to improve the poor living conditions of the working-class neighborhood. In a way, it all started in 1900, when the architecture firm Carrère and Hastings was commissioned to develop a recreational area of what was then the degree zero of the Jewish, Irish, and Polish immigrant community in New York. The architects, who had just won the competition for the main branch of the New York Public Library [32] with their idea to build the largest marble structure in North America turned toward Paris, as was usual for the American aristocracy. Inspired by the recently built Petit Palais and its "power to educate the mind while it pleases the senses," as one contemporary noted, they conceived the area as a square for the flaneur, filled with benches presumably to read on, patches of grass not to be used, and a Beaux-Arts-style gymnasium.[1] But there was friction over the import of Parisian modernity; the Francophile architects had simply underestimated their addressee. Within a year, the formal pathways and grass grounds on which the stroller was supposed to circulate were destroyed by the immigrant workers, a silent rebellion against the pressure to be assimilated by becoming a flaneur. Realizing the need to adjust Carrère and Hastings's bourgeois hallucinations, the city authorities succumbed to the demands of Lower East Side's community and reopened the park two years later, now with basketball courts, running tracks, and tennis courts. By the time Hamilton Fish Park Pool was inaugurated on that same square three decades later, it was only the Beaux-Arts-style gymnasium that remained, now something of a symbol of the failed attempt to equate immigrant workers with drifting flaneurs.

There is a sense of this negotiation between a hallucinated audience and a real addressee, of misguided imports and failed promises, in Benjamin Hirte's video *First Houses* (2020) [117–122]. In silently accumulating the destitute residues of post-New Deal public infrastructures—trash cans, public sculptures, gates, benches, gullies, playgrounds, fences, water hydrants, and doors—the video begs the question of how to encase these conflicts in a narrative structure. As the grand form of struggle and demise, the genre of melodrama appears to be most accurate: labor versus wealth, redistribution versus inheritance; the architectural objects are enlisted as silent actors brawling along the well-known lines dividing social democracies.

These architectural objects in Hirte's video index the social-democratic configuration that constructed these invisible infrastructures in the first place: the Keynesian consensus between labor and capital, the bipartisan support for the welfare state, the four decades of steadily declining inequality and social immobility.

1 – Herbert Butler, "The Palaces of Fine Arts," *Art Journal* 41 (1901), 44.

That is to say, what we get to see in *First Houses* is also what many of these objects have witnessed over time. By the time the Lower East Side "had become a congregating spot for drug dealers," as the *Times* reported in 1984 of Hamilton Fish Park Pool, New York's infamous 1975 fiscal crisis had shifted the power dynamics decisively, giving the melodramatic tale its necessary spin toward demise: debt was successfully weaponized to foster privatization and the dismantling of the welfare state, providing the first stages of a narrative we are all too familiar with.[2] In fact, there is a feeling that *First Houses* relays the immense distance separating us from a blossoming social democracy not yet cornered by the conservative counterrevolution of the 1980s and its austerity politics.

But how to look back at these residues of the welfare state without employing the by now well-rehearsed playbook of the social-democratic melodrama?

53

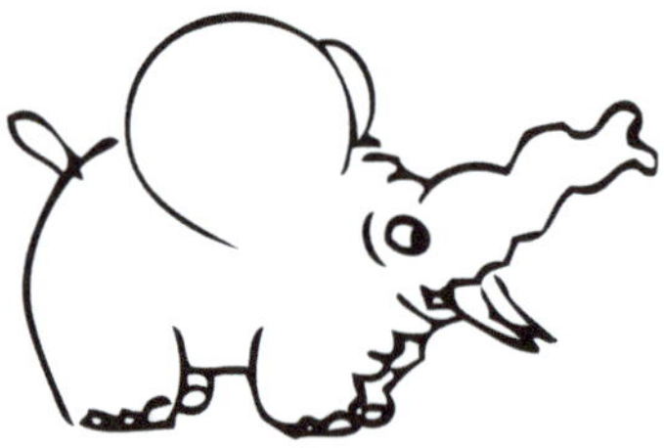

Hirte's red sandstone sculptures *Fountain for Erdbergstrasse* (2019) [52, 115] and *The Encounter* (2022) [58, 60] offer some hints. Based on *Nilpferd mit Jungem* (1963) [106] by Rudolf Schmidt, a hippo sculpture that is part of a historic *Gemeindebau* (social housing project) in Vienna's third district, as well as on the ubiquitous civic fountains surrounding those buildings, *Erdbergstrasse* reassembles two realities of public sculpture by transfiguring them into one suture-less unit that is cut in half. In *The Encounter*, a drain is also visible, but the way the cut operates is different. Instead of half an animal, we see what could be part of an arm with a slightly rolled-up sleeve and hints of two torsos and two buttocks. The violence of the cut is here replaced by the softness of two bodies rubbing against each other, the fragment of an expression of solidarity or conflict. The hole inserted in the tiny slot in between the two bodies then does the magical trick of filling space by emptying it out. This is less about the idea of the fountain, as in *Erdbergstrasse*, than that of a street gutter that absorbs rainwater—one that clogs in the fall when leaves fall from the trees. *The Encounter* thus appears to be a fragment of something that is not standing up but lying on the ground, waiting to be looked down upon. And even more than *Fountain for Erdbergstrasse*, *The Encounter* appears to deliberately reference the figurative language of the myriad public sculptures that were built between 1923 and 1934—the phase, usually designated as Red Vienna, when the Social Democratic government employed 190 architects who built over 400 *Gemeindebauten* [100, 101], managing to drastically improve the precarious living conditions of 200,000 from the working classes, often people who had only recently migrated from the rural periphery to the capital. But what is this recourse to the style of a long bygone era supposed to remind us of? Why provide a sectional cut, like in *Erdbergstrasse*, or a fragment, like in *The Encounter*, from a scene whose exact contours remain somewhat obscure? Are these the first two letters in a kind of alphabet of style? And are we, in turn, supposed to use these figurations in stone to piece together the world that they came from, making words out of letters, sentences out of words, and stories out of sentences?

In the case of the Gemeindebauten, the idea of style has a complicated legacy—frowned upon by intellectuals on both the Right and the Left. Manfredo Tafuri,

2 – Shawn G. Kennedy, "A Beaux Arts Playland on Houston St.," *New York Times*, January 8, 1984.

a Marxist who is often credited with being the most influential architectural historian of the twentieth century, famously designated these buildings as the emanation of an "exhaustion of style."[3] What he meant was that rather than following the modernist dogmas of "transparent construction" and abolition of ornament, as theorized by the Bauhaus, the Viennese Gemeindebauten veer toward a liberal pluralism that manifests itself in, among other things, eclectic facades that are too expressive, too monumental, too petit bourgeois, too symmetrical.

One of the guiding schools behind the Gemeindebauten was the Wagner School (named after the Austrian architect Otto Wagner), which openly criticized its Weimar peers about their rationalist modernism and their celebration of Taylorized forms such as serialization, standardization, and typification, as described in Eve Blau's *The Architecture of Red Vienna, 1919–1934*.[4] This antagonism is most palpable in the Wagner School's reliance on vernacular ornamentation that was first developed in the so-called Biedermeier style of the early nineteenth century and was then translated into the architecture of Red Vienna. These vernacular ornaments, understood as both regionally specific and historically formed, were supposed to convey domestic, anti-individualist family values, thus becoming media for channeling a continuation of the past rather than for preaching a dramatic rupture from it, as so many of the Wagner School's antagonists were doing. At least on the surface, the somewhat contested goal was to reconcile proletarian and Biedermeier (that is, petit bourgeois) values rather than pitting them against each other.

Architecturally, one effect of this vernacular focus was that the Wagner School distinguished neatly between core and surface, or between structure and facade (Otto Wagner himself designated the latter as a building's *Bekleidung*, or clothing, as if it were a kind of garment). This distinction afforded a division of labor whereby architects basically left slots within building complexes that could then be *bekleidet* (dressed), so to speak, by sculptors, resulting in the vast array of realist figurations surrounding the Gemeindebauten.

At the time, one of the most interesting defenses of the Wagner School's project came from the Marxist economist, museum director, and historian Otto Neurath[53]. After being the president of the Central Office of Economics for the Munich Workers' Council, which led the economic reform of the short-lived revolutionary government in Bavaria in 1919, Neurath moved to Vienna and became a prominent participant in the lively debates around urbanism. He composed an unrealized *Generalarchitekturplan* (general architecture plan)—which he conceived together with Adolf Loos and Oskar Strnad, and which would later serve as the blueprint for many of the megastructures built in the 1970s in Vienna (such as the Wohnpark Alt-Erlaa)—and he wrote numerous articles throughout the 1920s on urban development in which he addressed the romanticism of the vanguard (for instance, by chiding Bauhaus pioneer Peter Behrens for his "Würfelromantik").[5]

One of the most instructive of these critical articles is Neurath's "Rationalism, Working Class, and Building Form," in which he argues that the vanguardism of Bauhaus, Neue Sachlichkeit, and Constructivism "seems satisfied to make a spectacle of rationalism rather than to strive for a deeper engagement with its principle," thus

3 – Manfredo Tafuri, "Das Rote Wien," in *Vienna Rossa: La politica residenziale nella Vienna socialista, 1919–1933*, ed. Manfredo Tafuri (Milan: Electa, 1980), 134. Translation my own.

4 – Eve Blau, *The Architecture of Red Vienna, 1919–1934* (Cambridge, MA: MIT Press, 1999).

5 – Quoted in Blau, *Architecture*, 374. The original source is Otto Neurath to Franz Roh, letter, June 14, 1924, Roh Collection, GRI.

54

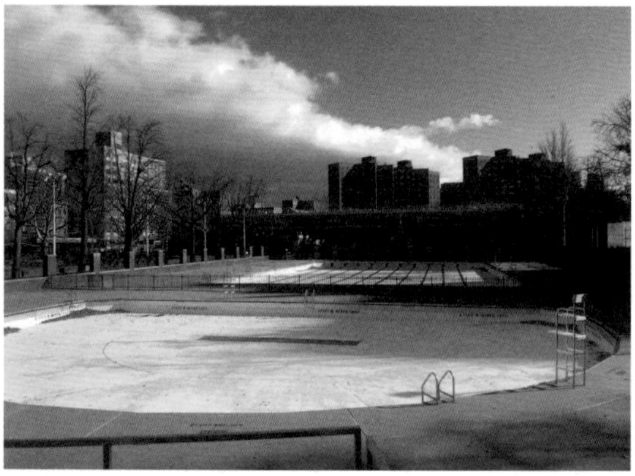

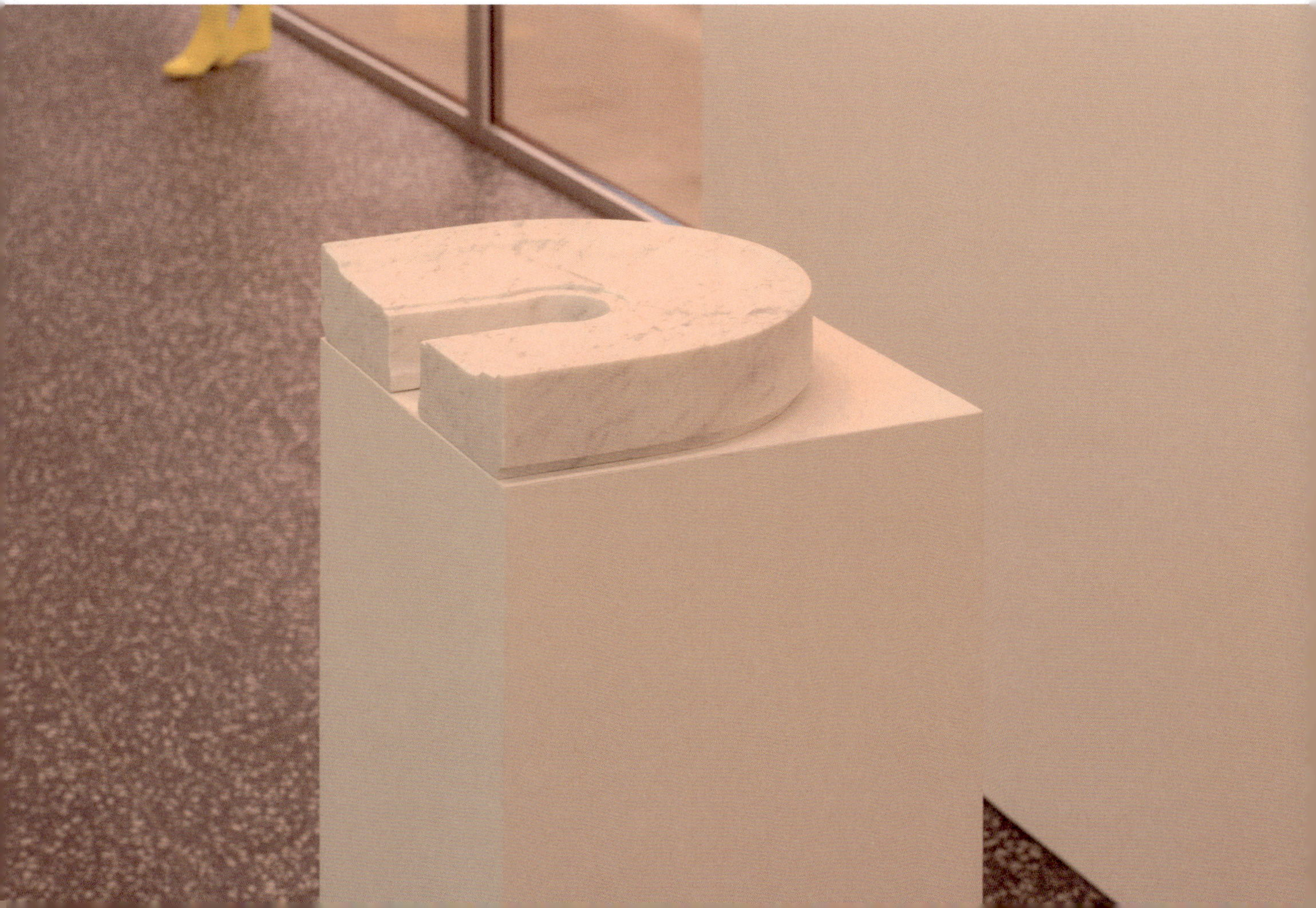

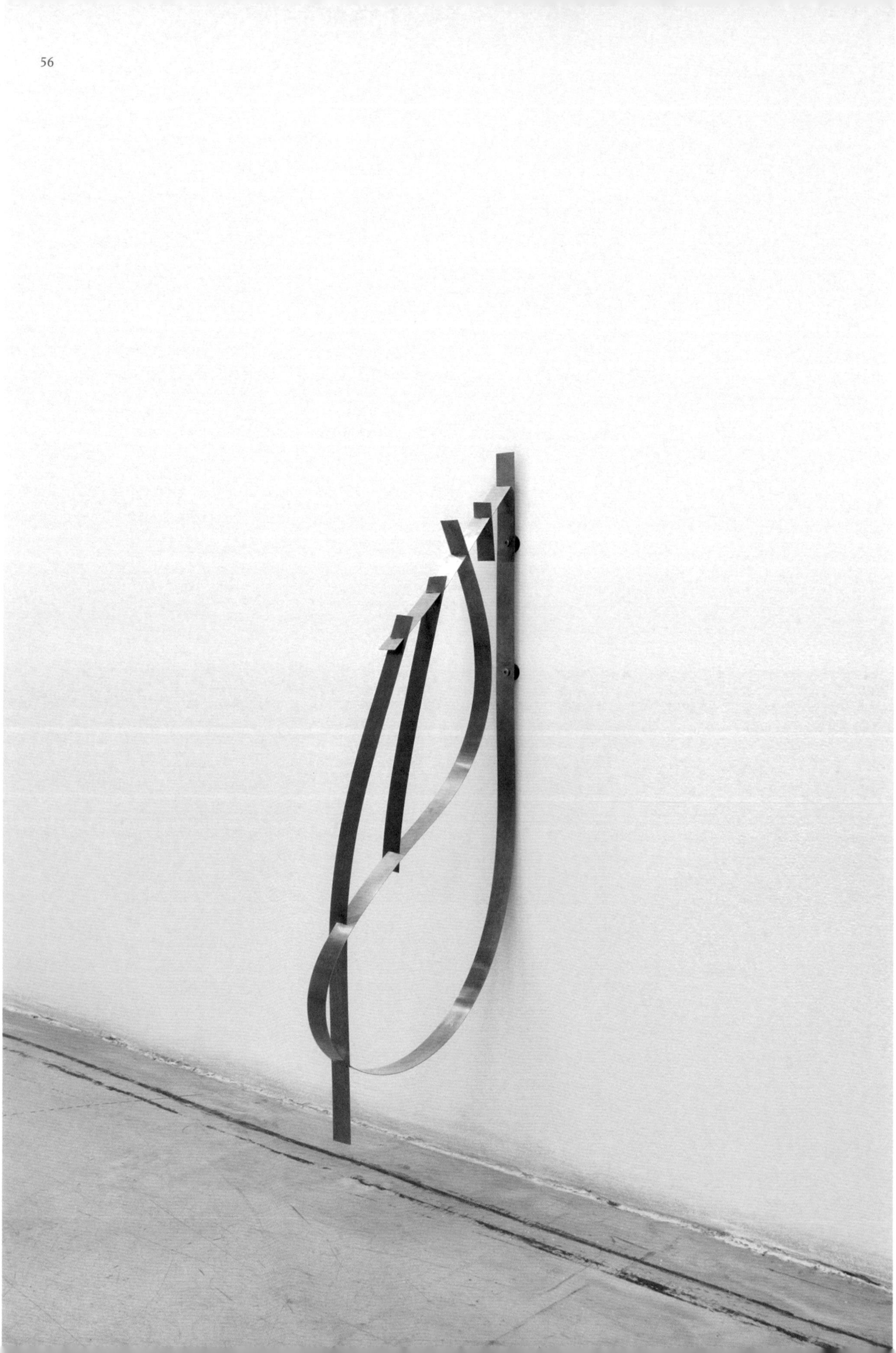

becoming a "romanticism that evades reality."[6] The point is crucial: just because it looks like rationalism—for instance, the presence of cubical glass windows framed by steel structures, thus mimicking the production methods of the Taylorized factory—does not mean that it follows what was at the time discussed as the "rationality of the proletariat." In this way, the vanguardist rhetoric to declare the difference between surface and structure obsolete may be understood as a confusion of terms, a sleight of hand by which the newly forming middle classes were transfiguring the logic of capital (Taylorization) into being the logic of the proletariat: rationalist surface was simply mystifying rationalist structure.

What is this proletarian rationality, then, and where can one find it according to Neurath? Structurally, there are two major differences between the Viennese Gemeindebauten and their German counterparts, the *Siedlungen* proposed in the numerous Werkbund exhibitions of the 1920s. For one, as much as the German modernists were surrounding themselves in their works with the rhetoric of Taylorism and prefabrication technologies, their solutions tended to be much more expensive and thus did not really address the proletariat they were aiming to educate aesthetically. By contrast, in the Gemeindebauten prefabrication technologies were only used for staircases, doors, and windows. For the facades and interiors, labor-intensive (rather than capital-intensive) production methods such as stucco-covered bearing-wall constructions, glazed tiles, and ornamental brick and metalwork were deliberately used. These elements were thus both materials and symbolic references to craft labor, since they were embedded in an ambitious employment program whose first priority was to use the state's capacities to ensure stable wages.

The German *Siedlungen* by the Werkbund advocated a highly individualistic lifestyle. The buildings were often outside cities and were not well-connected to urban spaces, and they thus prepared the ground for the exodus to the suburbs and their single-family homes—as occurred in the post-war decades in many industrialized nations—a process that would ultimately legitimize the defunding of public housing structures like First Houses, turning them into infrastructures of abandonment, as they are known today. Unlike the *Siedlungen*, the Gemeindebauten were explicitly designed to foster collectivity. Laundries, bathhouses, libraries, theaters, kindergartens, carpentry shops, cinemas, and clinics were all located within the Gemeindebauten, which thus drastically differed from the single-use constructions of the modernist vanguard. This collective aspect was spatially dramatized by turning the previously private interior of the blocks into semipublic spaces. Not neatly segregated into functional and individual zones, urban life, through the Gemeindebauten, was supposed to consistently reproduce collectivity.

So, let's return to the question posed by Hirte's *The Encounter*: in scaling up the details of Red Vienna's attachment to a kind of realist figuration, it is certainly something of a tentative reminder of the style wars of the interwar period, an allegorical allusion to a moment when form and politics had not been so neatly separated into distinct spheres. Red Vienna's sticking to the skilled labor of realism can here be understood not so much as a reactionary holding out against the modernist fetish for automation but, first and foremost, as part of a larger struggle against the attempt to split up production processes (and thus render labor cheaper, more precarious, and more easily replaceable, etc.). But in providing only a fragment, basically compressing

6 – Otto Neurath, "Rationalismus, Arbeiterklasse, und Gebäudeform," *Aufbau* (May 1926): 52.

the form of the class war into a stony excerpt, *The Encounter* stages the world of the Gemeindebauten as something irretrievable. Somewhat parallel to the melancholic melodrama of *First Houses, The Encounter* hints at a world whose relation to the present is tenuous at best. And yet, the melancholy is held at bay by the functional and figurative ambiguities of the fragments in both *The Encounter* and *Erdbergstrasse*. Where does the hippo's torso end and its throat begin in the latter sculpture? Is the *Fountain for Erdbergstrasse* supposed to source water like a fountain, or channel it like a drain, or contain it like a basin? Maybe the sculpture suggests that water, just like power, prefers to trickle down. How and where distribution is organized, however, remains part of the conflict to recompose our public infrastructures.

57

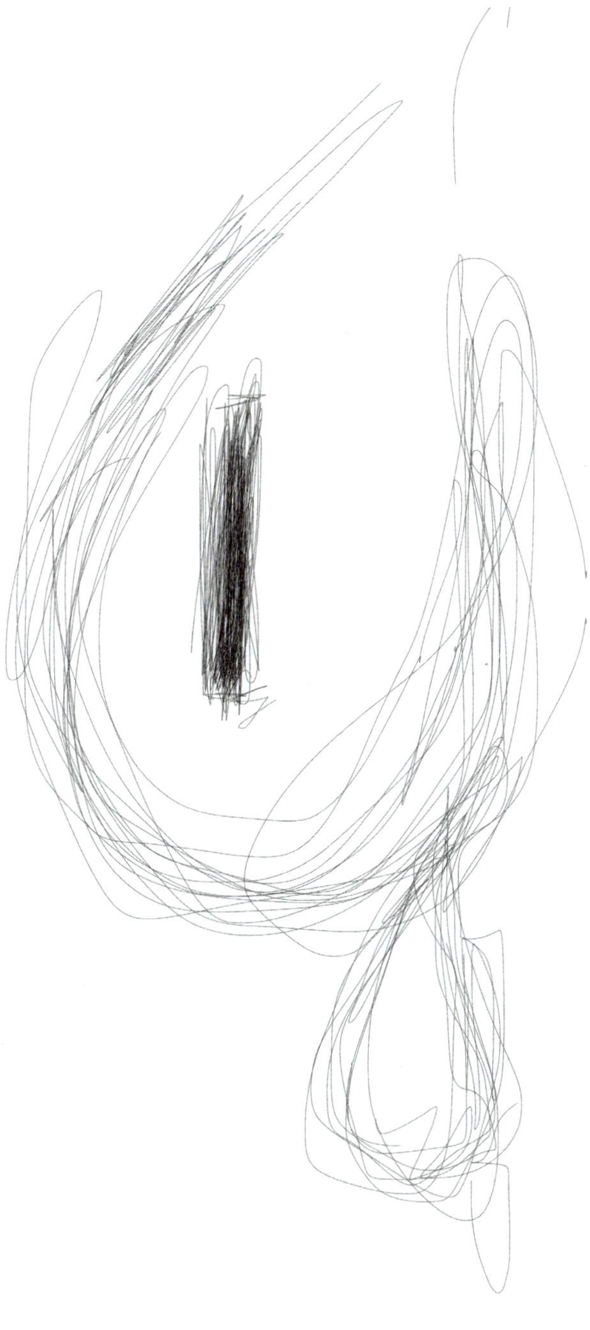

58

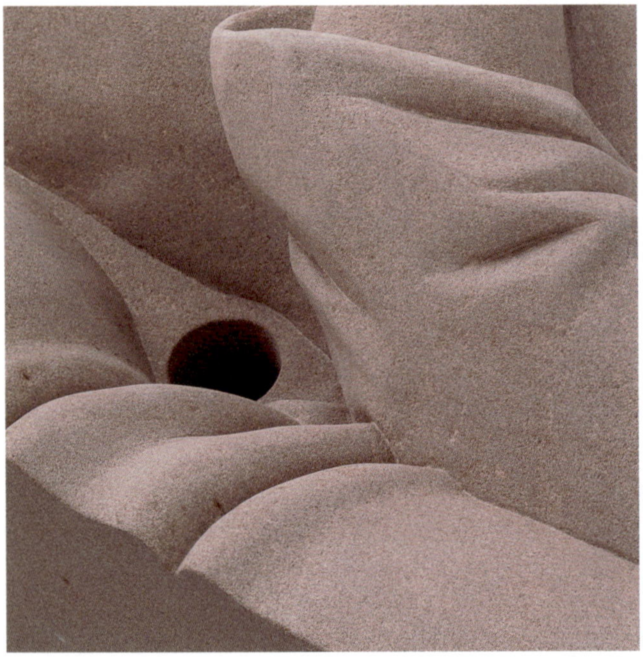

59

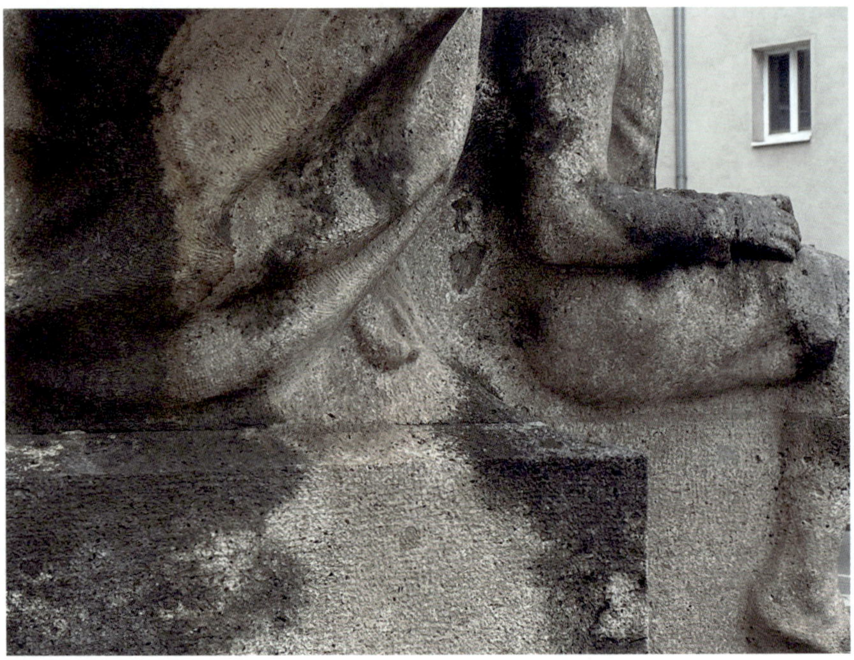

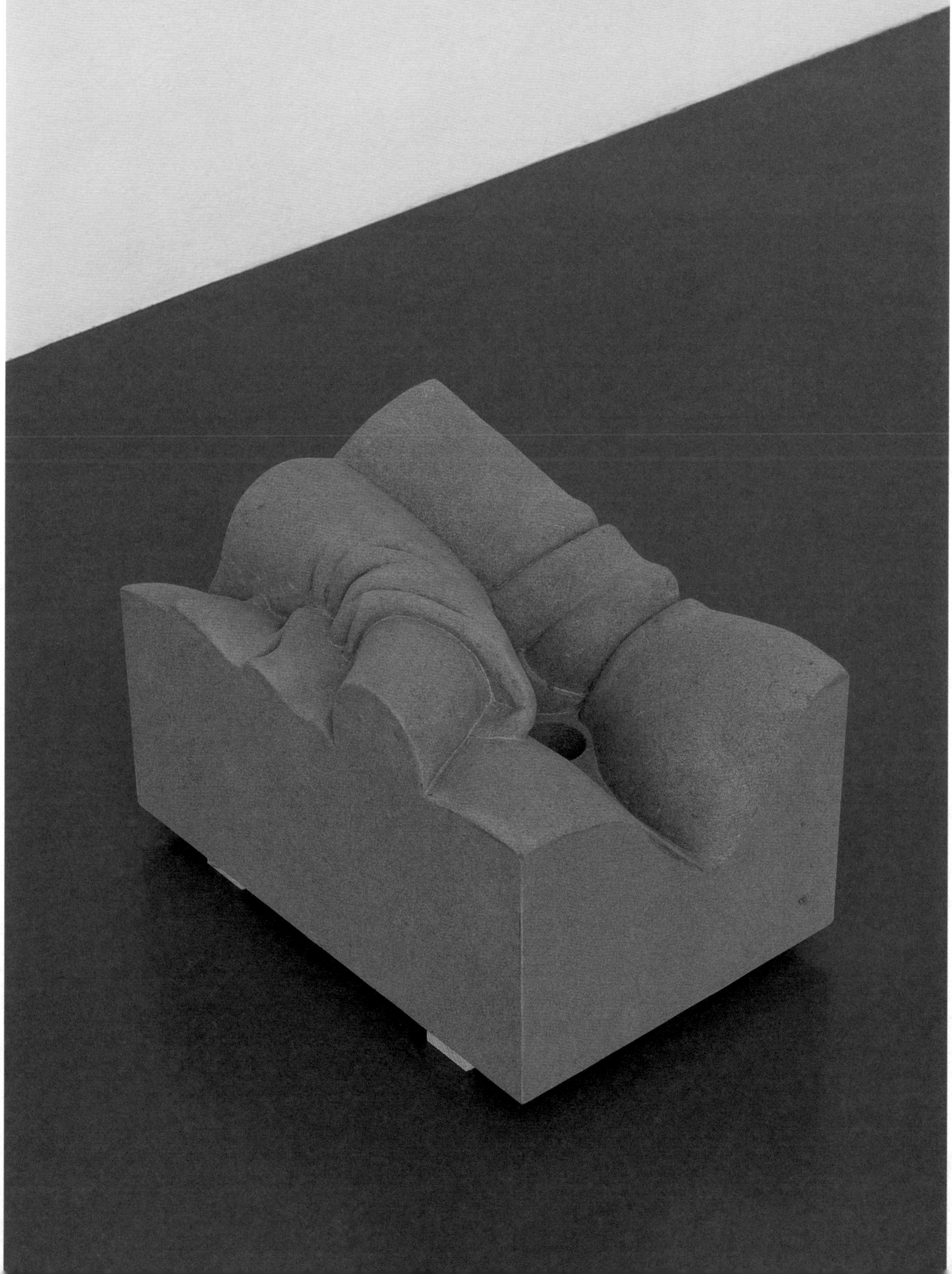

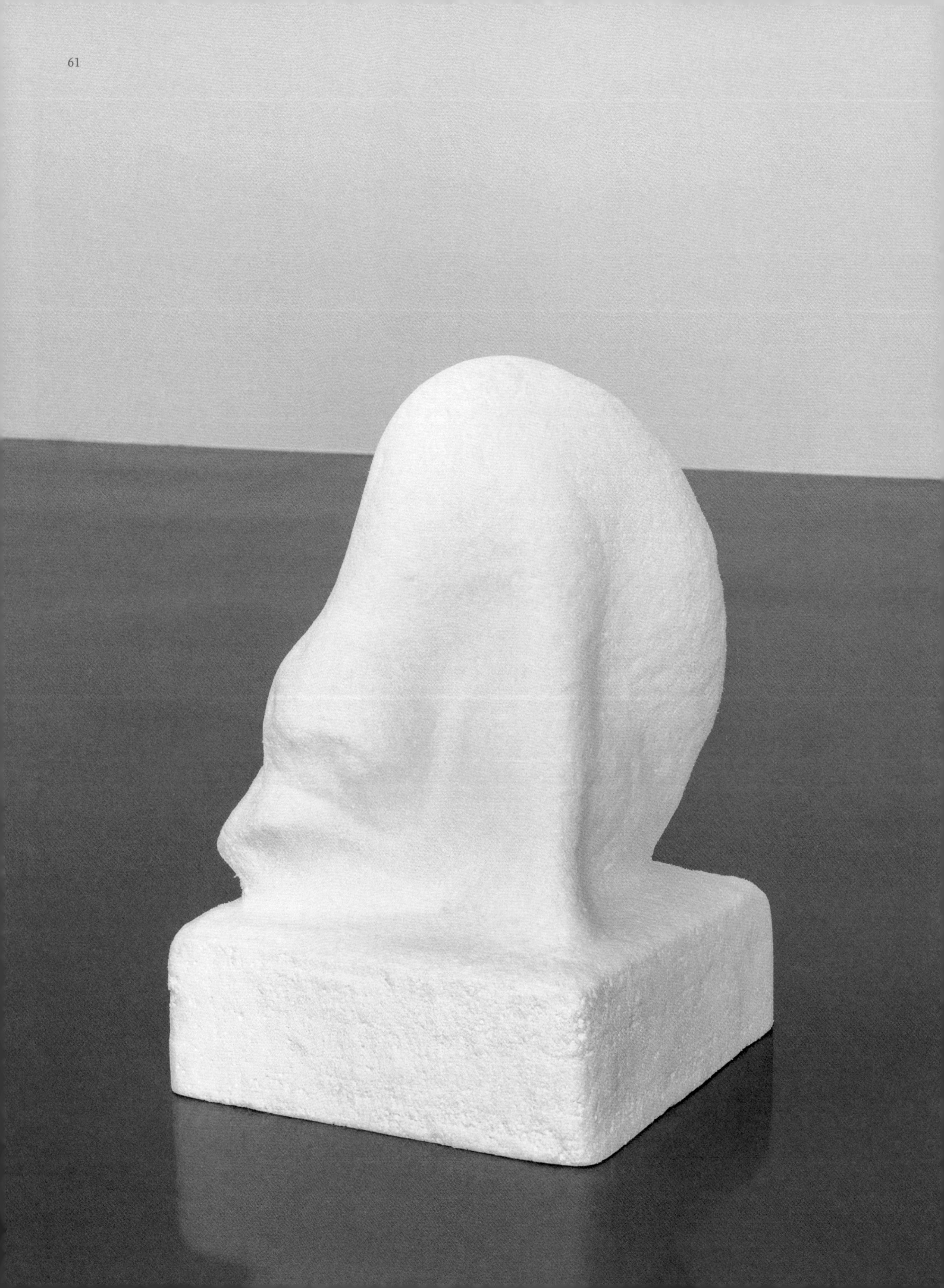

62

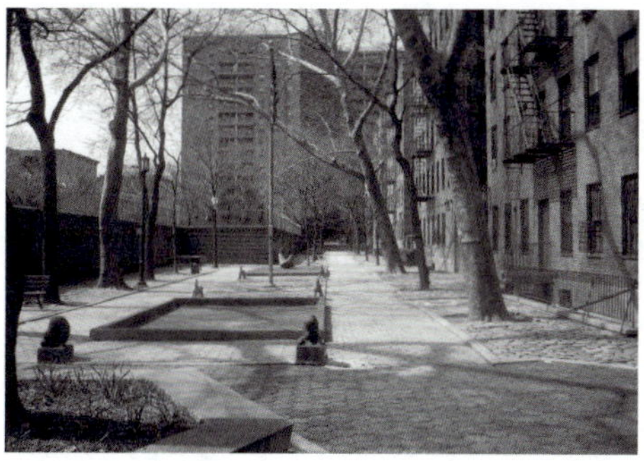

63

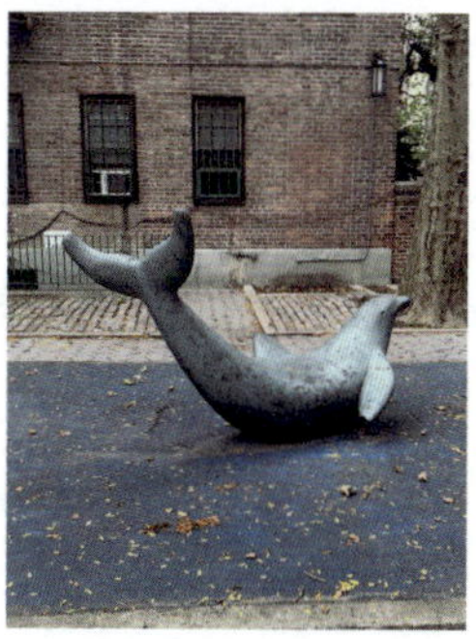

64

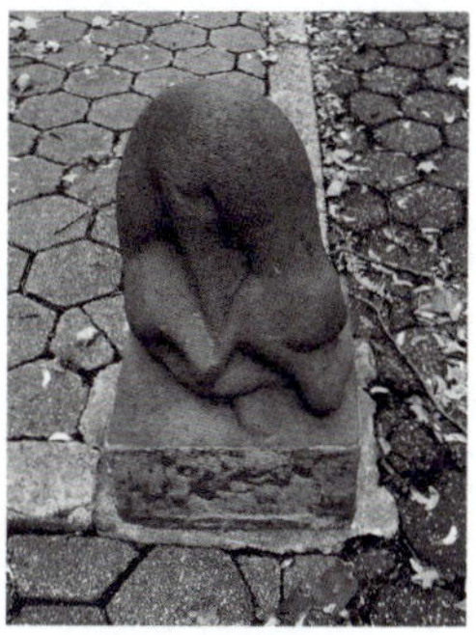

65

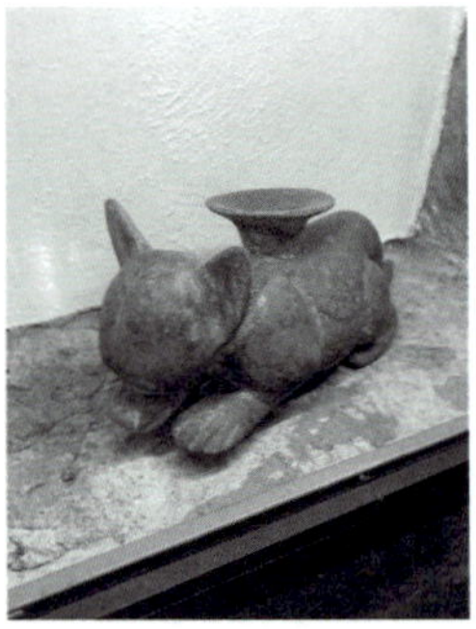

66

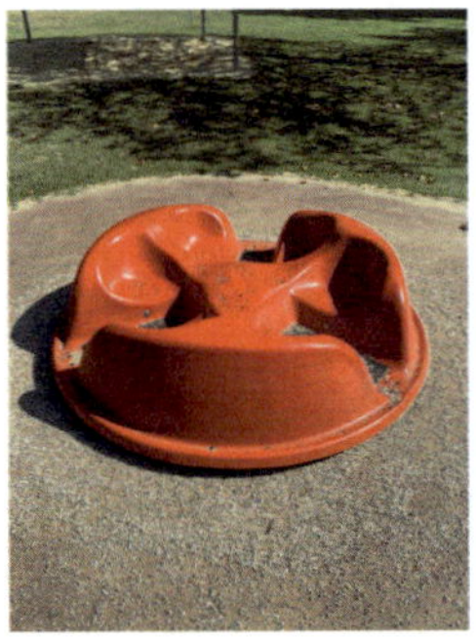

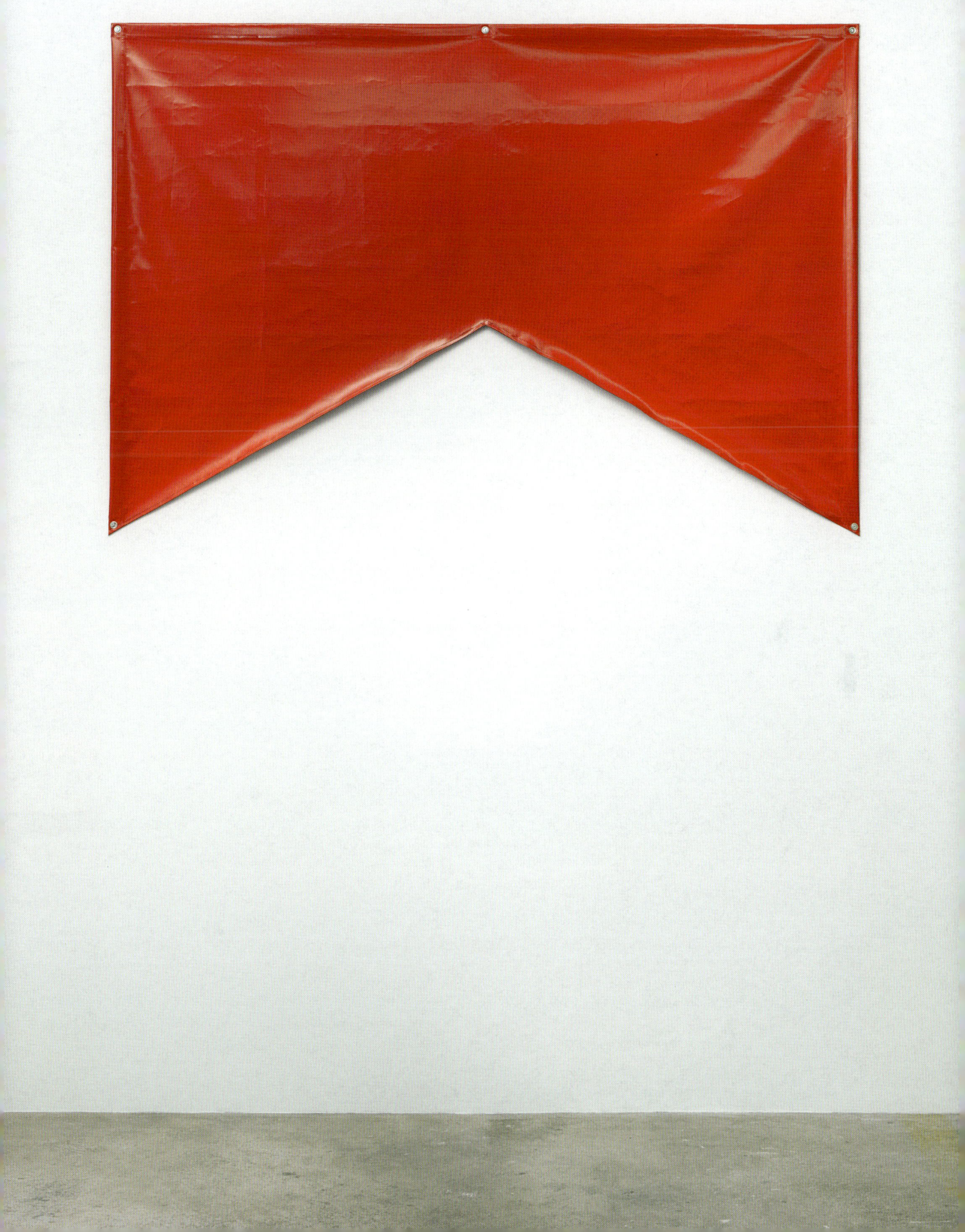

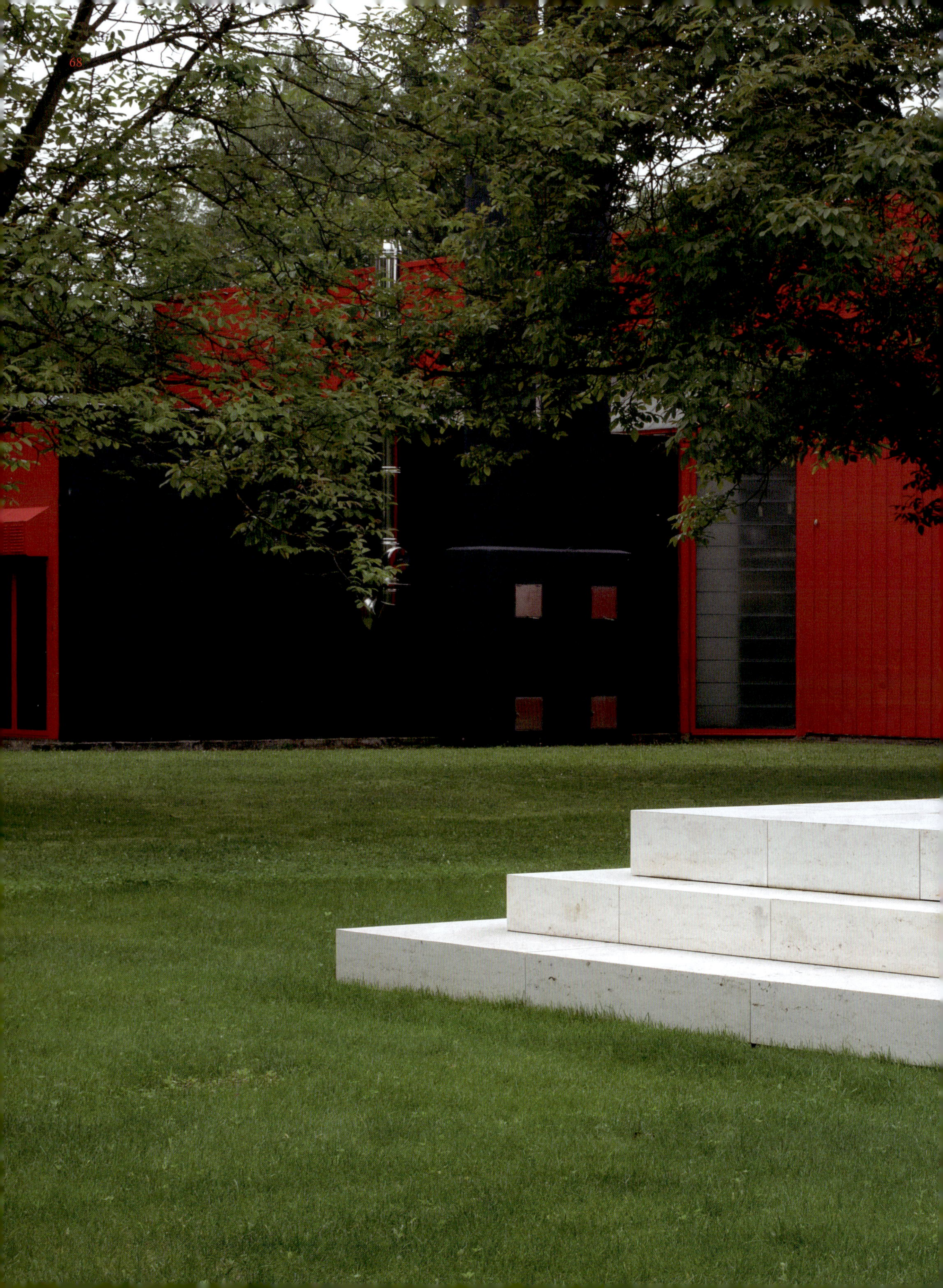

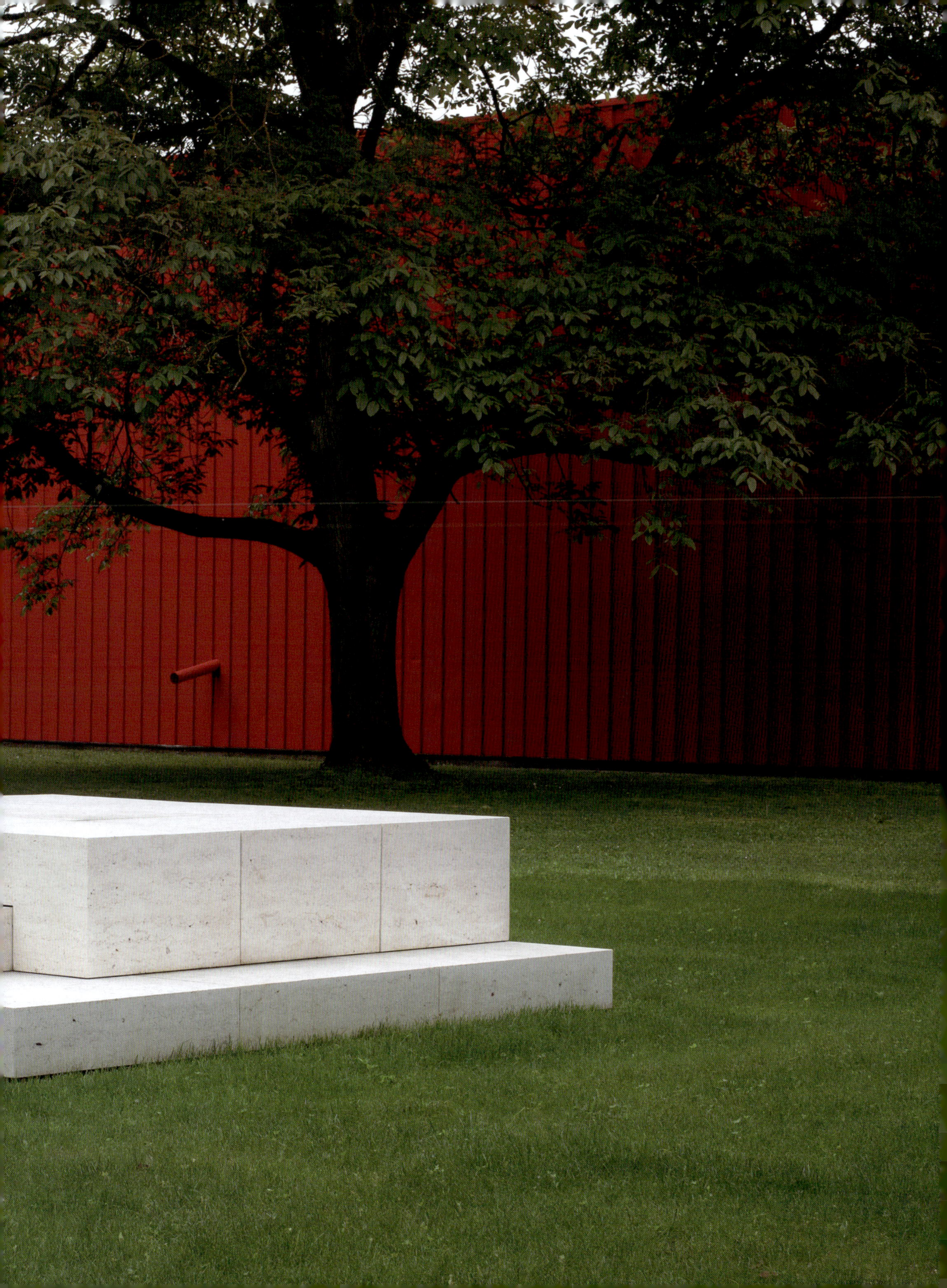

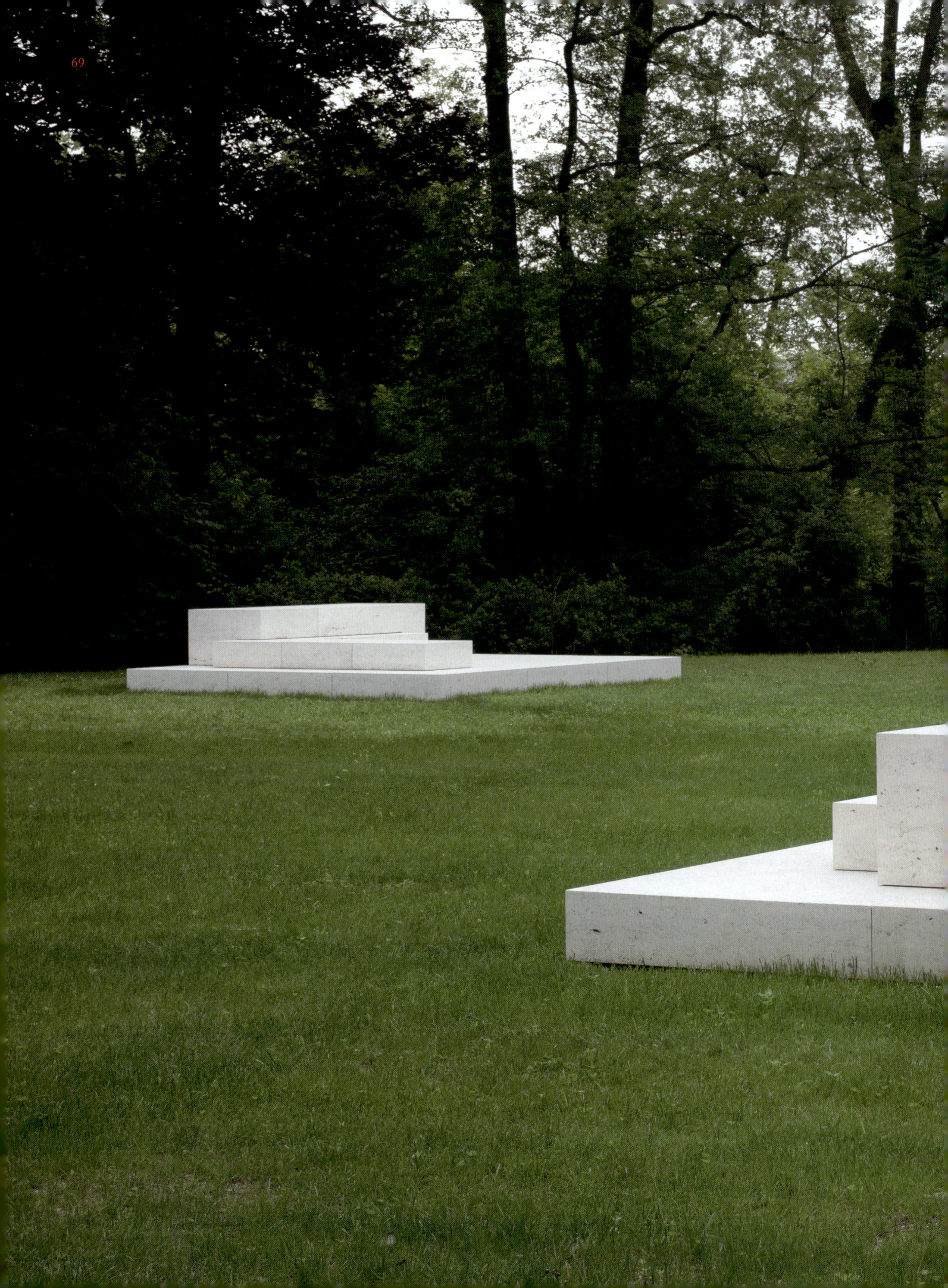

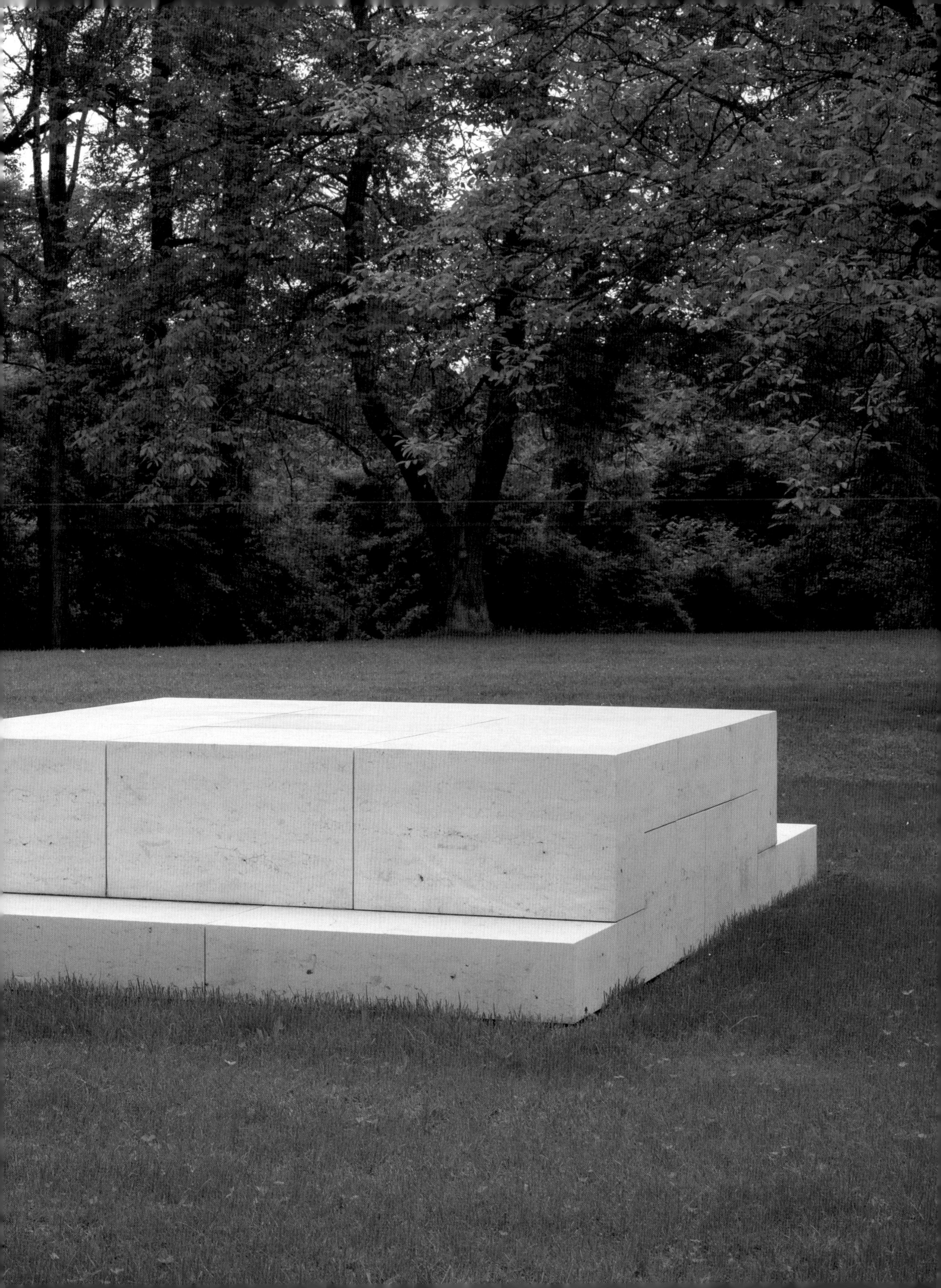

70

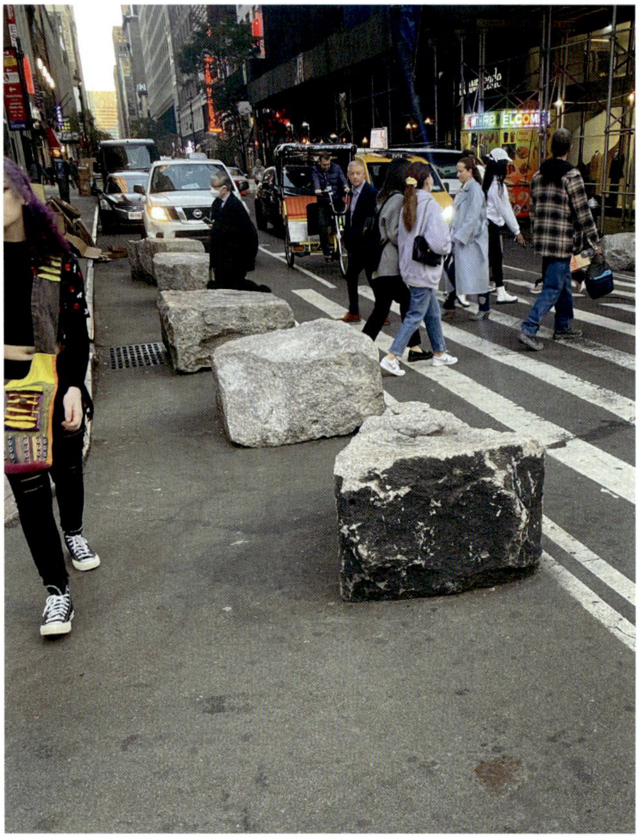

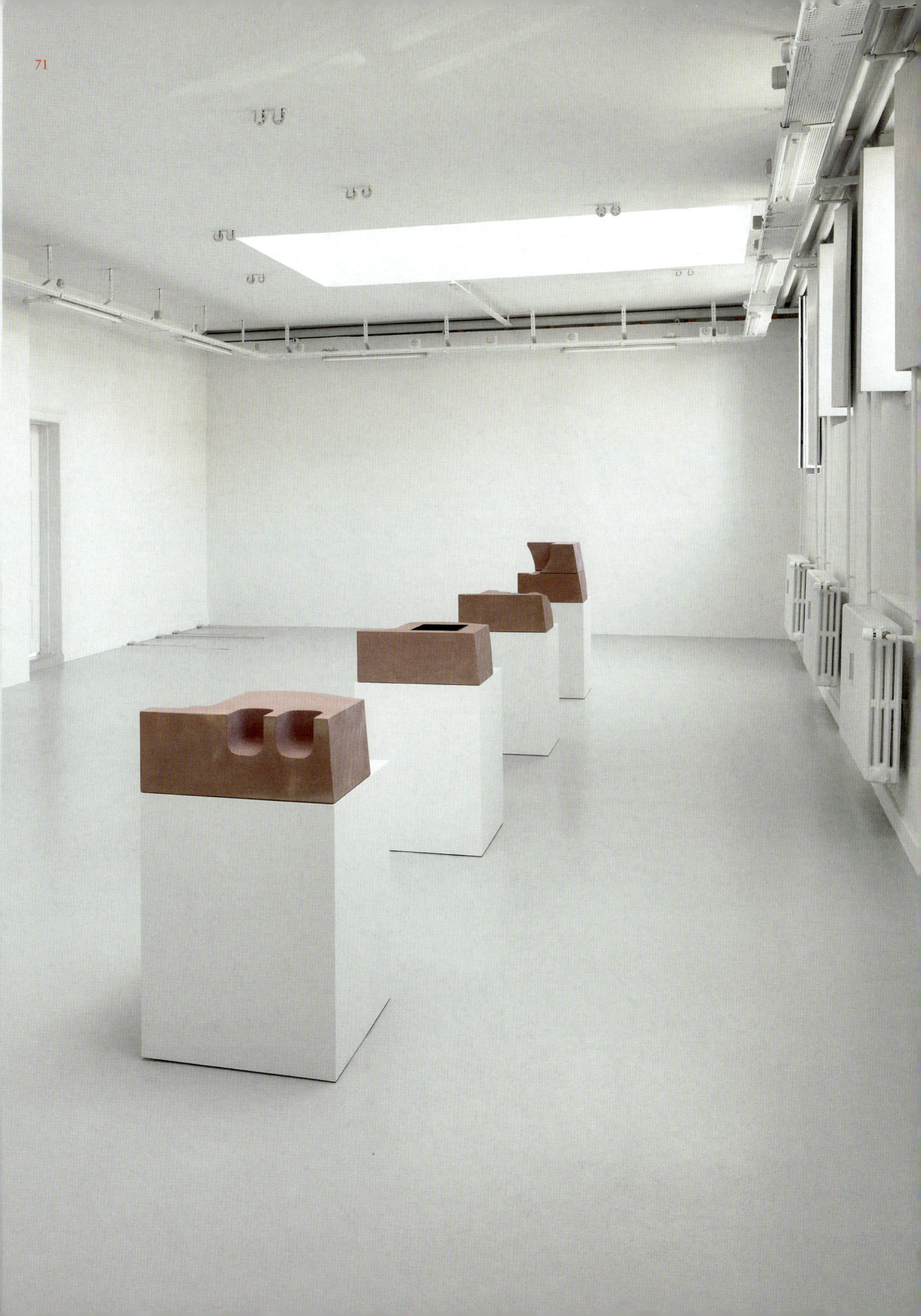

72

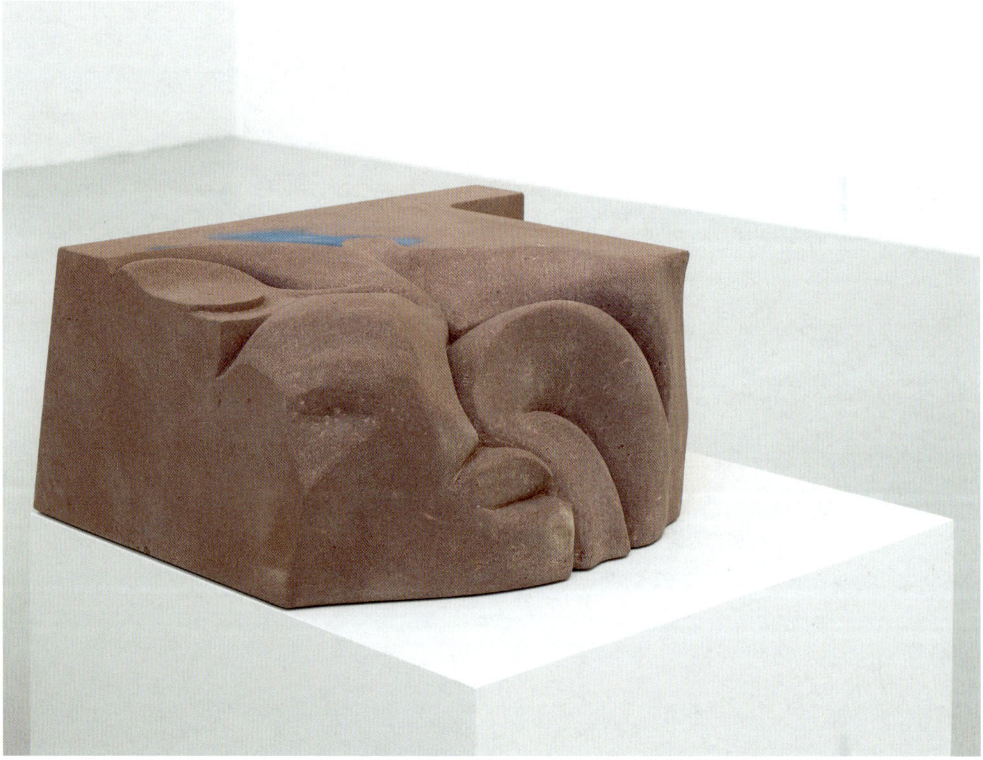

73

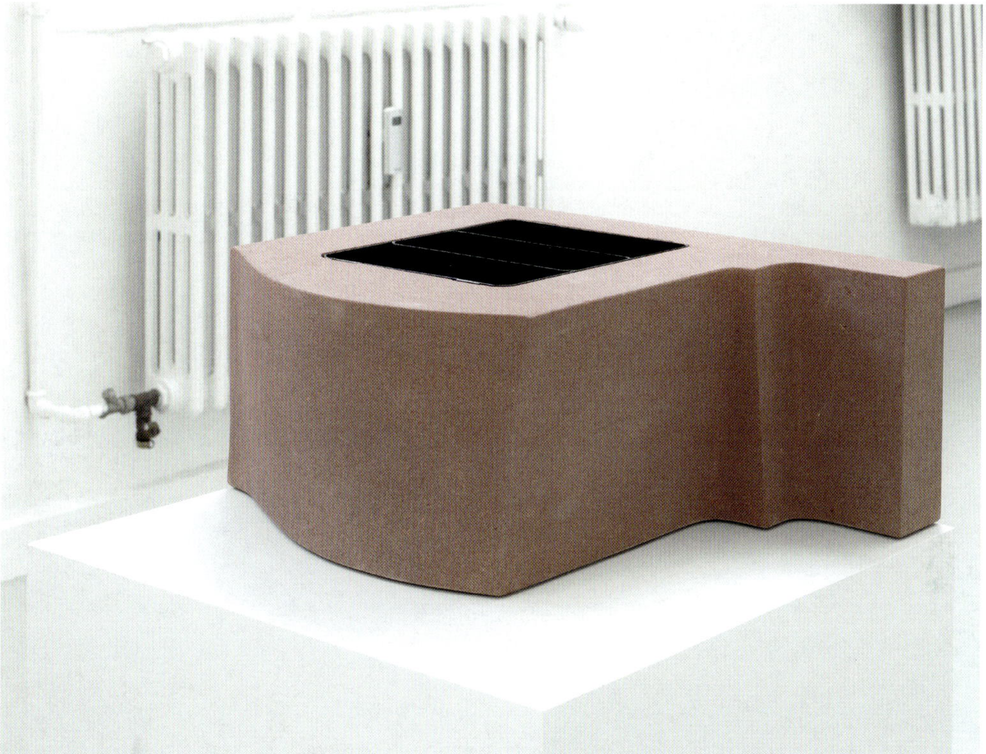

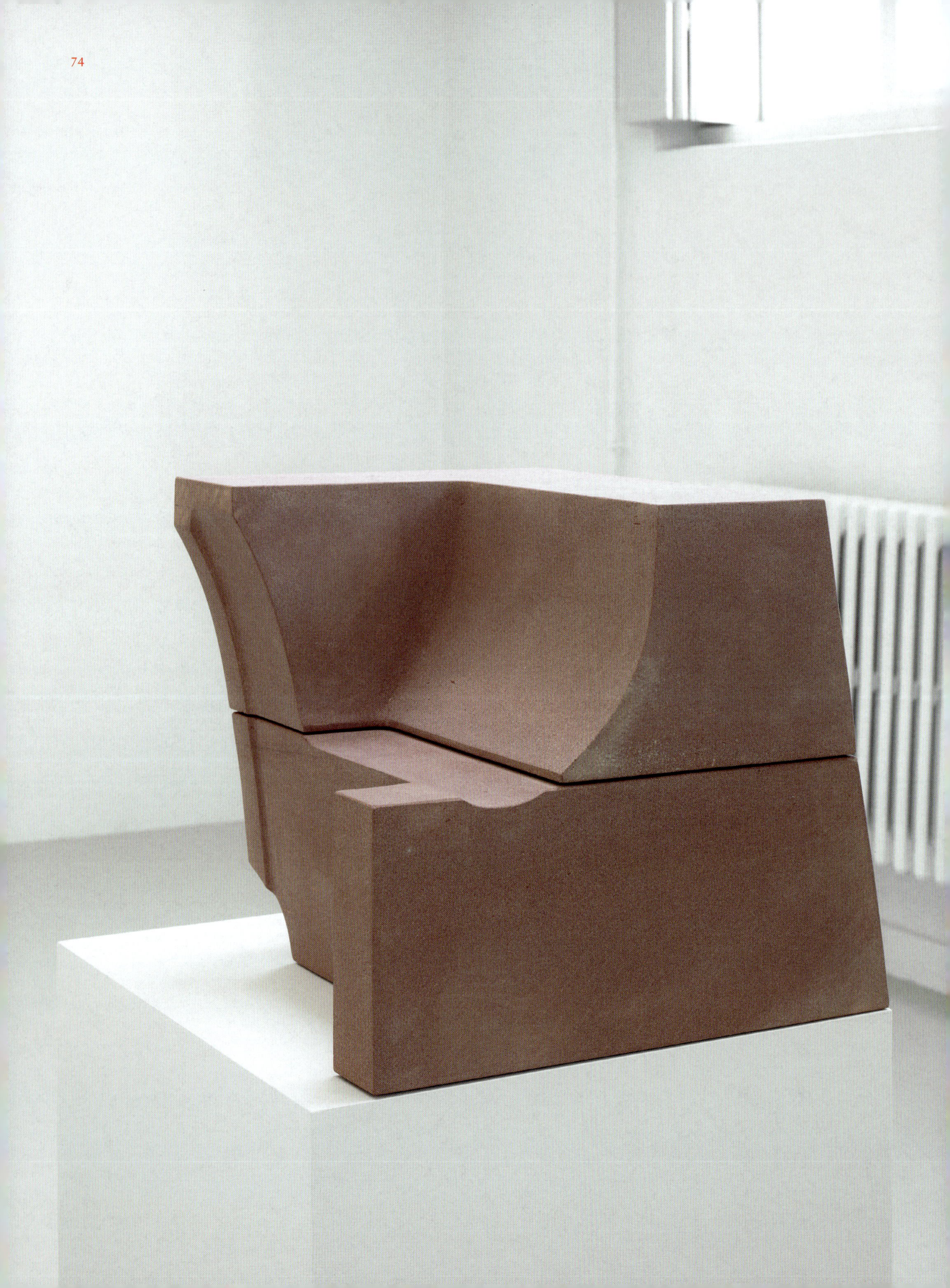

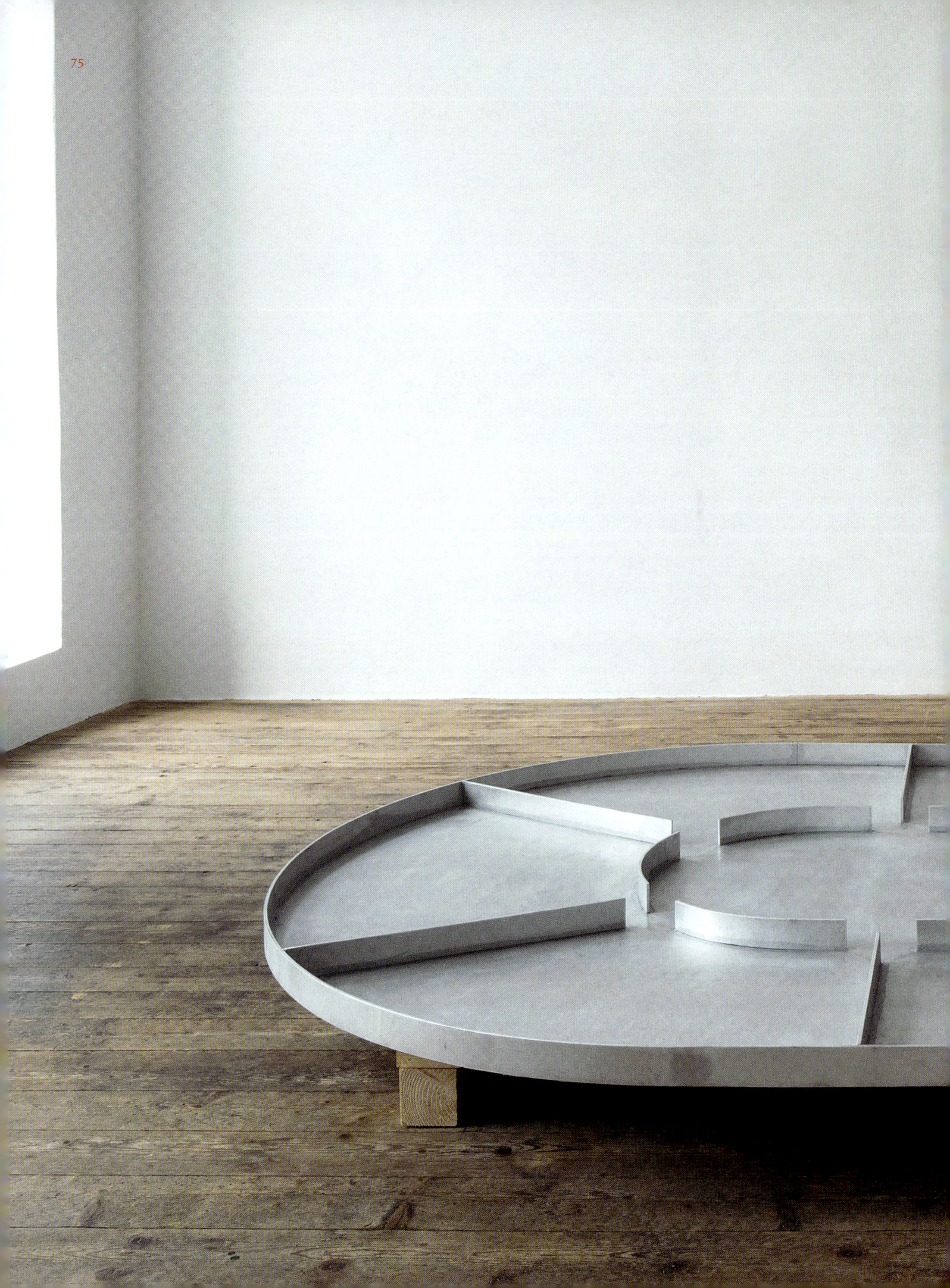

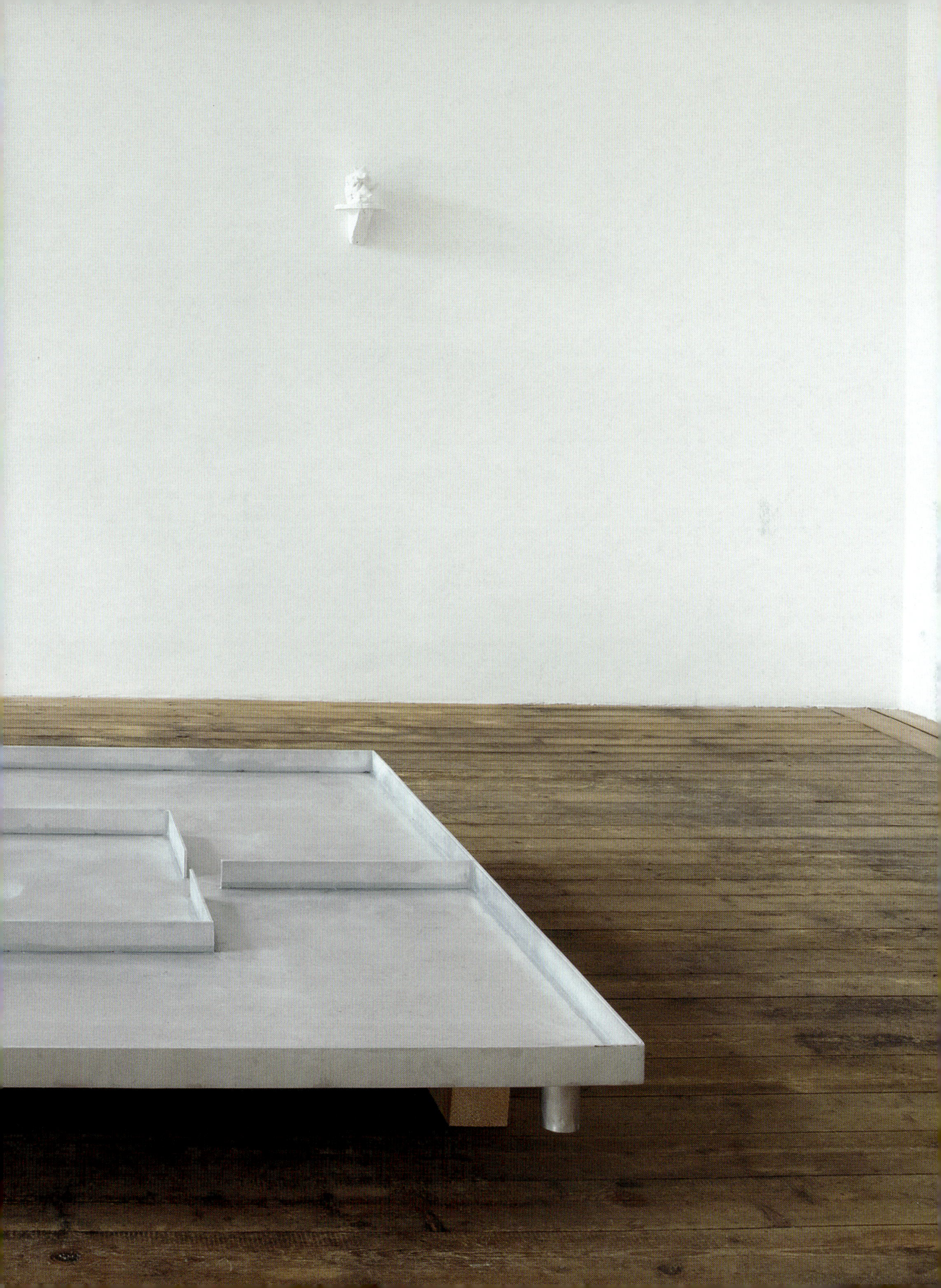

76

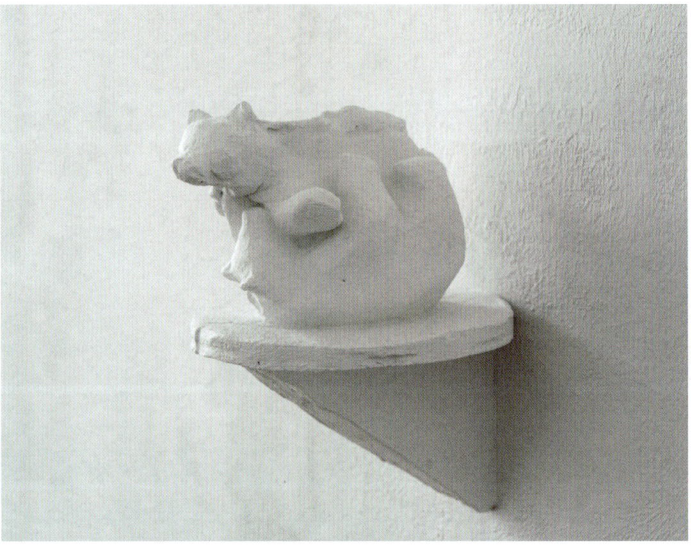

77

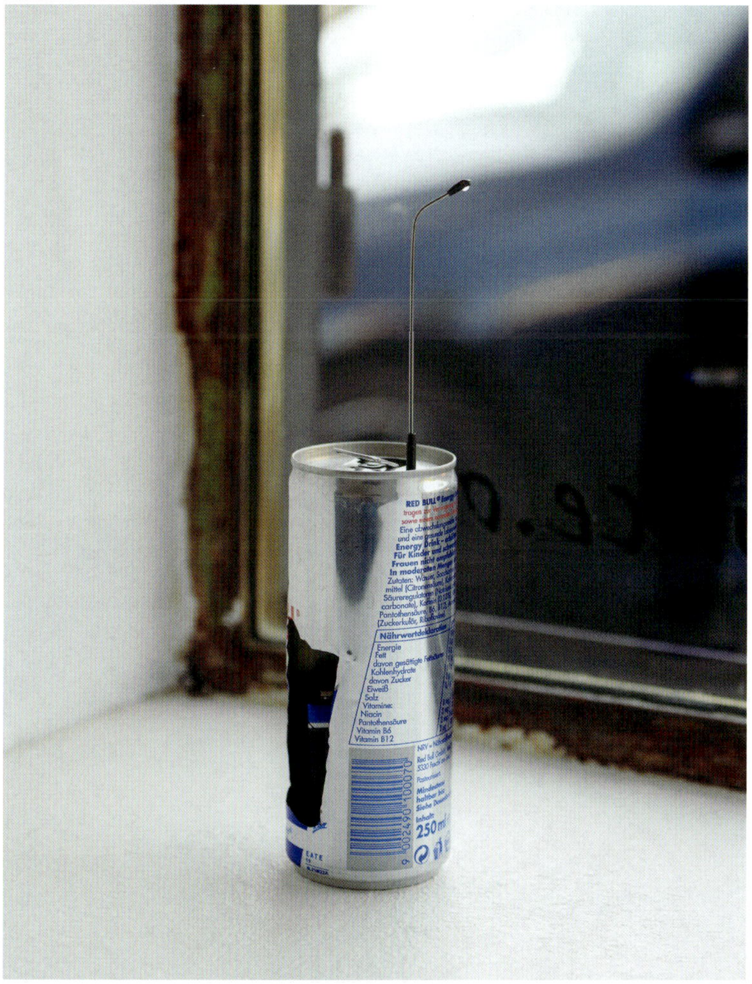
RED BULL®
Energie
Fett
Kohlenhydrate
davon Zucker
Eiweiß
Salz
Vitamine:
Niacin
Pantothensäure
Vitamin B6
Vitamin B12
250 ml

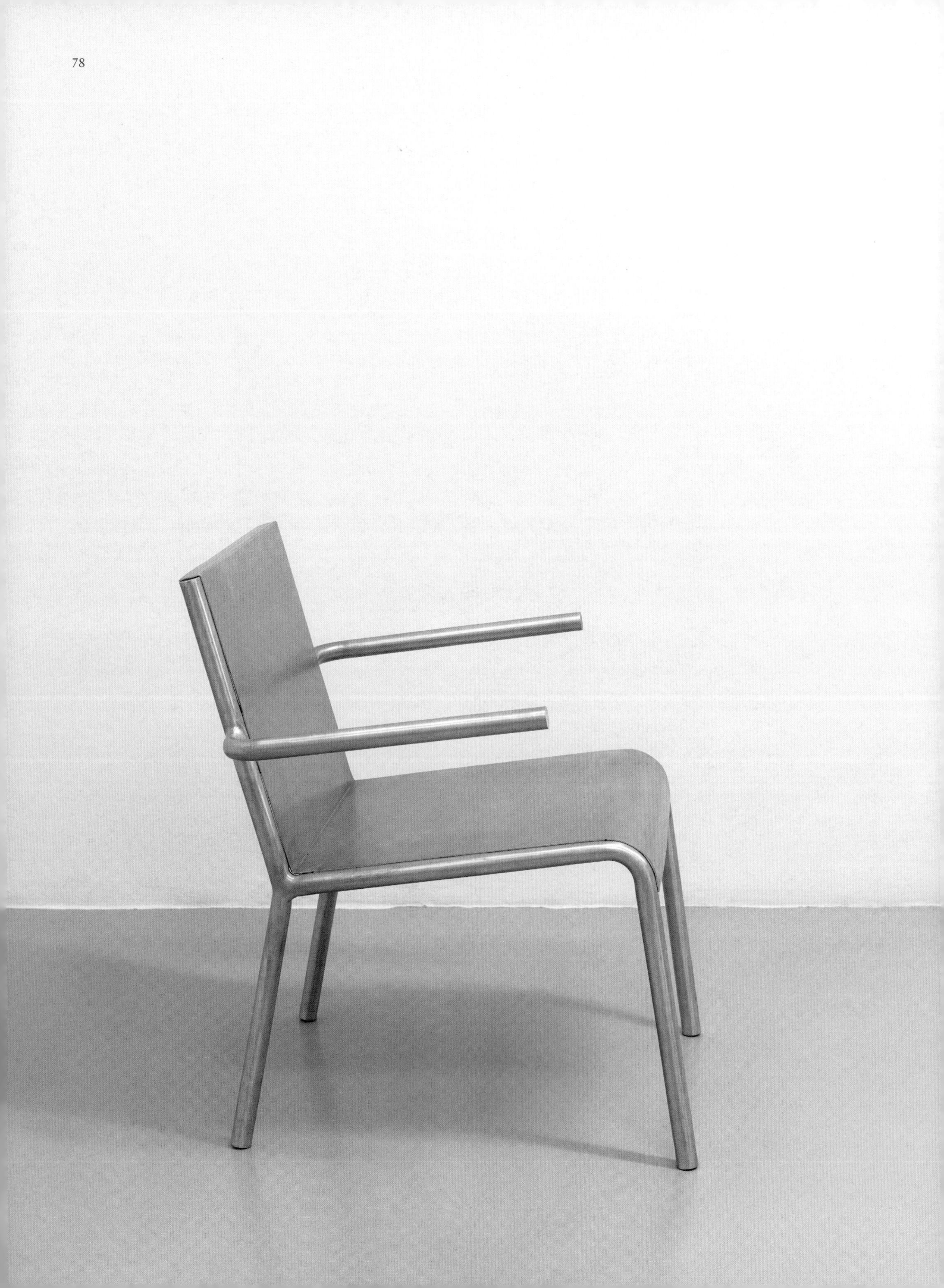

"But more important than dreams are the facts that our youngsters saw good housing in miniature"
A Conversation between Niloufar Emamifar and Benjamin Hirte

This conversation was recorded on May 21, 2022, in New York City.

BH We recently had a discussion about arts and crafts, which are in some way related to religious purposes.

NE It took me a while to appreciate applied arts or crafts again, let's put it that way. Maybe because the trace of totalitarian aesthetics was always more visible in applied arts. And the reverence for physical exertion in crafts was always religious to me. Some regimes viewed arts and crafts as a category of cultural production to portray majesty and virility. It was hard for me to get past the way they were utilized to represent someone's propaganda, and to pay attention to the aesthetic or the simple beauty of it or even the function of it—to remove myself and then appreciate it again, even with the abstraction.

BH A lot of art that relies on its political aims seems close to arts and crafts to me. To take as an example the mural as a format: if it has a clear political aim, it's functional. I guess public space plays a role, too—there is something "applied" about art in public and semipublic space, much more than in the white cube.

NE I feel like there is a different function to a mural than to a public sculpture, though it depends on how we define public sculpture. My definition is closer to Siah Armajani's manifesto on public sculpture[1] than, for example, to what a typical fountain in the middle of a square represents. There is supposed to be a social function, as he puts it, "based on concrete needs"—like a bench or a table.

BH True. If you have a mural or a statue with a clear political message, that's different from just a public sculpture or a bench with a defined purpose. Public sculptures generally are quite interesting. They have to have certain abilities, like robustness in their idea and in their material, to withstand weather and opinions. They must be able to take some beating. People might kick or vandalize it or, even worse, might not be interested at all. There is this moose sculpture[79] around the corner on Allen Street, for example. People basically just smashed it last night.

NE The Moose of the Lower East Side! It had a name ...

BH There was a lot of aggression toward this thing. And the moose sculpture was definitely not political; it was just trying to be a moose. The funny thing is, why would someone want to destroy that? You could destroy a window, you could destroy one of the benches, you could destroy anything in the street ... I think what makes people have aggression toward this kind of public art is that it wants attention from them. It claims that it is in some way more important than the bench, or the curbside, or the traffic light, or anything else.

NE You mean that when something asks too much attention from you, you start resisting? I rather think it's a message to send to the whole temporary public art program of NYC parks, for instance. It was not even someone taking a piece of

1 – "Manifesto: Public Sculpture in the Context of American Democracy" (first published 1978), Siah Armjani

the wood or something. They just decapitated the moose, and the head was left on the side. And now there is caution tape around it.

BH It is a crime scene!

NE What about other elements in public space, like a fountain?

BH A fountain has a function; it is a utility. It originates from the tradition of having a well in the center of a village. By now, the fountain is mostly just decorative, or provides a motif. Still, its original function of offering water is a very soothing idea.

NE This might sound a bit cynical, but I find them to be hostile to the public in certain socio-spatial contexts. In Iran, there are so many public fountains, most of which occupy squares: a public fountain can occupy the entirety of or more than two-thirds of a square. In that case, the sole function of the fountain, similar to most of other public art strategies implemented by state, is to counteract or prevent public gatherings[80, 81]. When I moved to Orange County, urban fountains had a different purpose[82, 83]. They were still purely for decorative purposes, but they were designed and put in specific locations to sell an idea of a desirable social class.

BH I would imagine they're pretty much fake historical monuments in Orange County.

NE Often, architects and urban planners have this weird rendering fetish for imitating natural space in the built environment but in such a fake-looking way. They love it.

BH They're real estate props, which makes their placement different than if one would really want people to gather around or use it. Prime real estate is not interested in real public space.

NE But that's what I mean. With public space, there's always the question of the architecture of engagement. Is the public element there to devour space or to offer you more space? I feel like it's quite tempting for authorities to use these public elements—which have a history of bringing the public together—to do the exact opposite: to either divide or push the public aside.

BH I wouldn't say this is true, at least not yet, in most parts of Europe. Public spaces are still quite dedicated to an actual public. Also, let's not forget that you can drink alcohol in public in Europe—that's a whole different approach. Every large city has these squares, where mostly young people sit and drink in the evening. Vienna's Karlsplatz has a huge round fountain basin—with a large, bony Henry Moore sculpture[84]. It's very crowded in summer and spring; people go around and sell beer unofficially. During Covid, they started having raves there; the police came with riot gear and cleared it. You could still say that the

79

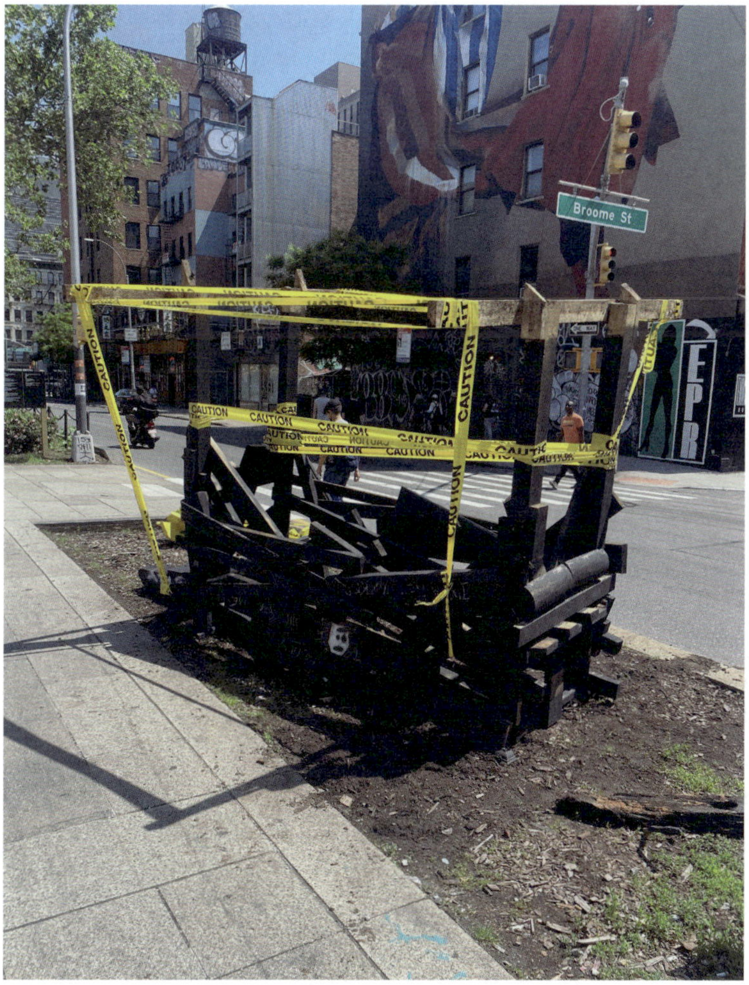

central basin is so large that it breaks up real crowds. I think you are right—it seems like something the state in general has no interest in, unless in a totalitarian sense, where the square is designed to be so vast that no one would gather there voluntarily.

NE I've never been to Europe.

BH It has a lot of imperial fountains.

NE The imperial fountain [85, 86] and the totalitarian fountain [87], which are again two different fountains. I had a studio at the Glassell School of Art, which is part of the Museum of Fine Arts in Houston. There is the Cullen Sculpture Garden [88] next to it, designed by Isamu Noguchi. So, in between the building where our studio was and the sculpture garden, there was an open space that was still privately owned, but the public had access to it. There was this extensive fountain [89], designed by the architect. It was basically sprinklers, and its sole purpose was to keep the homeless from camping there.

BH Why would they spray water? To make it steamy and uncomfortable?

NE It is a tactic to prevent loitering. The art school and the museum also had the right to call the police if someone camped there because it was a privately owned public space—which is a contradictory term in itself. The sculpture garden in that area is the only gated part, which is funny because someone (and I'm not sure about this) mentioned that the land itself belongs to the city.

BH When talking about these semipublic spaces, it sounds almost like we're discussing theological problems. For instance, trying to explain the absurdity of the foreclosure rules in New York and of "vendor culture"—the leasing of public spaces to private corporations and individuals. It's like a complex theological problem that is in some theoretical sense logical but that is very absurd on a practical level. I guess law develops similarly to religion over a very long period of time. It gets twisted and layered.

NE It's also designed to be that way. The majority of the discourses in urban studies are focused on gentrification as the key factor of forced displacement in the United States. Gentrification is the more visible part of the problem. But it also has to do with the ongoing expansion of the public-private sphere that is characterized by various sorts of pseudo-public spaces, from mass private properties or MPP (the private properties that are open to the masses) to privately owned public spaces or POPS. The ongoing effects of such invisible transactions are much harder to trace since they do not have the heavily made-up face of gentrification. The invisible system of discipline used for the spatial control of pseudo-public spaces is implemented by "guards" instead of police. The merging of service and surveillance in these spaces makes them difficult to map.

BH Yes, the process is very sneaky; its symptoms are not supposed to show. If they do, it looks like a bad joke. We already spoke about this grotesque fenced-off ventilation on the corner of Grand and Essex Street[90].

NE The property corner of Seward Park is part of NYCHA (New York City Housing Authority). It's called Seward Park Extension Project. There was a homeless camp on the adjacent corner. It was a perfect spot to camp because there was all this warm air during winter from a vent. The community also knew the people camping there, until suddenly the space was blocked off by black metal fencing. It's like trapping empty air.

BH It looks very carceral. It's a cage for air now.

NE I asked the administration of Seward Park Extension Community Center about what happened, and they responded that they had made a hygiene complaint to the city about the encampment there.

BH Yes, and your initial information was that the NYCHA made a complaint to the city about hygiene, and they found a vendor to fence off the corner.

NE ... which is not an uncommon practice. It is the way these problems get outsourced ... but I was in contact with NYCHA, the city, and even the DCAS (Department of Citywide Administrative Services), because the vent might not even be NYCHA property. It might be, say, part of the metro system, which makes it even more complex. Nobody was able or wanted to give me a concrete answer, at least so far. Usually in these cases, the city does not sell the ownership; it sells a bundle of rights and obligations. As an example, let's say there is a new Prada store right in the middle of Chinatown. The store owners go to the city and get the right to put big planters on the sidewalk in front of the store.

BH New York also has a lot of urban design strategies to deal with such matters—which are quite common now in most large and midsize cities, including in Europe. The often good-looking but uncomfortable design of benches, for instance, makes them impossible to sleep on. The common feature is dividers, some more prominent than others, between individual seats. The accommodating gesture of the bench in public now usually comes with a prohibitive design[91–93].

NE Where do we even start with benches?! [*laughs*]

BH Benches can be very "pushy"—they come with a set of conditions. There is a melancholy to someone sitting alone on a bench for three or, even worse, a bench for two. I think that's why people really like sitting on stairs. It's because stairs have another kind of expectation from you. You are supposed to walk on them. You can do a lot of things with them, but they don't have this kind of clear framing for you to sit there.

80

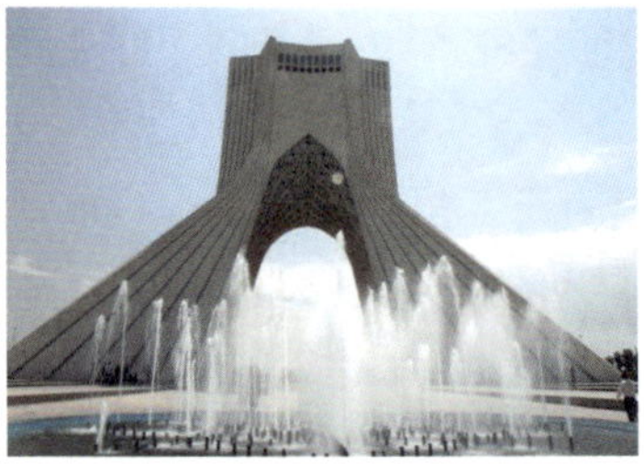

81

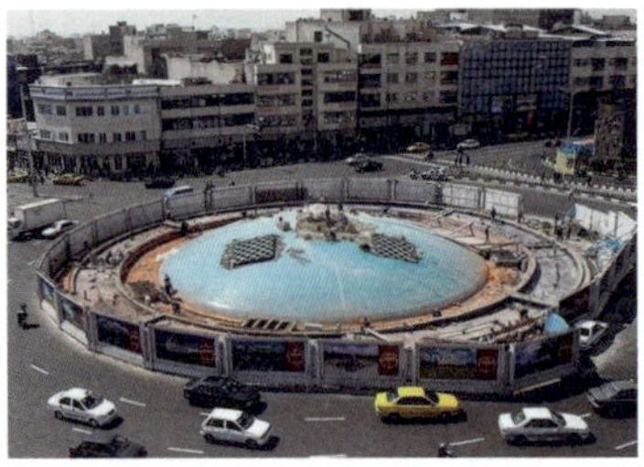

82

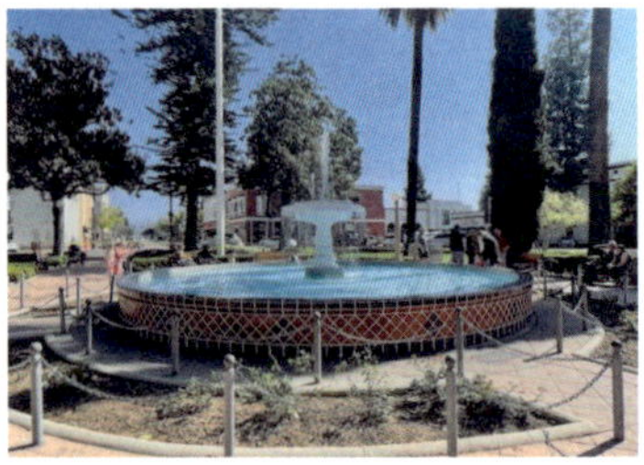

83

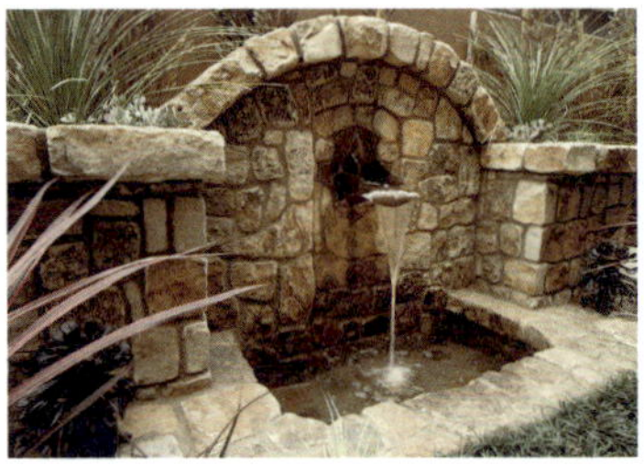

84

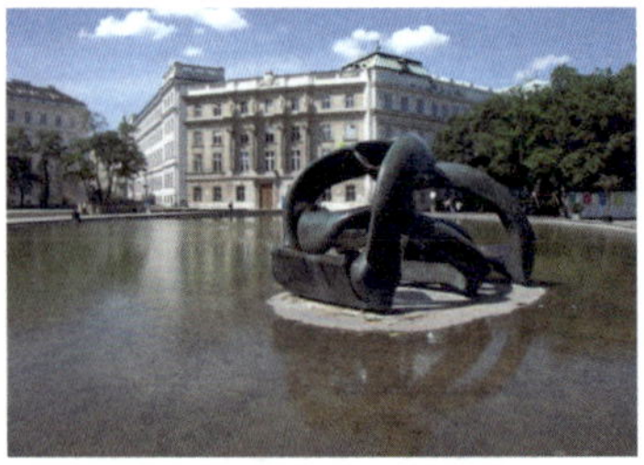

85

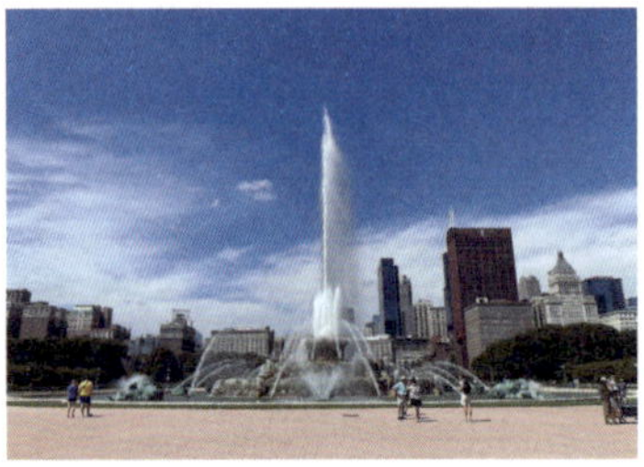

86

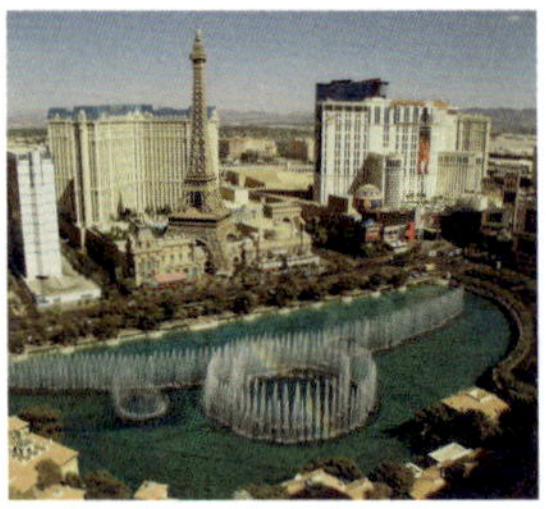

87

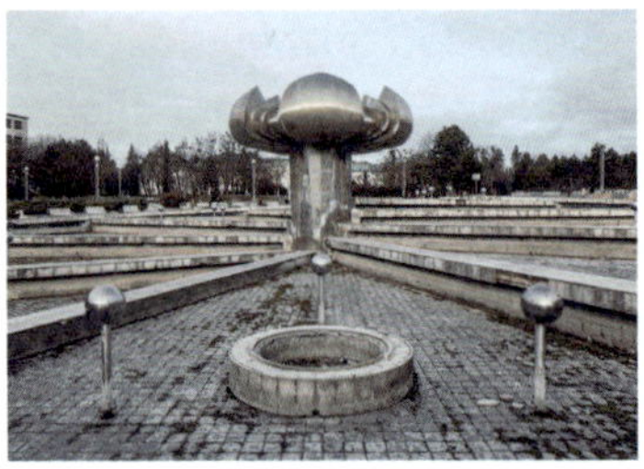

NE Which could lead us, again, to ideas about public sculpture and its audiences, and how different public sculpture is from sculpture shown in a context explicitly dedicated to art. Have you ever made something unofficial in public, like put a work somewhere to see if someone would remove it?

BH No, I never did, but I understand the interest in doing something like that. Like, who is it for? With graffiti, there's a similar problem and also a similar thrill. First of all, you would probably say that it's for everybody, that it's just out there to be seen by any kind of public. But then there's an inner logic, especially with graffiti: it's in and for your own community, who know who you are, and they appreciate it in the most particular way[94]. I am not sure if I would want to do it—maybe it's too subversive for me. Of course, there's a particular beauty to it. Again, it is out there for everyone to see, while its actual logic is for the people in the know.

NE Graffiti and sculpture still occupy different spaces for me, even if both share the "public view with no permission" quality. And a commissioned public sculpture is still more difficult to pull off.

BH An actual public sculpture in some way has to answer to everyone. If you get a commission for a public sculpture in a public space or in a publicly accessible location, one that will stay there long-term, it needs a certain amount of pop—it can't be too smart. A popular solution is if people can sit on it or use it in any way. As long as people can sit on it, the rest of the sculpture can be very opaque and complex. You can create a really weird work, and as long as it is offering some kind of common use, it's going to be fine. Maybe even a water dispenser or, of course, a fountain.

NE You can never determine these things. I'm 100 percent with Armajani in that sense—about how and what a public sculpture should be, if the sculpture is intended to have some practical use ...

BH Siah Armajani made the bridge sculpture at the Walker Art Center[95].

NE He built a lot of bridges, and you can walk on most of them! I remember an interview he did years ago: there was a point where the interviewer asked him about his reading rooms[96]. From what I remember, she said, "I was looking at your reading rooms you made over the years. I was wondering how many people would actually go and read in these rooms. If people don't sit in these rooms and read, then what would be the function of these rooms?" He responded, "Nothing! Public art is 90 percent illusions. A dream. I've been making public art for forty-five years, but at the end of the day ... Nothing ... We haven't been successful."

BH I mean, people can use it in one way or another, just like the Lower East Side Moose. Seems like they wanted to use it in some way, and the only way was to destroy it.

NE I think the problem was the location, to be honest. It was the worst place to put a sculpture. It took up, like, one-fourth of the sidewalk and took up space for the cyclists. So, they put it in the wrong spot; they put it literally in the walking area.

BH It was not considerate.

NE Speaking of considerate public elements, what was the last public sculpture you saw that anticipated and incorporated your movement as a viewer?

BH I remember the Bruce Nauman piece at Skulptur Projekte Münster[97]—which is, of course, a very specific context for public sculptural projects. He built these kinds of triangles out of concrete that form something like a pit. You can go down into it and walk around. It's weird. It has a certain bluntness that is still playful—highly intelligent and also very simple. Still, it doesn't really have much of an aim; it's even called *Square Depression*. Depression is also a technical term for a pit, besides its psychological meaning.

NE How about public art in Vienna—I remember that some of your work relates to that?

BH I documented a lot of public art from Vienna's social housing. The city has a long tradition of public housing, most of it built in the 1920s and '30s[100, 101]. In the inner or outer area of such buildings, there is usually one or more sculptural works. I made 3D scans or just photos. Most of the sculptures are figurative, some are memorials, and some function as fountains. None of them seems particularly contemporary or radical for the time it was made. Vienna had a socialist government in the 1920s and beginning of the '30s; it was not really avant-garde in its art, but politically it was a radical time. The funny thing is that most of the sculptures from this period are figurative in a socialist realist manner[102–105]. After the war, the Social Democrats were again in charge in Vienna, and have been from the '50s till now, but most of the public sculptures are just cute and popular animals. They're not supposed to carry any political message anymore. They are just friendly decoration. The post-war social housing complexes are generally quite plain, square, and non-decorative. And then a nice, cute animal would be placed in front or in the courtyard that makes it easier to swallow. Like a mascot[106–108].

NE I'm always suspicious of beautification policies. Sometimes it feels manipulative. It's like when Tehran municipality's so-called bureau of beautification started painting hundreds of murals that were surreal or that presented an idealized view of nature—the blue sky and the countryside, for instance[109]. And you're like, what are you trying to sell? Nazgol Ansarinia did an interesting project about this years ago.

BH The sweet beautification of modernist housing projects! It's almost slapstick. Advertising does a similar job now.

NE There's an involuntary dark humor to it of course.

BH It's funny because it doesn't understand itself anymore.

NE Exactly. My favorite story in your book, *The Robbers*, is "The Old One." You said it is somewhat inspired by the controversy over Diego Rivera's mural, *Man at the Crossroads*, at the Rockefeller Center [110].

BH Yes, somewhat. In this case, the contradiction of having the socialist mural in the capitalist cathedral was too much. Nelson Rockefeller himself ordered it to be taken down before the lobby was open to the public.

NE It existed, but nobody saw it. Was it painted over or chiseled off? Because I don't think they could take it down. It's directly on the wall, so it's technically still there.

BH I think they chiseled it off, but it is a nice thought that the Rockefeller Center is still haunted by Rivera's mural. Rivera had a Brechtian approach: it is very explicit, it includes popular imagery, and it has a certain message. Rivera's work is didactic, but up-front about it.

NE Rivera, or one of his assistants, added a portrait of Lenin to the mural, which had not been apparent in the initial sketches. I like that he added the Lenin portrait after they were already upset with the painting.

BH The Rockefellers then wanted Picasso to do it. He was interested but would not negotiate from his stated price of $32,000.

NE Of course, the problem for him was the money.

BH The question in general is whether Rivera's socialist mural should have been there in the first place. From an ideological standpoint, probably not, although Rivera must have had his reasons.

NE It's kind of like putting lipstick on a mouth full of blood. That would be my responding imagery, particularly in New York. It sounds intense, but that's how I perceive many of the solutions of modernism and philanthropy in the United States.

BH The social housing in Vienna, a project of modernism, is much more intact than it is in the United States, for example, or in Germany, where there has been basically no investment in social housing over the last forty years. This housing is in ruins, and nobody wants to invest in it, and nobody has done anything new with it. In Germany, I would say the Social Democrats have sold it off by now. Germany only has something like 4 percent state-run housing, while Austria has almost 25 percent. I think if the ideology leaves these buildings or even if the state simply stops believing in it, then the people will too. In Vienna, there is still a little pride left in the still-functional social housing complex. I'm not saying it's perfect—there are real problems and more on the horizon. So, I wouldn't say "mouth full of blood," but there's definitely some teeth missing. In New York, the "mouth full of blood" analogy makes absolute sense, I agree.

NE Maybe because social housing is still a radical concept in the United States, and when you talk about government-funded housing, my mind can't help but think of crumbling apartment towers with enormous maintenance backlogs. But even in New York, what you see in the First Houses [62, 111] is radically different from the changes that happened to NYCHA properties post-1969. In the First Houses, you see that there is deliberate attention to how the light works and the generous space between each unit.

BH Yes, I think the luxury is that the space and the courtyard are generous, even though they seem like very ordinary brick houses. There is space in between the single buildings, which also means that the apartments are brighter. In Vienna, when they started the social housing projects in the '20s, one of the main goals was to lift the very basic standards of living of the working class. They came up with a certain amount of light that has to be there, the size of the windows, and even the location of toilets in the apartment—not in the hallway anymore. The ceiling had to have a certain height, etc. The new standards they set then are still valuable for the people living there now, and these buildings are better than some of the newer ones. I would say that the First Houses have that, too. And, of course, they have cute animal sculptures in the courtyard! They're original from the 1930s [63, 64, 112].

NE There are people still living there from decades ago, also because of rent control. Just from looking at the playground and the backyard, you can tell that this is different from what you see in other places.

BH This type of housing represents real care—to use that word. New Deal care. You remember the quote from the film *Modest Homes*: "But more important than dreams are the facts that our youngsters saw good housing in miniature."

NE Oh, yes, it was at that architecture exhibition at MoMA. Care can also easily transition to chaos in some contexts: when state-funded housing becomes, as Hashem Shakeri wrote, "ghost towers," or when it becomes dystopian and an embodiment of what, in the view of the government, those who can afford only low-income housing deserve [113, 114].

BH I think one of the important aspects of Vienna's municipal housing is that if you begin to earn more money, they do not throw you out. You also don't have to be completely precarious to qualify for these apartments, which allows for a demographic that is slightly more diverse in terms of income. Also, such housing was built all over the city, which prevents ghettoization—this is one of Jane Jacobs's better arguments.

NE So, to move in, you cannot be wealthy.

88

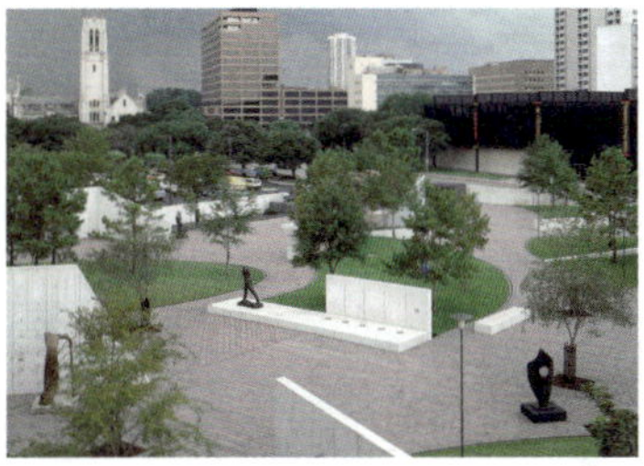

89

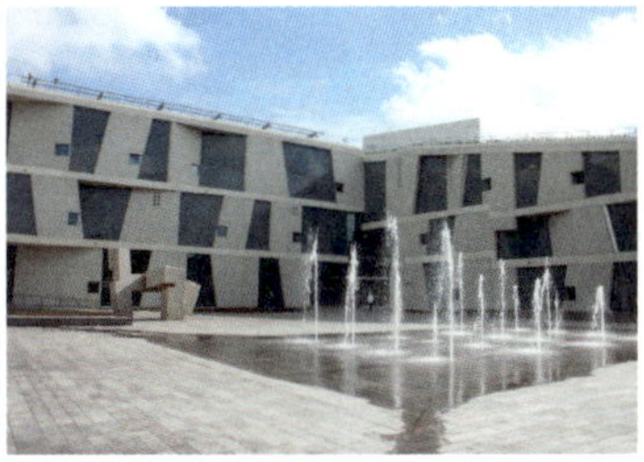

90

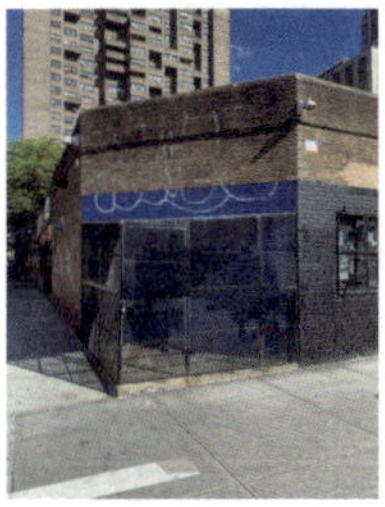

91

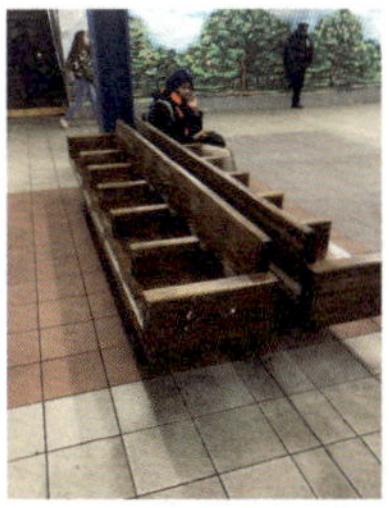

92

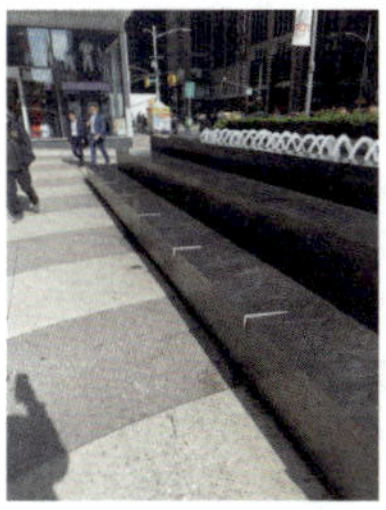

93

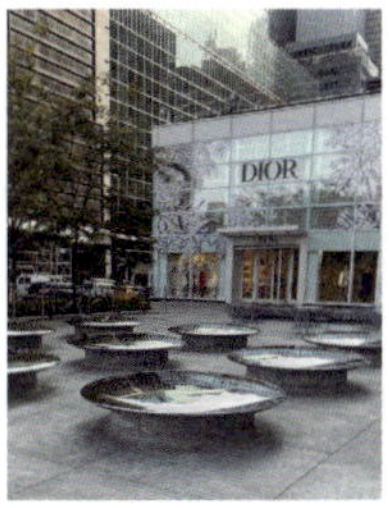

94

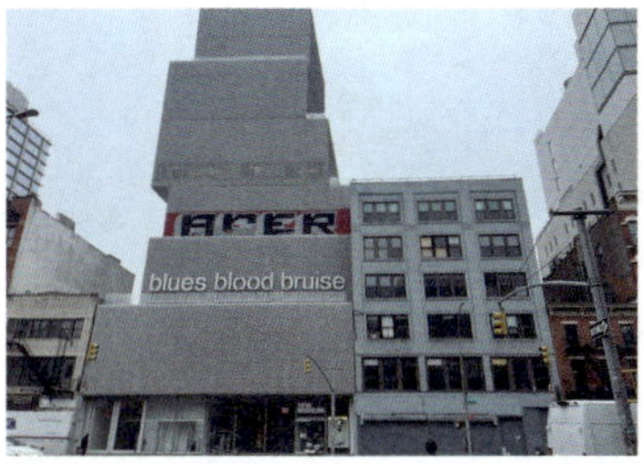

95

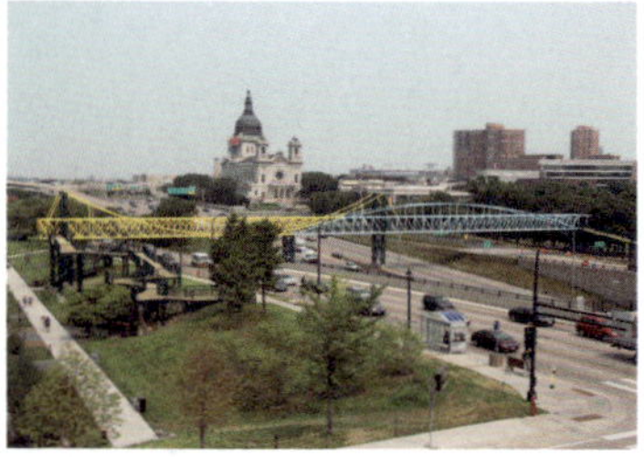

96

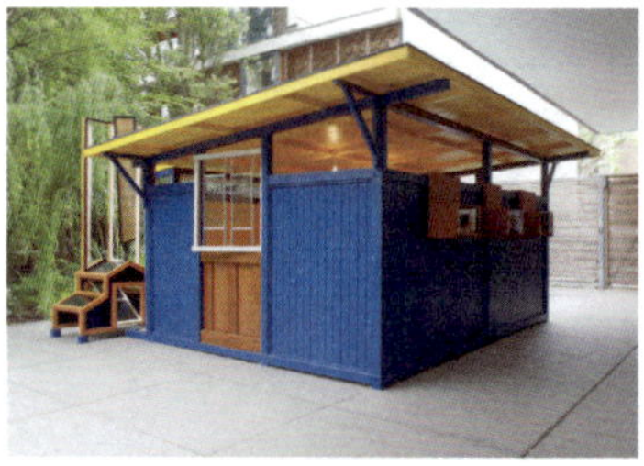

97

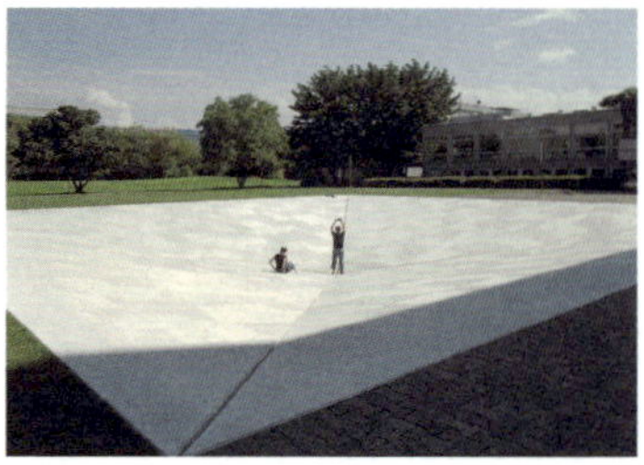

98

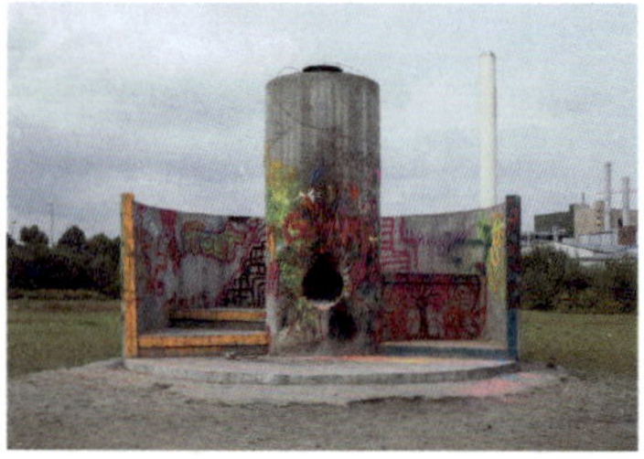

99

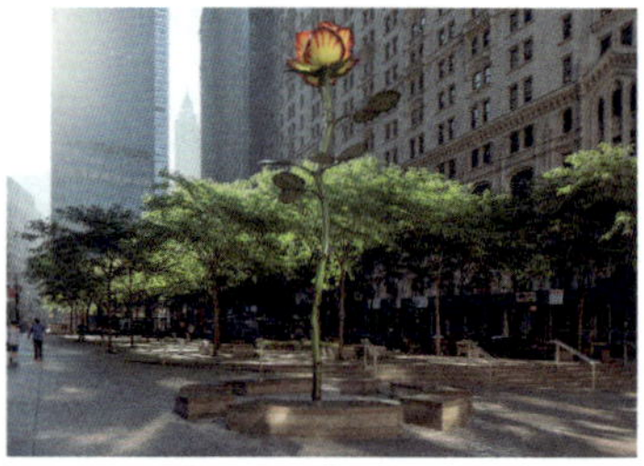

100

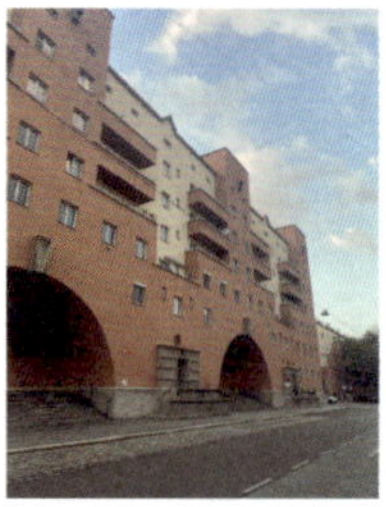

101

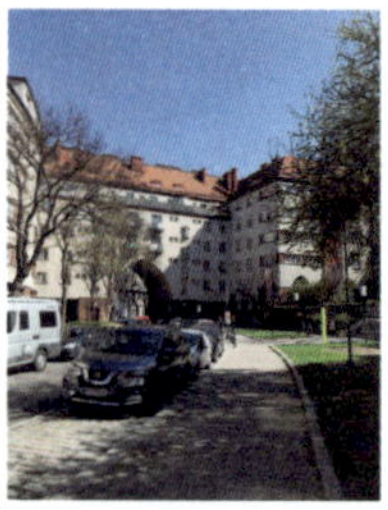

102

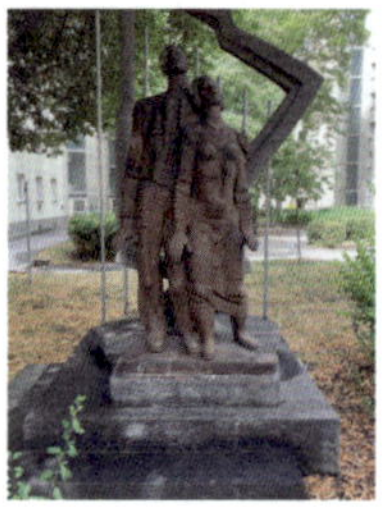

103

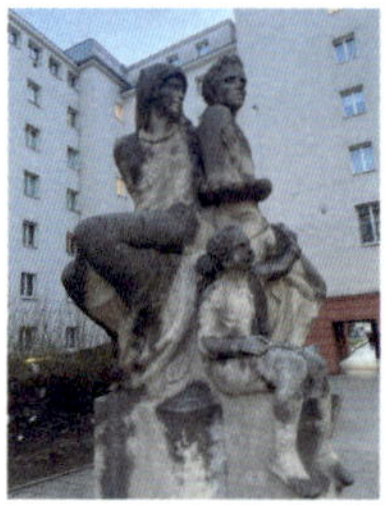

104

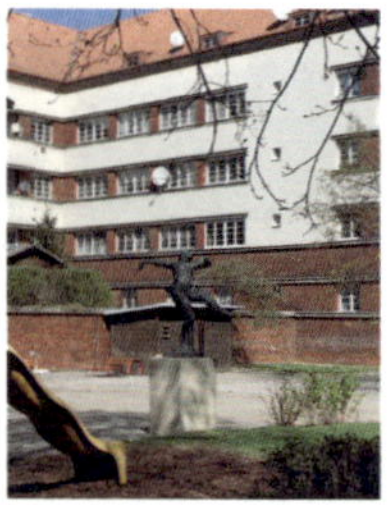

105

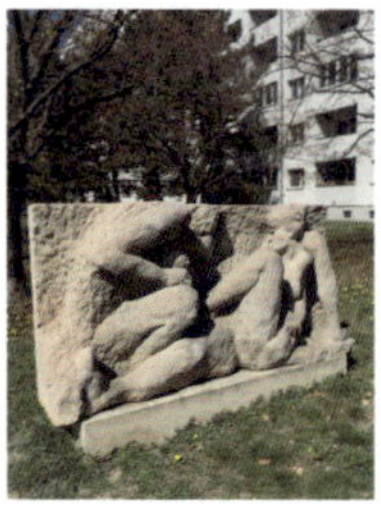

106

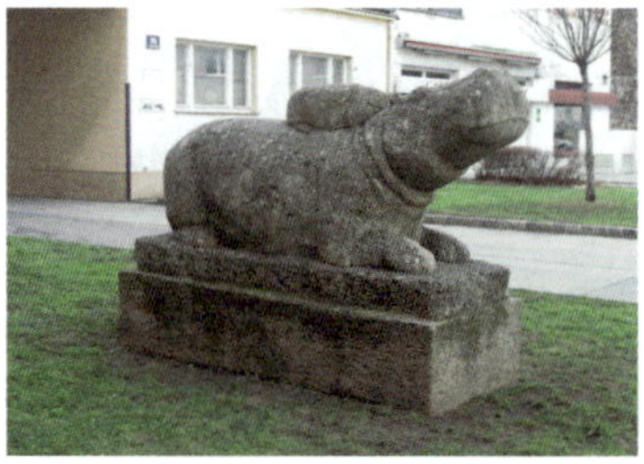

107

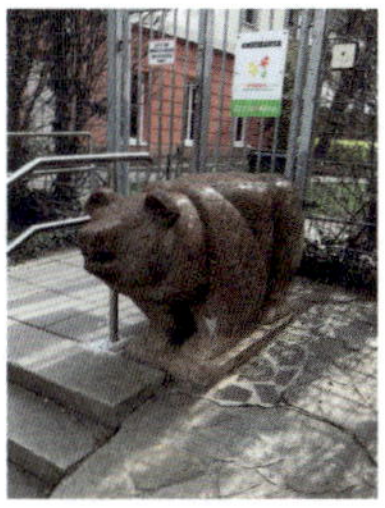

108

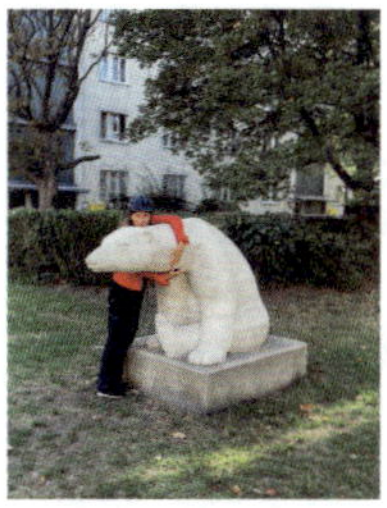

109

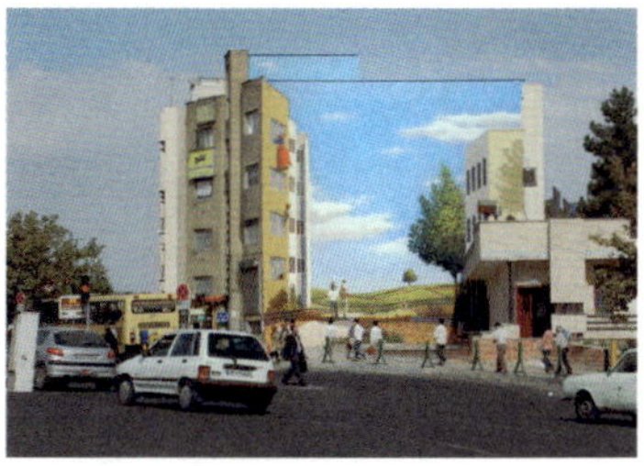

110

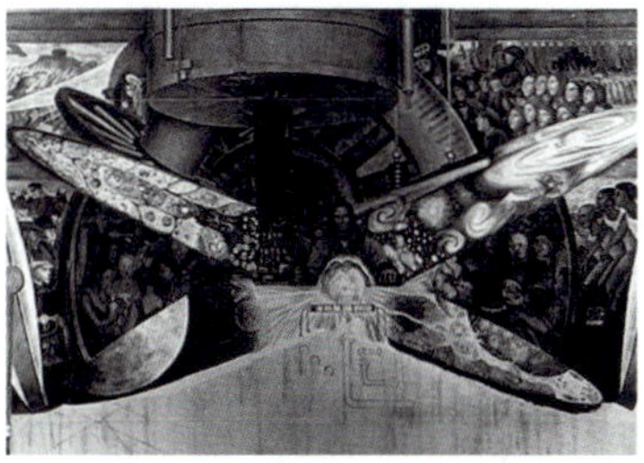

111

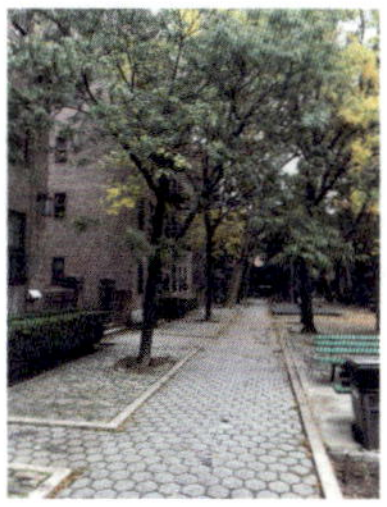

112

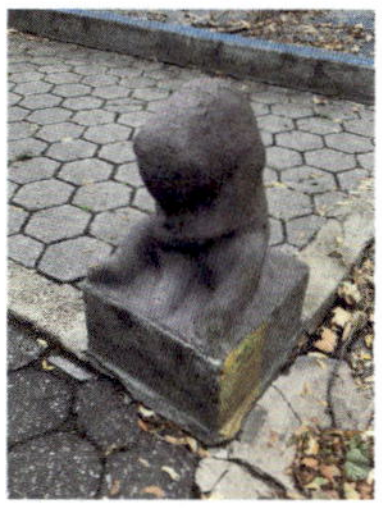

113

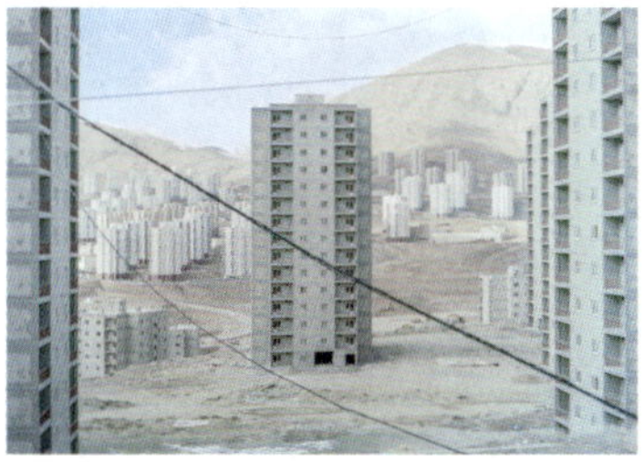

114

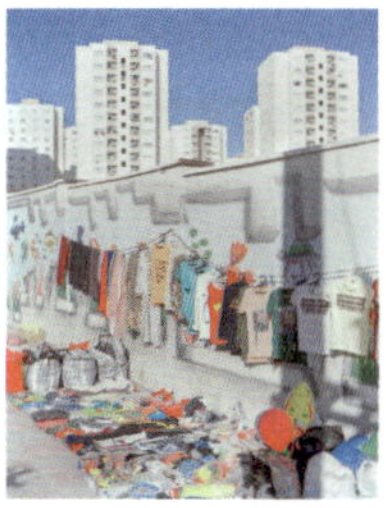

115

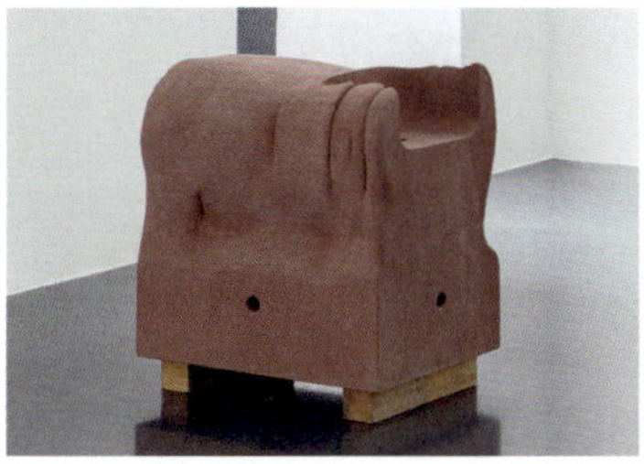

BH That's right, but you don't have to be poor either.

NE There's this sculpture of yours called *Fountain for Erdbergstrasse* [52, 115]. From what I understand, it is related to a municipal housing complex in Vienna.

BH I used to live in the third district of Vienna. Around the corner was a smaller social housing complex with a hippo statue in front [106]. The sculpture was from the late '60s. It was just a very cute stone hippo, with some of those thick skin folds hippos have. I used some elements for a stone sculpture, but I didn't replicate it completely. It's more like a torso. So, it's somehow this middle part of the hippo with thick skin folds, but it became a weird fleshy thing, which looks as if it's a part of something bigger.

NE And then the holes ...

BH Well, then I added a sink, a drain, and outlets to all sides. We've already spoken about my interest in animal sculptures in public space, and my ideas about public art and some kind of utility or usefulness of such art. In the front of the sculpture, I carved out a very basic form of a bathroom sink—which is just like making the whole thing a utility. It also looks a bit like a maw, but it's also offering something on a symbolic level, in this case the idea of offering water. You can still drink from some older fountains in Vienna—it's a very generous gesture in public space to offer water for free, especially as the concept of water becomes more and more contested.

NE I have only seen images of the work in the gallery. Would you see this also as a functioning public sculpture? Would you install it in public?

BH Yes, absolutely. It can be outside, and the water can run all the way through it if it rains. There would be visible traces of the water running through the sculpture after a while. The work was sold to Wien Museum – Museum of the City of Vienna, which cares for everything concerning the city's history. It's a very layered institution. They're expanding, building a new museum, and I hope they might put it somewhere outside there, but I'm not sure.

NE I like that the sculpture can go outside. For me, it's easier if sculptures can either go back to their spaces or be in some way "used."

BH All my recent stone sculptures have a drain or some kind of sink or outlet. The sink is such a common utility. It's quite dramatic, actually—leading into some kind of hidden, dark world. [*laughs*]

NE ... one that you can't predict—that's true.

BH That's why sculptures should have drains.

NE Yes, sculptures have to have drains.

116

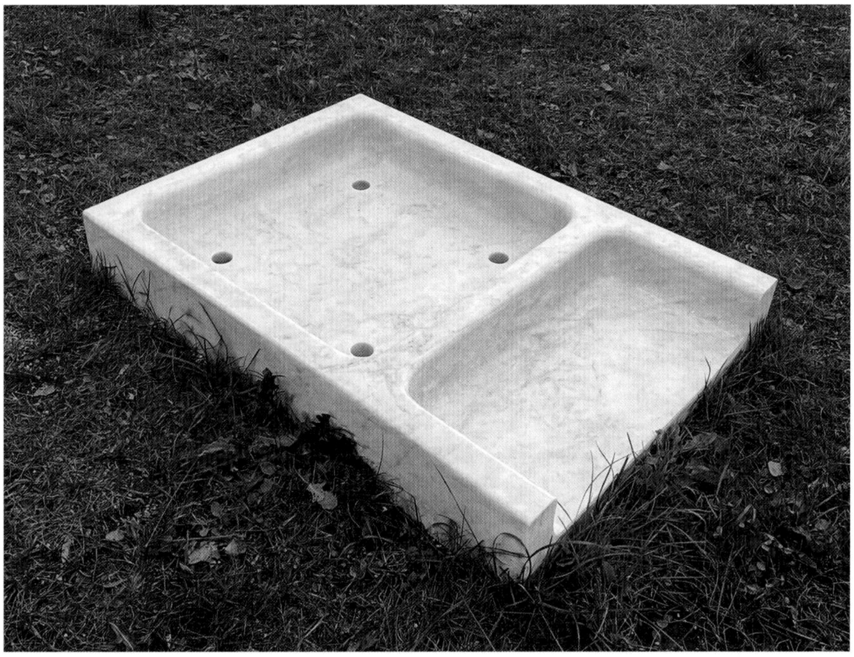

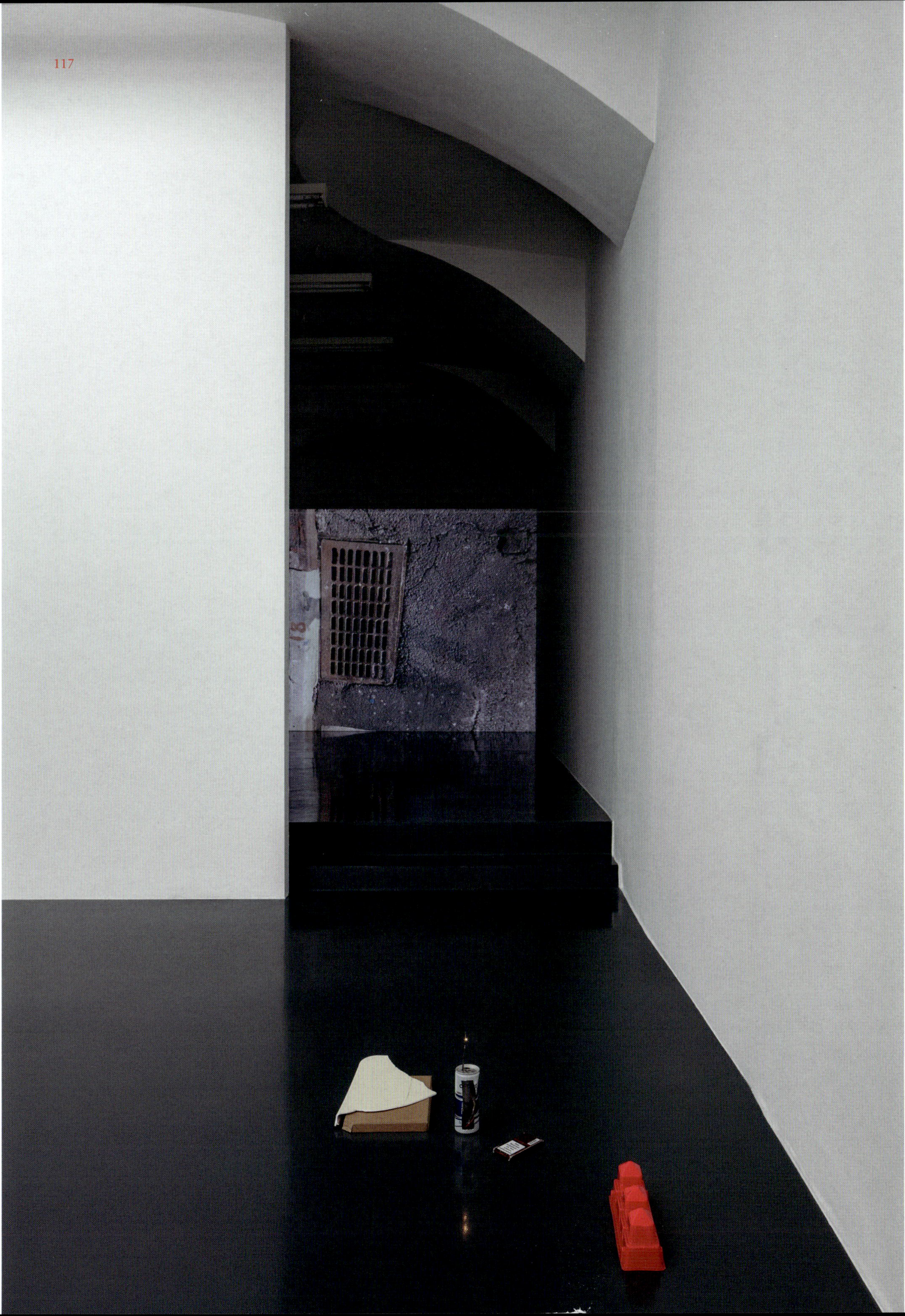

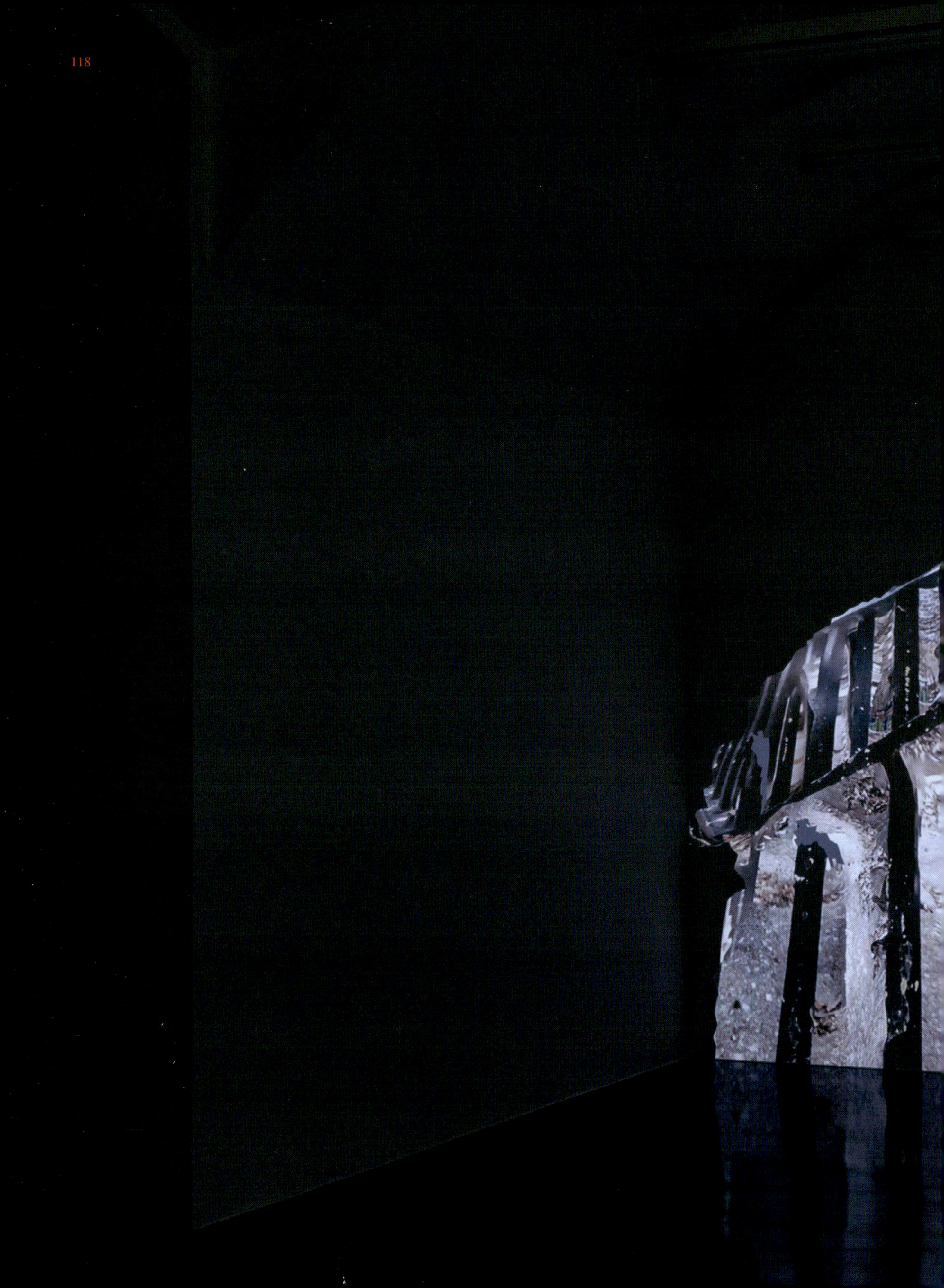

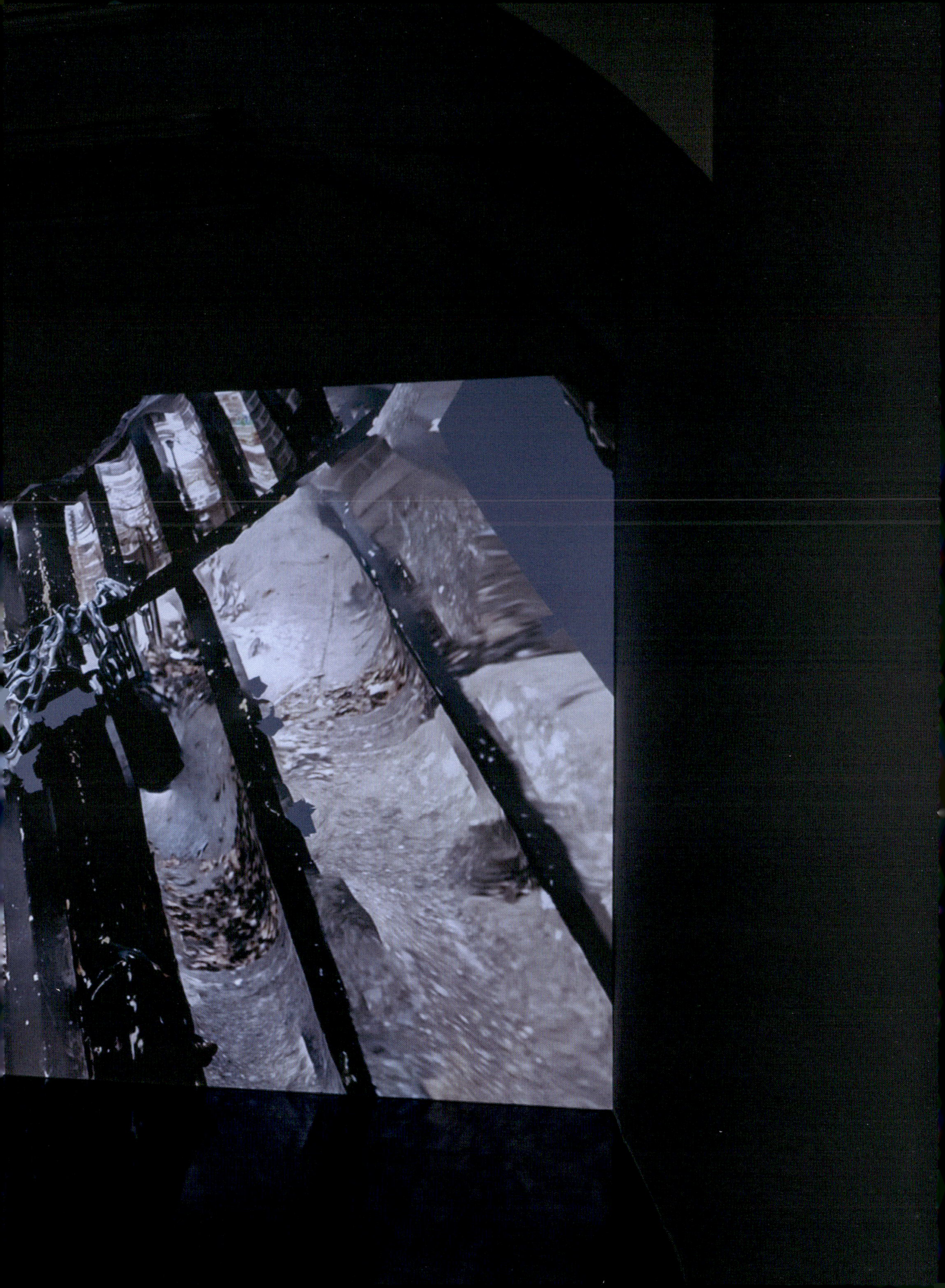

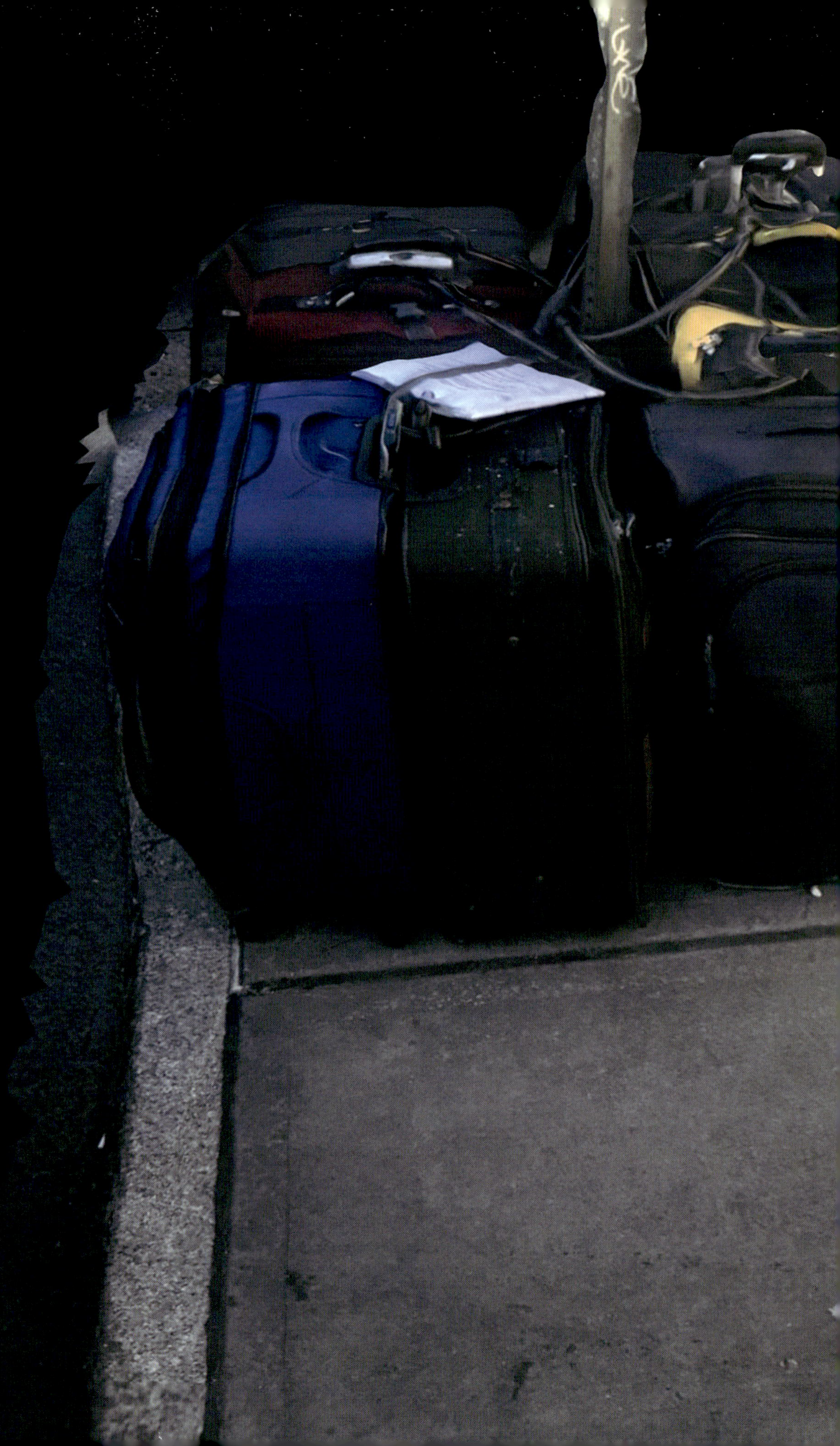

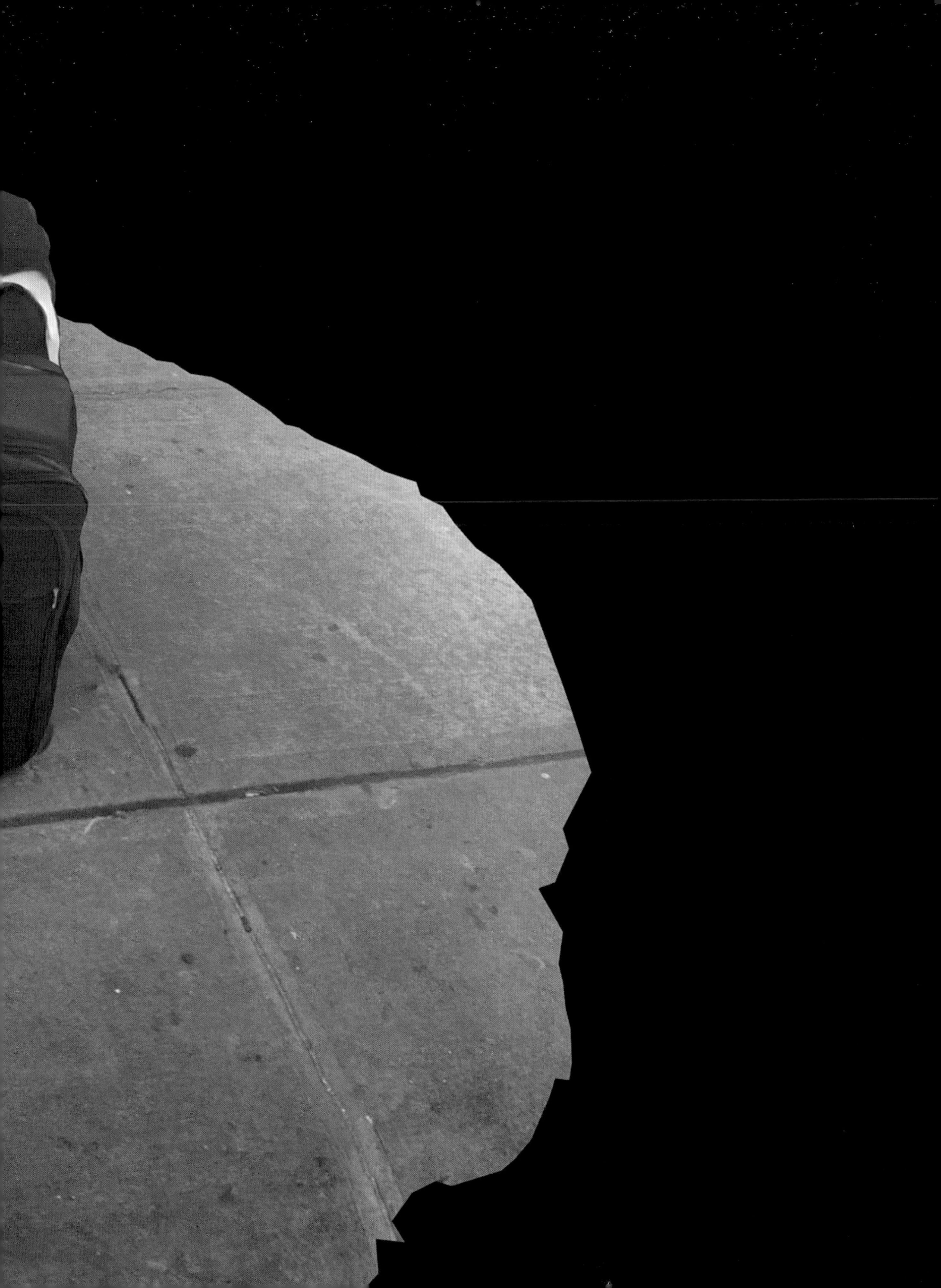

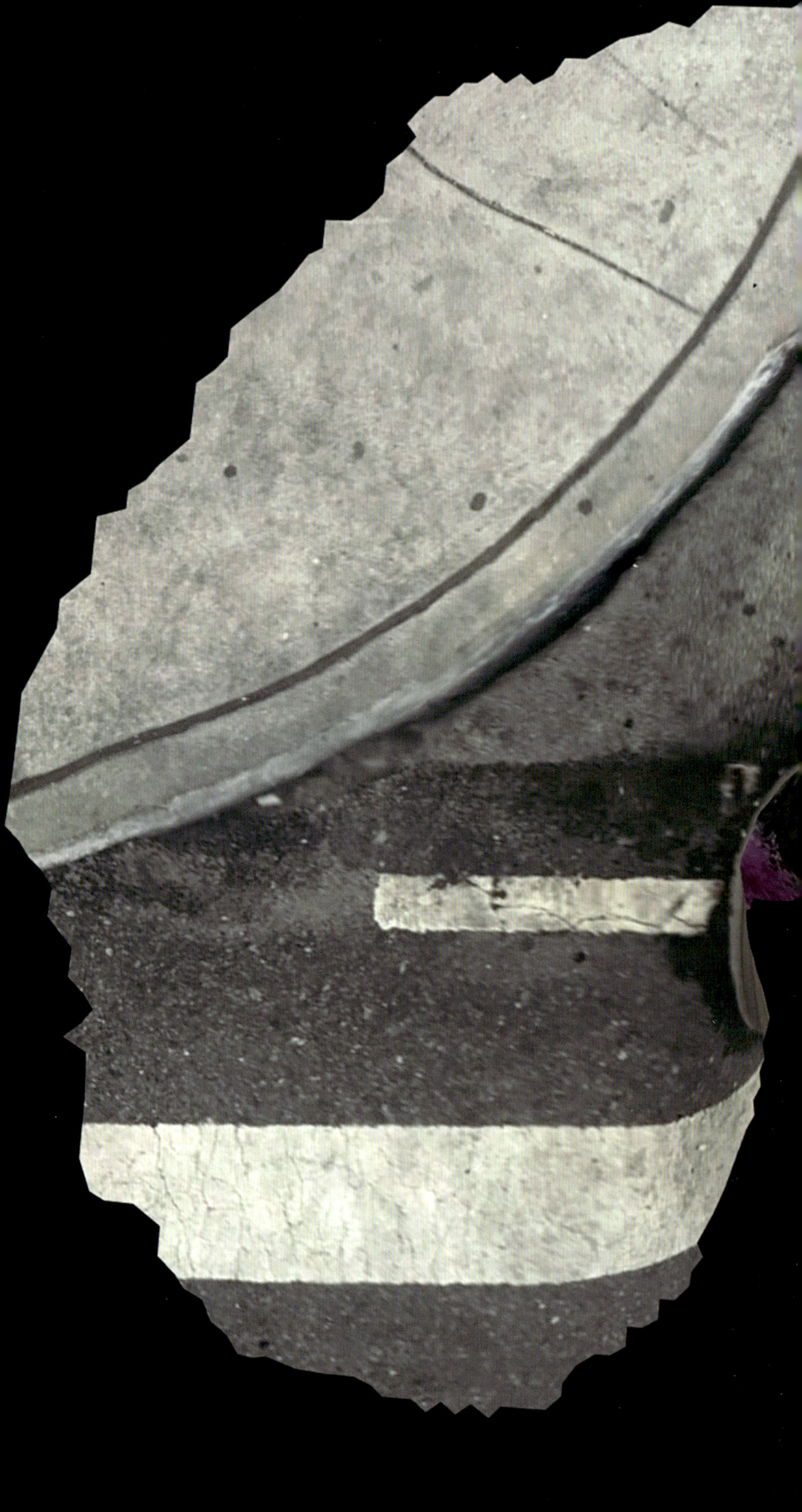

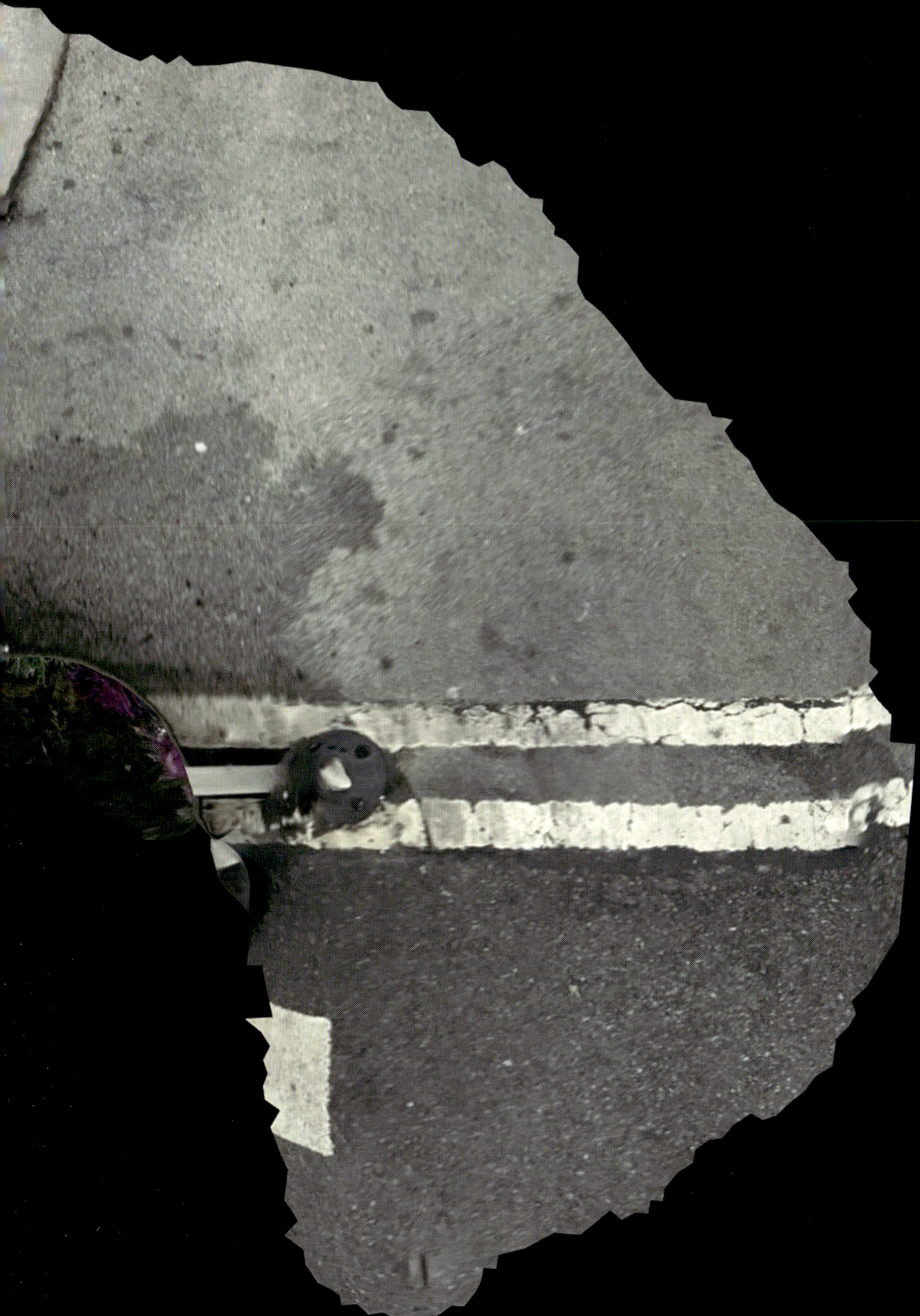

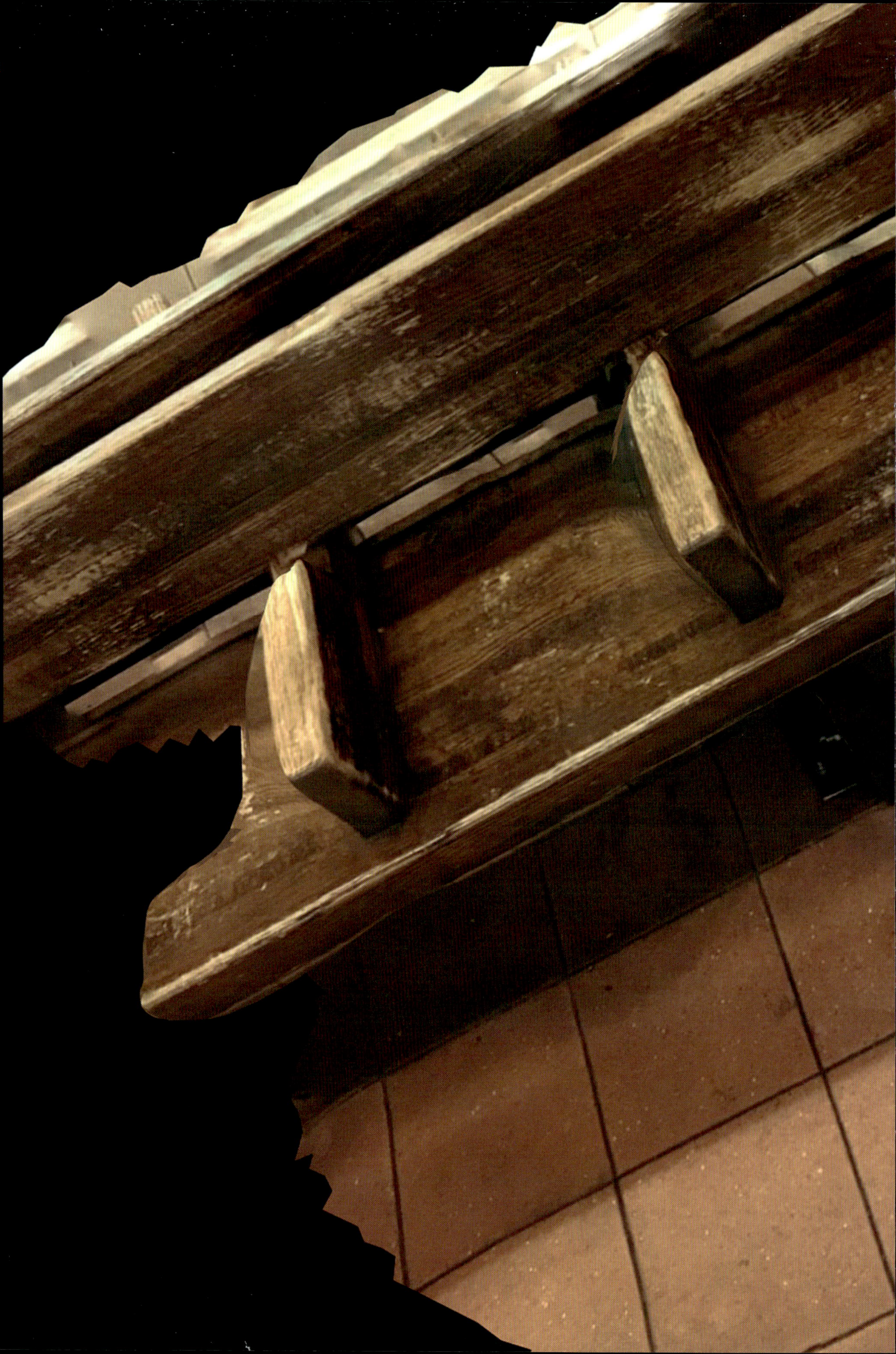

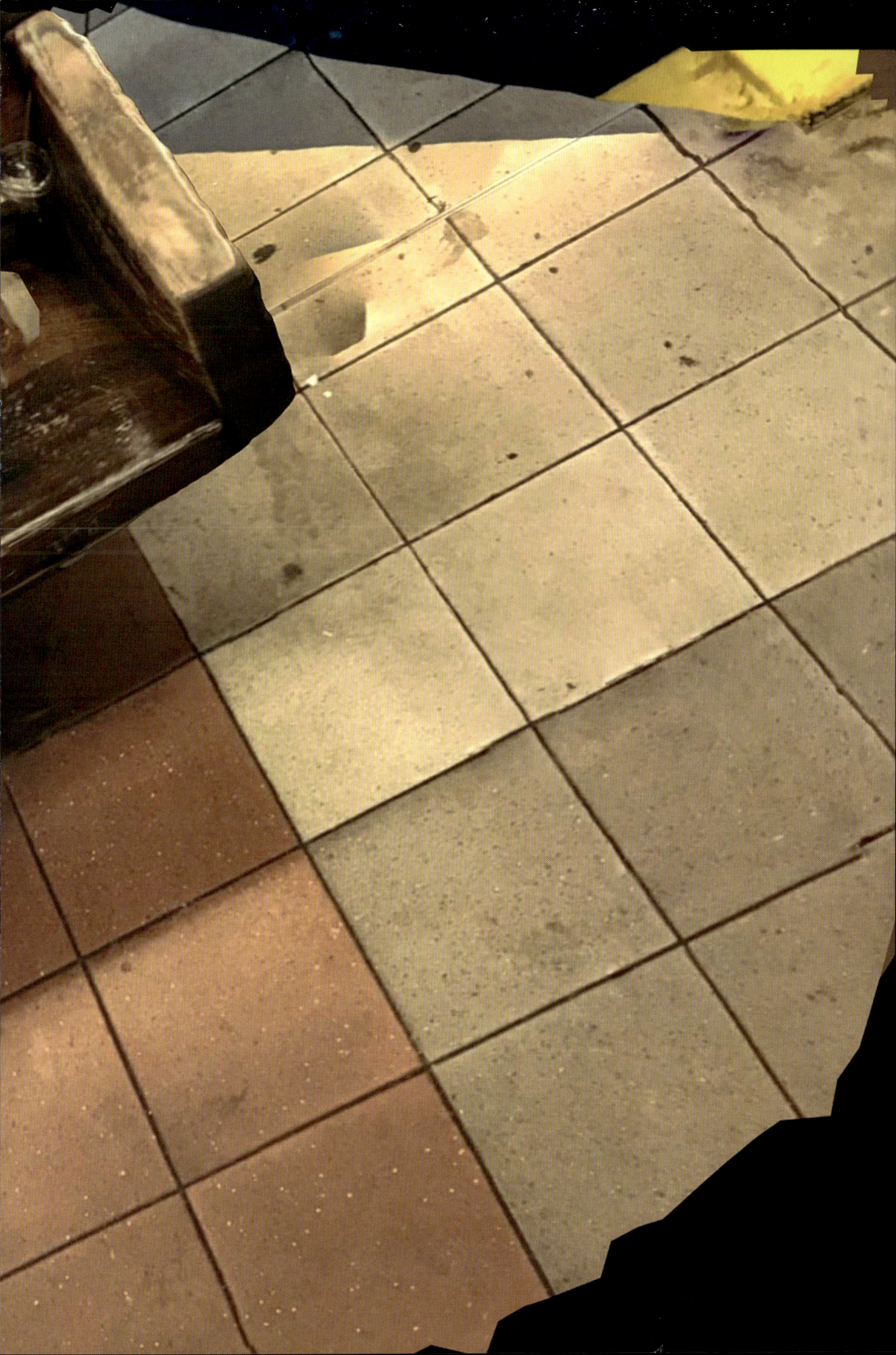

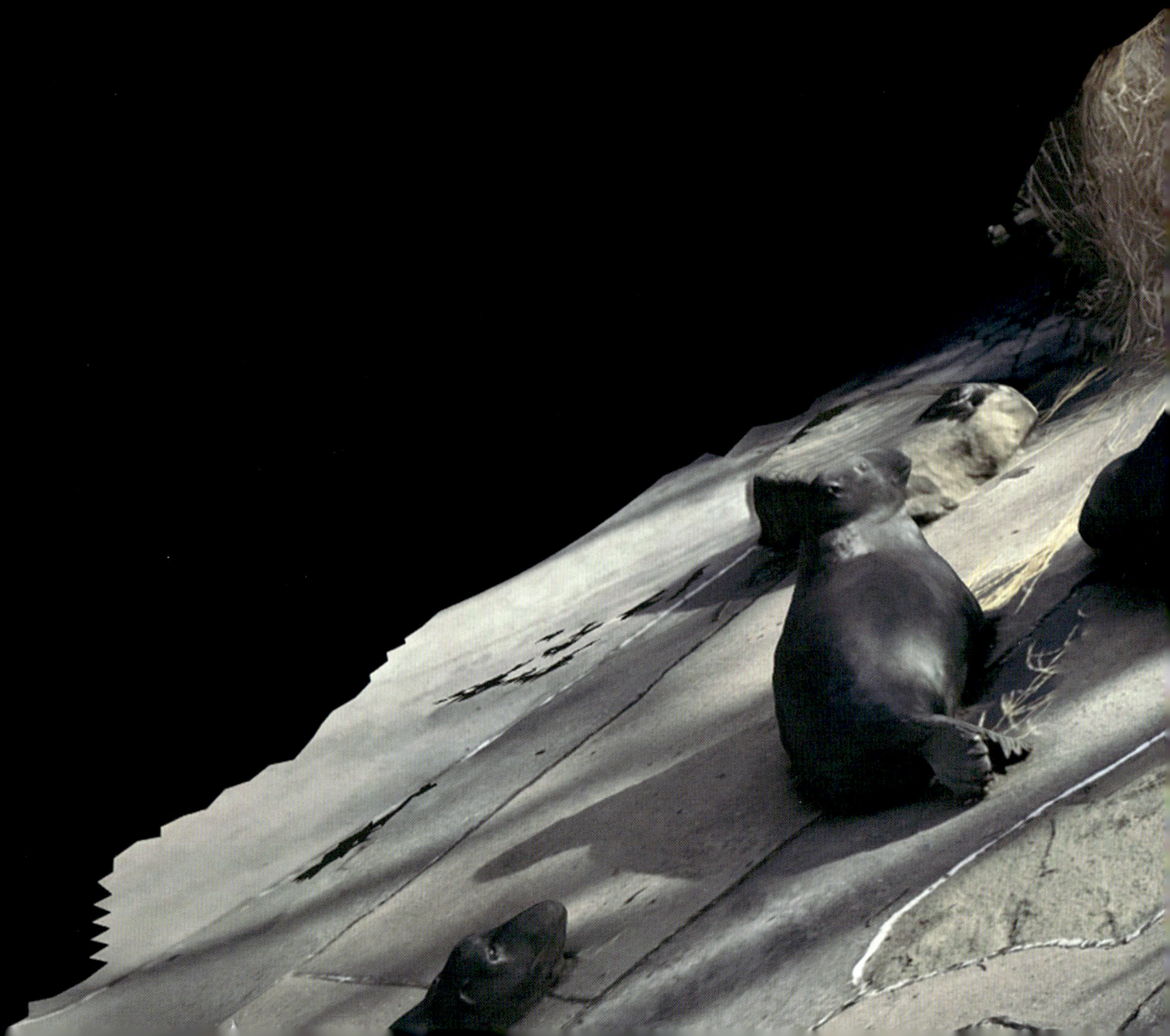

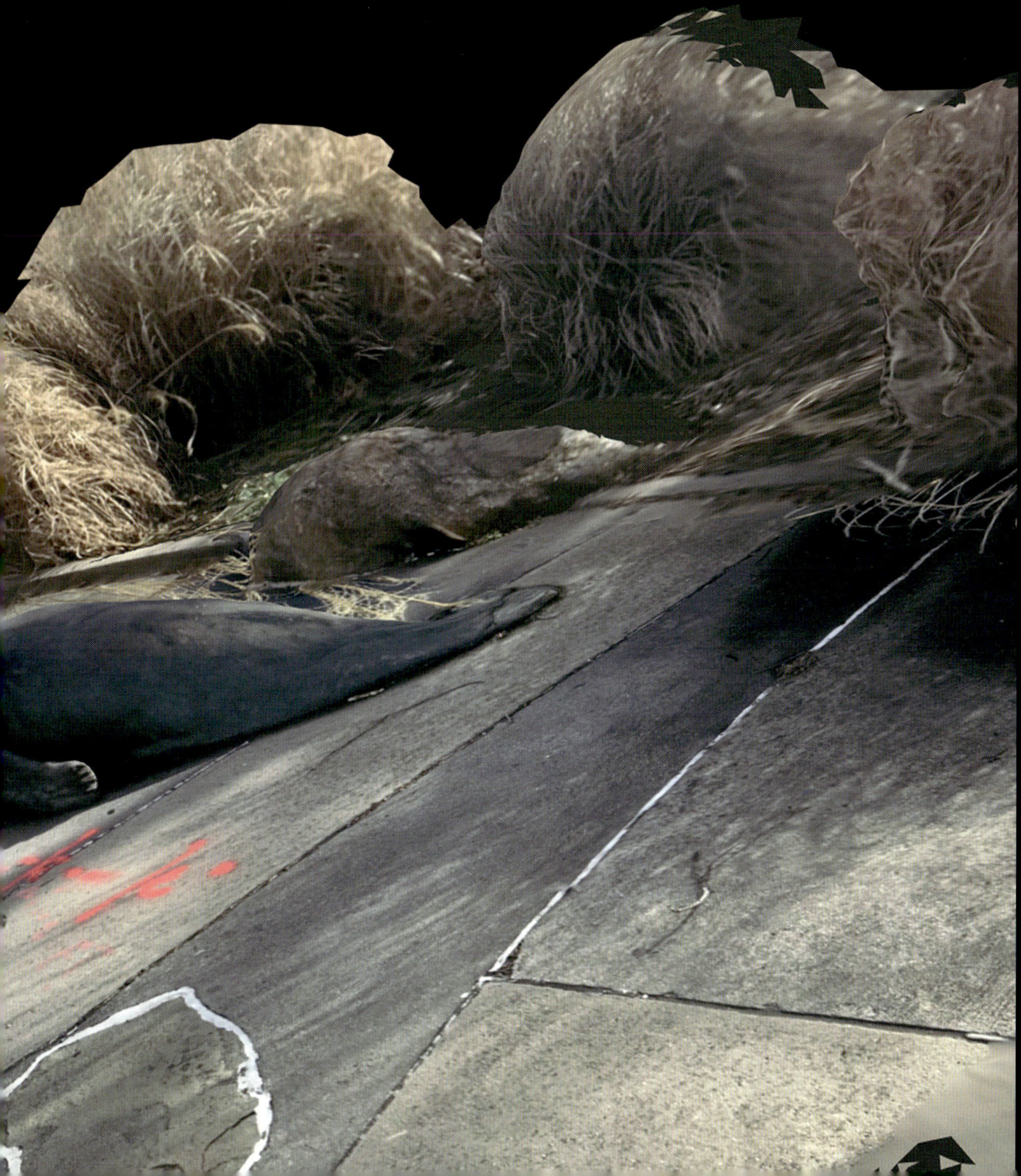

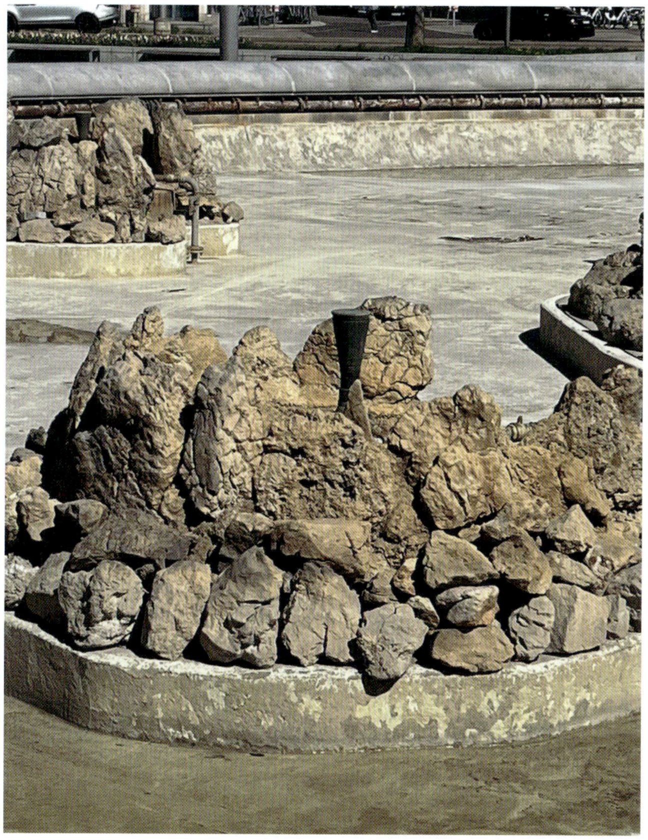

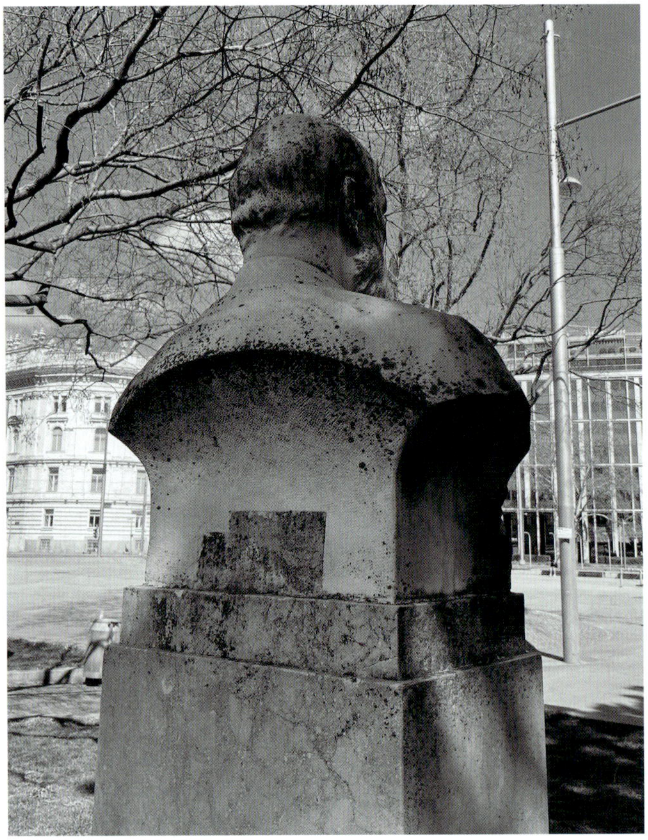

Alphabet und Abfluss: Die Dinge das Laufen lehren
Katharina Hausladen

Infrastrukturen sichern die funktionalen Abläufe in einer Gesellschaft. Die Versorgung mit Gütern und Dienstleistungen gehört dazu ebenso wie die Gewährleistung symbolischer Handlungen der Kommunikation und Distribution. Besonders im Zuge der wachsenden Aufmerksamkeit für sogenannte „kritische", da lebensnotwendige Infrastrukturen zeigt sich, dass diese „auf sichtbare und unsichtbare Weise [...] unsere Gegenwart formen"[1]. Sei es die Energie- und medizinische Versorgung, sei es die Lebensmittelproduktion und -verarbeitung, seien es die Medienberichterstattung, das Transportwesen oder der Zahlungsverkehr – Infrastrukturen halten die Gesellschaft funktionsfähig, und zwar sowohl, indem sie bestimmte Verhaltensweisen ermöglichen, als auch, indem sie bestimmte andere kontrollieren, unterbinden oder unter Strafe stellen. Wem welche Infrastruktur nützt und wer von den infrastrukturellen Instanziierungen des Dürfens, Könnens und Sollens direkt oder indirekt ausgeschlossen bleibt oder in besonderem Maße von ihnen reglementiert wird, ist also immer auch Ausdruck ganz bestimmter Mehrheitsverhältnisse und insofern ideologisch konstruiert.

Objekte zweiter Ordnung

Die Aspekte des Funktionalen und Nützlichen, die Infrastrukturen begleiten, treten in den Arbeiten von Benjamin Hirte vor allem als Werkzeug hervor: einerseits als Werkstoff oder Material, andererseits als Instrument oder Methode. Für seine Ausstellung „Hamilton Beach"[7, 15, 40, 41], die 2018 von Hirtes Wiener Galerie Layr im Rahmen des Galerienfestivals „CONDO New York" in den Räumen der New Yorker Galerie JTT gezeigt wurde, produzierte er eine Installation, bestehend aus den Arbeiten *Factory*, *Apotheke / Pharmacy*, *Barrel* und *Water tower* (alle 2018), die sich auf den ersten Blick wie ein Bauchladen des täglichen Lebens liest. Die vier Objekte, die auf einem weißen Tisch[41] wie Utensilien aus der Sammlung eines technischen oder stadtgeschichtlichen Museums angeordnet sind, erinnern an Modelle von Gegenständen, die unterschiedliche Nützlichkeitsversprechen kommunizieren: die mit Seegrasschnüren umspannten Rohre in *Factory* könnten Teile eines größeren Kanalsystems sein; das gotische A als Erkennungszeichen für Apotheken in Deutschland, das in *Apotheke / Pharmacy* aus Aluminium gefräst eine Plexiglasbox[7] im Format eines Erste-Hilfe-Kastens ziert, signalisiert gesundheitliche Fürsorge; und *Water tower* wirkt wie die aus Baumarktelementen wie Wellblech und Holz archetypisch zusammengezimmerte Miniatur eines Wasserturms. Spätestens beim Anblick des vierten Objekts, *Barrel*[15], das aus einer grob abgeschliffenen Getränkedose besteht, die mit Stroh gefüllt ist und von der so etwas wie kleine Abzugsrohre abstehen, stellt sich die Funktionalität der hier präsentierten Objekte als Projektion heraus: Was repräsentiert das kleine Fass? Ein Feuerrohr, eine Art Heizsystem oder Verbrennungsanlage? So oft das Auge den Gegenstand auch abtastet, so wenig vermittelt sich dessen Verwendungszweck. Dies hat den Effekt, dass auch die anderen Dinge mit einem Mal unter Verdacht stehen, keine Kleinstnachbildungen bestehender Gebrauchsgüter zu sein, keine Darstellungen von Infrastrukturen im alltäglichen Sinne. Die Plexiglasbox *imitiert* einen Erste-Hilfe-Kasten, die Rohre *suggerieren* ein Kanalsystem, der überdachte Trichter im Holzgitter *kopiert* einen Wasserturm. Doch sind dies keine naturalistischen Abbildungen funktionaler Ensembles, sondern Abstraktionen von diesen. Hirte zitiert zwar einzelne Details aus infrastrukturellen Umräumen, setzt sie aber zu Objekten zweiter Ordnung zusammen. Der Betrachter*in fällt deshalb nicht sofort auf, dass die wiedererkannten optischen Zeichen in ihren spezifischen Verbindungen gar keine Entsprechung in der Realität haben.

1 – „Einrichtung und Gegebenheit: Infrastruktur als Form und Handlung", kuratiert von Martin Beck, Sabeth Buchmann und Stephanie Damianitsch, Exhibit Galerie, Wien, 9. März bis 22. Mai 2022, https://www.akbild.ac.at/de/museum-und-ausstellungen/Exhibit/ausstellungen-veranstaltungen/aktuelle-ausstellungen/2022/einrichtung-und-gegebenheit-infrastruktur-als-form-und-handlung.

Was als postmodernes Spiel der Kombination und Rekombination von Elementen, die Benutzbarkeit suggerieren und diese zum Teil auch erfüllen, im Anschluss an österreichische Nachkriegsarchitekten und -künstler wie Hans Hollein, Walter Pichler [14] und Franz West verstanden werden kann, legt Hirte, anders als diese, nicht partizipativ an. Zumindest gehen Skulpturen wie *Untitled (stool)* (2010) [1] – eine seiner frühesten Arbeiten, die in dieser Linie stehen – nicht in ihrer Benutzbarkeit auf. Für diese Arbeit hat er in Anlehnung an einen von Arne Jacobsen designten Holzstuhl aus den 1950er Jahren einen Hocker gebaut, der zwar als solcher zu gebrauchen ist – es lässt sich auf ihm Platz nehmen. Die visuellen Einschreibungen von dessen Funktionalität hat Hirte allerdings so verschoben, dass man nicht sicher sein kann, ob auf dem Stuhl auch tatsächlich Platz genommen werden soll. Die Rückenlehne in Form des dänischen Design-Klassikers hat er so abgesägt, dass das Rund der Biegung am hinteren Ende der Sitzfläche und damit die ursprüngliche Gestalt des Stuhls noch angedeutet bleiben. Dazu hat er die Beine eines weiteren Stuhls so an die Unterseite der Sitzfläche montiert, dass die Schraublöcher der originären Stuhlbeine an der Oberfläche noch zu sehen, aber nicht mehr deckungsgleich mit den neu verschraubten sind. Nur der geschulte Blick erkennt, dass Hirtes Version des Jacobsen-Stuhls Teile aus insgesamt drei verschiedenen Stühlen enthält.

Realismus und Readymade

Solche Verfremdungen von Produktformen und infrastrukturellen Zeichen des Konsums werden bei Hirte als Reflexionen der Konstruktion von Normalität verständlich. Als solche sind sie keine Entwürfe einer erst zu realisierenden Wirklichkeit; Hirte geht es, mit anderen Worten, nicht darum, alternative Welten zu bauen, die zur Interaktion mit den ausgestellten Objekten, ob funktional oder dysfunktional, einladen. Eher handelt es sich hierbei um Kommunikationsangebote, die die visuelle Wahrnehmung auf die formale Qualität eines Dings lenken und dadurch Codes aufrufen, die auf etwas Bestehendes in der Welt verweisen. Das Modellhafte, der Schablonencharakter, durch den Hirte seiner Darstellung der erkennbaren Welt Objektivität verleiht, dient folglich der Illusion von Realität, so als spräche ein Ding über sich selbst. Dieser Realismus gelingt ihm vor allem durch meist einfache Sujets wie Stühle, Rohre oder Becken, durch geometrische Klarheit und Strenge, die Funktionalität suggerieren, sowie oftmals durch kühle und widerständige Materialien wie Aluminium und Stein. So scheint es, als hätten die überdimensionierten Alu-Haken (*1.1*, *1.2* und *1.3*, 2014) [17], die an riesige Tackerklammern erinnern und skulptural im Raum platziert sind, aufgrund ihrer figurativen Spuren ein Eigenleben. Gleiches gilt für die zementgebundenen Spanplatten (*Untitled [tags]*, 2014) [8, 35], die Hirte wie monströse Produktverpackungen, teils an die Wand gelehnt, teils senkrecht aus ihr herausstehend, montiert und in die er Löcher, u. a. in Form von sogenannten Eurolochaufhängern, mit denen Waren zum Verkauf an Haken präsentiert werden können, geschnitten hat: Von diesen Verpackungsriesen geht eine Souveränität aus, die sie nicht nur durch ihre Größe, sondern auch durch die figurative Rhetorik, mit der sie scheinbar der realen Dingwelt entnommen sind, erhalten.

In gewisser Weise ähnelt Hirtes Spiel mit figurativen Operationen wie diesen dem von Filmemacher John Wilson in dessen HBO-Comedy-Dokuserie *How To with John Wilson* (2020–22). Durch die Straßen von New York ziehend, nimmt Wilson einen schier endlosen Bilderstrom von meist unfreiwilligen Slapstick-Momenten im öffentlichen Raum auf, die häufig durch vorgefundene Objekte ausgelöst werden. Dadurch, dass und wie die Kamera diese Objekte festhält, erlangen sie den Status öffentlicher Skulpturen, treten sie als Readymades in Erscheinung, was der Situationskomik zugleich eine sozialanthropologische Komponente verleiht. Indem sie öffentliches Leben als ästhetische Erfahrung, „die der Betrachtung wert ist", einsichtig werden lassen, wie Kevin B. Lee argumentiert, schreiben sich Wilsons „Aufnahmen – eine Brottüte baumelt in einer U-Bahn an einem Handgriff, eine Frau lockt eine Taube in eine Einkaufstüte – das Gewicht von Ort und Zeit" ein.[2] Auch Hirtes Arbeiten leben von dem verunklärten Verhältnis der Artefakte zu ihrem realen Kontext; und auch bei Hirte bewirkt die narrative Verfasstheit sowohl der Verknüpfung irritierender Details eines Dings (weshalb ist die

2 – Kevin B. Lee, „Wie macht man Internet-Comedy (ohne das Internet)?", in: *Texte zu Kunst*, #121, Berlin 2021, S. 49–55, hier: S. 51.

Bowlingkugel in *Gamebreaker*, 2013[21], nicht rund, sondern beschnitten?) als auch von dessen eigensinniger Neukontextualisierung (die Gewinde und Rohre in ~, 2013[16], bilden die Form einer Pistole) eine Komik, die einen Abstand zum bestehenden physischen wie symbolischen Tauschwertuniversum westlicher Gesellschaften markiert. Nicht das Regelhafte, also die Bezugsmöglichkeit auf jegliche Regel der Sinnproduktion, wird hier verunsichert. Es ist die Berufung auf etablierte Regeln der Unterscheidung zwischen Fundstück und künstlerischer Bearbeitung, die in Hirtes Werk an Stabilität verliert.

Kalkül der Niedlichkeit

Eine wesentliche Rolle spielt in diesem Zusammenhang Hirtes Umgang mit Proportionen in Kombination mit einer Distanz erzeugenden Ästhetik der industriellen Herstellung. Beide Verfahren machen seine Werke anschlussfähig an die Praxis von einerseits (post-)minimalistischen Künstler*innen wie Cady Noland, abzüglich der Noland-typischen Brutalität, sowie andererseits Vertretern der Pop Art wie Claes Oldenburg. Während für die Nähe zu Noland vor allem Hirtes Einsatz von metallischen Oberflächen, eine reduzierte Formensprache sowie ein Interesse für die institutionellen und kommerziellen Manifestationen von Öffentlichkeit sprechen – etwa dann, wenn er Americana wie das rote Marlboro-Dach als großformatige PVC-Plane inszeniert (*Vector [Marlboro theme]*, 2016)[67] –, ist der Bezug zu Oldenburg vor allem einer der räumlichen Dimension. Der Sprühkopf etwa, den Hirte aus weißem Marmor übergroß nachbildet (*Untitled*, 2012)[24], und der Hocker, den er in Gestalt eines Rückenwirbels aus Kunstleder, Filz und Schaumstoff fertigt (*Backbone*, 2017)[25], scheinen unmittelbar aus dem Oldenburg'schen Repertoire monumentaler Skulpturen von Alltagsgegenständen entnommen zu sein. Sieht man Hirtes Knochen-Hocker genauer an, fällt zudem auf, dass die Wirbelfortsätze ebenso gut die zu eng aneinandergenähten, klatschenden Hände einer Cartoon-Figur sein könnten, so wie auch die spiegeleigelbe Sitzfläche Assoziationen an Pikachu, Emoji, die Simpsons und Co. aufkommen lässt.

Überhaupt nimmt das ästhetische Vokabular von Hirtes Werk zunehmend niedliche, runde Formen in die weitgehend nüchterne visuell-installative Sprache auf. Schon frühere Arbeiten wie *wig* (2012)[22] – ein Leinen-Siebdruck, der die Disney-Version einer barock anmutenden Perücke zeigt – greifen physische und symbolische Materialisierungen von populären Figuren und sprachlichen Zeichen auf. Allerdings thematisieren aktuellere Skulpturen Hirtes wie *The Robbers* (2019)[9], das eine Art Totem darstellt und sich wie beim Papierknickbildspiel aus so unterschiedlichen Elementen wie dem Rumpf einer bauchigen Cartoon-Figur, einem Macaron, der comichaften Parodie eines Totenkopfes sowie einer gestauchten Variante von Snoopy mit kindchenschemahaft großem Kopf zusammensetzt, den Warencharakter des Niedlichen, wie er im Rückgriff auf Sianne Ngai bestimmt werden kann, *ausdrücklich*: als Wunsch nach einer intimeren, sinnlicheren Beziehung zu den Waren, die wir konsumieren; als Begehren, die Dinge, die wir als niedlich empfinden, in die Hand zu nehmen oder zu streicheln und damit die kognitive Distanz zugunsten einer affektiv-taktilen Nähe zum begehrten Objekt zu überwinden.[3]

Zeichen und Affekt

Es sind solche Momente der Affizierung und scheinbaren Aufhebung des Abstands zwischen Betrachter*in und Werk, die Hirtes Arbeiten inzwischen häufiger durchziehen. Dies mag auch daran liegen, dass er seit einiger Zeit vermehrt „weichere" und weniger beharrliche Materialien wie Gips, Styropor und Kunststoff verwendet. So etwa auch bei *Solace* (2021)[2], einer eigens für den Wiener Kunstverein angefertigten Arbeit, für die Hirte erneut ein Möbelstück variiert hat: ein Sitzrondell aus lackiertem Styropor und glasfaserverstärktem Kunststoff, an dessen Außenseite er vier knubbelige Füße angebracht hat. Zum Loch in der Mitte der kreisrunden Sitzbank hin hat Hirte zudem ein Gewinde oder eine Nut ausgespart, so als ließen sich – in der Logik von *The Robbers* – weitere Körper- oder Objektteile auf diesen Unterkörper stecken. Interessant ist diese Arbeit auch deshalb, weil sie verschiedene,

3 – Vgl. Sianne Ngai, *Our Aesthetic Categories: Zany, Cute, Interesting*, Harvard University Press 2012, besonders S. 13, 27 und 54.

in Hirtes Werk wiederkehrende Elemente in sich vereint. Dazu gehört zum einen das „Flansch-Prinzip", wie man diese Methode des Ineinandersteckens und der modular erweiterbaren Verschraubung, mit der Hirte bereits seit den frühen 2010er Jahren arbeitet, nennen könnte, und die sich im wiederholten Einsatz von Rohren, Rinnen und Abflüssen als Orte des Durchlaufens, Aufbrauchens und Auswerfens ausdrückt. Das Rohr oder der Ablauf hat außerdem den Effekt, dass hinter der zweidimensionalen Frontansicht immer schon eine Bewegung in den Raum angelegt ist, eine Vertiefung oder Ausdehnung nach hinten oder unten hin, die im Falle des Abflusses sogar unendlich gedacht werden kann. Das Flansch-Prinzip als eines, das den Raum strukturiert und gestaltet, ist also prototypisch skulptural. Ein anderes für Hirtes Werk zentrales Motiv, das sich in *Solace* entschieden artikuliert findet, ist das der angewandten Dimension des Sitzmöbels: Anders noch als bei *Untitled (stool)*[1] lädt diese Arbeit dezidiert dazu ein, sich – dem titelgebenden Versprechen gemäß, darin Trost zu finden – auf ihr niederzulassen und zu verweilen, so als handle es sich um eine Bank in einem Park oder im Foyer eines repräsentativen Gebäudes. Das Potenzial der Benutzbarkeit, das bei Hirte stets eine wichtige Rolle gespielt hat, bekommt hier noch einmal deutlich mehr Gewicht, ja, es werden die Bereiche der angewandten und der bildenden Kunst, von denen seine Praxis sich gleichermaßen beeinflusst zeigt, noch stärker miteinander in Beziehung gesetzt. Schließlich verbinden sich in *Solace* auch noch zwei weitere Aspekte: Die Niedlichkeit, evoziert durch die runde Form und die Füßchen, die auf massenkulturell Figürliches verweisen, bewirkt in Ergänzung der Funktionalität einer Sitzbank, die es so im öffentlichen Raum tatsächlich geben könnte, dass diese als öffentliche Skulptur wahrgenommen werden kann. Es würde nicht verwundern, wenn die Arbeit, die sich gleichermaßen aus Überlegungen über den angewandten Status wie über das knuffig Maskottchenhafte eines Objekts des täglichen Lebens in einer Stadt wie Wien speist, dorthin rücküberführt würde, wo sie konzeptionell herkommt: in den öffentlichen Raum.

Damit erhält die Frage nach dem Wie der Bezugnahme auf infrastrukturelle Zeichen in heutigen Massenkulturen bei Hirte eine genuin erzählerische oder allgemeiner: sprachliche Verfasstheit. Anders gesagt kehrt das Flansch-Prinzip hier auf der Ebene des sprachlichen Zeichens wieder. Denn der prinzipiell endlos erweiterbare semiotische Zusammenhang von Gefundenem und selbst Hergestelltem, Readymade und Multiple, für den Hirtes künstlerische und gestalterische Praxis steht, legt die der Rezeption zugrundliegenden ästhetischen, politischen, sozialen etc. Gebrauchs- und Funktionszusammenhänge frei, die deren „Alphabet" bilden – und zwar nicht erst dann, wenn er Buchstaben der von ihm entworfenen, die formale Struktur von Lochbändern aufgreifenden Schriftart *Plumbers Font*[20] installativ integriert (etwa mit Werken wie *C*, 2017[46], und *untitled (A)*, 2015)[44]. Ein Gitterbecken ist ein Springbrunnen ist eine Treppenstufe ist ein Fußballfeld. Hirtes Skulpturen sind niemals ganzheitlich vorhanden, niemals identisch mit dem Zeichenmaterial, aus dem sie gemacht sind. Mehr noch rücken sie als Materialisierungen sozialen Lebens immer auch die infrastrukturelle Bedingtheit ihrer eigenen Produktion in den Blick.

Im Falle von Hirtes Arbeit *We labour but not for ourselves*[27], die er für seine gemeinsam mit Nancy Lupo 2021 in der Mackey Garage am MAK Center in Los Angeles konzipierte Ausstellung „Antwerp" produziert hat, heißt dies vor allem die ökonomische Logik der autoritären bzw. internalisierten Ausbeutung der Arbeitenden. Die aus Polyurethan gefräste Skulptur stellt einen Bienenkorb dar und ist an das Emblem[26] jener österreichischen Genossenschaftsbauten angelehnt, die nach dem zweiten Weltkrieg aus Mitteln des Marshall-Plans finanziert wurden. Wie die Biene im Bienenstaat, so ließe sich analogisieren, beinhaltete Arbeit im historischen Sozialismus Österreichs eine Form des sozialen Handelns, das auf kooperative Wirtschaft gerichtet war. Im gegenwärtigen Spätkapitalismus dagegen ist Arbeit zwar immer noch auf die soziale Welt gerichtet, aber hochgradig individualisiert. Ökonomische Rationalität herrscht demnach auch und gerade dort, wo Identifikationsangebote bei gleichzeitiger Vereinzelung der Subjekte und Inwertsetzung von Individualität behauptet werden. Hirtes Realismus ist es zu verdanken, dass seine Bezugnahme auf den Bienenkorb als Symbol für sozialistisches Wirtschaften und Wohnen einerseits ikonisch, nämlich als Bild gewordene Politik, andererseits dialektisch, nämlich als offener Widerspruch zu der gesellschaftlichen Realität, der sie entstammt, erkennbar wird. Im Zeichen der Sprache zu handeln, heißt so gesehen, die Dinge das Laufen zu lehren.

Es war ein wichtiges Jahr für die New Yorker Lower East Side. 1936 entstand in dem Stadtteil mit den First Houses nicht nur das erste Projekt des sozialen Wohnungsbaus in den Vereinigten Staaten. Dieselben New-Deal-Maßnahmen, die dafür verantwortlich waren, hatten auch den Bau eines neuen öffentlichen Schwimmbads ermöglicht. Die Ausstattung des Hamilton Fish Park Pools [54] war nach den Maßstäben von 1936 üppig: eine Hightech-Filteranlage, Unterwasserbeleuchtung, blau glasierte Terrakottafliesen, Ablaufrinnen, ein Badehaus mit einer Kapazität von 2.200 Besucher*innen, ein Hauptbecken mit olympischen Dimensionen und zwei angrenzende Tauch- und Planschbecken. Tatsächlich bildeten die drei Schwimmbecken in der ursprünglichen Anordnung einen Halbkreis, wodurch so etwas wie ein Gefühl halber Inklusion entstand.

Dies war allerdings bereits die dritte Phase staatlicher Maßnahmen, die eine Verbesserung der schlechten Lebensbedingungen des Arbeiterbezirks zum Ziel hatten. Begonnen hatte alles um das Jahr 1900, als das Architekturbüro Carrère and Hastings damit beauftragt wurde, die Freizeitanlage im damaligen Zentrum der jüdischen, irischen und polnischen Einwanderer-Communities zu gestalten. Nachdem sie mit der Idee, die größte Marmorstruktur Nordamerikas zu errichten, den Wettbewerb für das Hauptgebäude der New York Public Library [32] gewonnen hatten, richteten die Architekten, wie es in der amerikanischen Aristokratie üblich war, ihr Augenmerk auf Paris. Angeregt von dem erst vor Kurzem fertiggestellten Bau des Petit Palais, das von der Presse wohlwollend aufgenommen worden war als ein Objekt, das sowohl „den Verstand bildet als auch die Sinne erfreut", planten sie die Fläche als einen Platz, der prädestiniert war für die Figur des Flaneurs: mit Bänken, auf denen man sich zum Bücherlesen niederlassen konnte, Grasflächen, die nicht genutzt werden sollten, und einer Turnhalle im Stil der Beaux-Arts-Architektur.[1] Die importierte Pariser Moderne sorgte aber schnell für Reibungen, denn die beiden frankophilen Architekten hatten den Eigensinn ihrer Adressat*innen unterschätzt. Innerhalb nur eines Jahres waren die angelegten Wege und Grasflächen zerstört, auf denen die Spaziergänger*innen ihre Kreise ziehen sollten. Den Behörden wurde klar, dass die bürgerlichen Fantasien von Carrère and Hastings einiger Anpassungen bedurften. Also folgten sie den Forderungen der Lower East Side Community und eröffneten den Park zwei Jahre später erneut. Jetzt fanden sich hier unter anderem Laufbahnen, Basketball- und Tennisplätze. Als drei Jahrzehnte später der Hamilton Fish Park Pool an diesem Ort entstand, war von den ursprünglichen Plänen nur die Beaux-Arts-Turnhalle übrig geblieben – ein Symbol für den gescheiterten Versuch, eingewanderte Arbeiter*innen mit herumschlendernden Flaneuren gleichzusetzen.

Das Video *First Houses* (2020) [117–122] vermittelt einen Eindruck dieser architektonischen Aushandlungsprozesse zwischen imaginiertem Publikum und wirklichen Adressat*innen, von fehlgeleiteten Bezügen und enttäuschten Versprechen. Durch die stille Montage der Reste öffentlicher Infrastrukturen aus der Post-New-Deal-Ära – die Mülleimer, Skulpturen im öffentlichen Raum, Tore, Parkbänke, Gullys, Spielplätze, Zäune, Wasserhydranten und Türen – wird die Frage aufgeworfen, wie diese Konflikte in eine narrative Ordnung eingebettet werden können. Als etablierte Form der Erzählung von Kampf und Niedergang scheint das Melodram hier am besten geeignet: Arbeit versus Wohlstand, Umverteilung versus Erbschaft. Die architektonischen Objekte werden als stille Akteure in einem Streit entlang der wohlbekannten Trennlinien der Sozialdemokratie rekrutiert.

Und tatsächlich erschließen sich anhand der architektonischen Objekte bestimmte Konfigurationen der Sozialdemokratie, die diese unsichtbaren Infrastrukturen überhaupt erst hervorgebracht haben: der Keynesianische Konsens zwischen Arbeit und Kapital, der parteiübergreifende Rückhalt gegenüber dem Wohlfahrtsstaat, die vier Jahrzehnte rückläufiger Ungleichheit und sozialer Immobilität. Was wir in *First Houses* zu sehen bekommen, ist das, was viele dieser Objekte im Laufe der Zeit miterlebt haben. Als die Lower East Side

1 – Herbert Butler, „The Palaces of Fine Arts", *Art Journal* 41 (1901), S. 44.

zu einem „Sammelpunkt für Drogendealer" geworden war, wie die *New York Times* im Jahr 1984 in einem Bericht über den Hamilton Fish Park Pool schrieb, hatte die Finanzkrise von 1975 bereits zu einer maßgeblichen Verschiebung der Machtverhältnisse in New York geführt, wodurch die melodramatische Erzählung ihre zwangsläufige Wendung zum Niedergang nahm: Schulden wurden zur effektiven Waffe für die voranschreitende Privatisierung und den Abbau des Sozialstaats. Dies sind die ersten Stufen eines uns allen wohlbekannten Narrativs.[2] In der Tat hat man das Gefühl, dass *First Houses* die enorme Distanz zu vermitteln vermag, die uns heute von jener Blütezeit der Sozialdemokratie trennt, die sich noch nicht von der konservativen Gegenrevolution der 1980er Jahre und ihrer Pionierarbeit in Sachen Austeritätspolitik in die Enge getrieben sah.

Doch wie soll man auf diese Residuen des Wohlfahrtsstaats zurückblicken, ohne auf das inzwischen eingeübte Skript des sozialdemokratischen Melodrams zurückzufallen? Hirtes Skulpturen aus rotem Sandstein *Brunnen für die Erdbergstraße* (2019) [52, 115] und *Die Begegnung* (2022) [58, 60] geben einige Hinweise. *Erdbergstraße* basiert auf Rudolf Schmidts *Nilpferd mit Jungem* (1963) [106], einer Nilpferd-Skulptur aus einem historischen Gemeindebau in Wiens 3. Bezirk, sowie auf den in diesen Gebäudekomplexen allgegenwärtigen öffentlichen Springbrunnen. *Erdbergstraße* fügt so zwei Realitäten der öffentlichen Skulptur neu zusammen, die erst in eine nahtlose Einheit transfiguriert werden, um diese dann in Hälften zu schneiden. In *Die Begegnung* ist auch ein Abfluss zu sehen, aber der Schnitt hat hier eine andere Funktion. Statt eines halben Tieres sehen wir etwas, das aussieht wie der Teil eines Arms mit umgeschlagenem Ärmel, Ansätze von zwei Torsi und zwei Hintern. Die Gewalt des Schnitts wurde hier durch die Weichheit der sich aneinander reibenden Körper ersetzt – ein fragmentierter Ausdruck der Solidarität oder des Konflikts. Das Loch, das sich in dem winzigen Spalt zwischen den Körpern befindet, füllt paradoxerweise den Raum, indem es ihn leert. Es geht hier weniger um die Idee des Springbrunnens wie in *Erdbergstraße* als um die eines Rinnsteins, der das Regenwasser aufnimmt, um im Herbst von Blättern verstopft zu werden. *Die Begegnung* funktioniert damit als Fragment von etwas, das nicht aufrecht steht, sondern auf dem Boden liegt und darauf wartet, dass jemand herabschaut. Noch mehr als *Brunnen für die Erdbergstraße* scheint *Die Begegnung* sich absichtlich auf die figurative Sprache der Unmengen von öffentlichen Skulpturen zu beziehen, die zwischen 1923 und 1934 errichtet wurden – in der Phase des Roten Wiens, als die sozialdemokratische Regierung 190 Architekten mit dem Bau von mehr als 400 Gemeindebauten [100, 101] beauftragte. Durch diese Initiative wurden die prekären Lebensbedingungen von 200.000 Angehörigen der Arbeiterklasse, die häufig erst vor kurzer Zeit aus der ländlichen Peripherie in die Hauptstadt migriert waren, drastisch verbessert.

Aber woran soll uns dieser Rekurs auf den Stil einer längst vergangenen Ära erinnern? Warum einen Querschnitt zeigen, wie in *Erdbergstraße*, oder ein Fragment, wie in *Die Begegnung*, eine Szene, deren genaue Konturen unklar bleiben? Handelt es sich dabei um die ersten beiden Buchstaben eines neuen Stil-Alphabets? Und sollen wir aus diesen steinernen Figurationen jene Welt wieder zusammenzusetzen, aus der sie kamen, Worte aus Buchstaben, Sätze aus Wörtern und Geschichten aus Sätzen formen?

Im Fall der Gemeindebauten ist das stilistische Konzept mit einem komplizierten Erbe verbunden, ein Erbe, das von rechten und linken Intellektuellen gleichermaßen geschmäht wurde. Manfredo Tafuri, ein Marxist, der als einer der einflussreichsten Architekturhistoriker des 20. Jahrhunderts gilt, bezeichnete diese Art des Bauens als „Erschöpfung des Stils"[3]. Er meinte damit, dass die Wiener Gemeindebauten, statt den durch das Bauhaus propagierten modernistischen Dogmen des „transparenten Bauens" und der Abschaffung des Ornaments zu folgen, einem liberalen Pluralismus nachkamen, der sich, unter anderem, in eklektischen Fassaden manifestierte, die zu expressiv, zu monumental, zu kleinbürgerlich und zu symmetrisch wirkten. Eine der prägenden Architekturschulen hinter den Gemeindebauten war die nach dem österreichischen Architekten Otto Wagner benannte Wagner-Schule, die, wie Eve Blau ausgeführt hat,[4] kritisch gegenüber dem rationalen Modernismus

2 – Shawn G. Kennedy, „A Beaux Arts Playland on Houston St.", *New York Times*, 8. Januar 1984.

3 – Manfredo Tafuri, „Das Rote Wien", in *Vienna Rossa: La politica residenziale nelle Vienna socialista, 1919–1933*. Hg.: Manfredo Tafuri, Milan: Electa, 1980, S. 134.

4 – Eve Blau, *The Architecture of Red Vienna, 1919–1934*. Cambridge, MA: MIT Press, 1999.

ihrer Weimarer Kolleg*innen eingestellt war und deren Huldigung Tayloristischer Ideen von Serialität, Standardisierung und Typisierung ablehnte. Am deutlichsten wird dieser Antagonismus in der Rückbesinnung der Wagner-Schule auf vernakuläre Ornamentik, die zuerst im Biedermeier-Stil des frühen 19. Jahrhunderts entwickelt worden war und dann in den Architekturstil des Roten Wiens übersetzt wurde. Diese volkstümlichen Ornamente, die als spezifisch für eine Region und historisch geformt galten, sollten häusliche, antiindividualistische Familienwerte transportieren und so zu Medien einer Fortsetzung der Vergangenheit werden, statt einen dramatischen Bruch zu proklamieren, wie es so viele Gegner*innen der Wagner-Schule taten. Zumindest oberflächlich ging es dabei um das umstrittene Ziel einer Versöhnung proletarischer Werte mit der kleinbürgerlichen Welt des Biedermeier, statt sie gegeneinander auszuspielen.

Einer der architektonischen Effekte dieser Fokussierung auf das Volkstümliche war, dass die Wagner-Schule zwischen Kern und Oberfläche und zwischen Struktur und Fassade trennte (Otto Wagner selbst erklärte letztere zur *Bekleidung* des Gebäudes). Diese Unterscheidung bedingte eine Arbeitsteilung, bei der Architekten Flächen innerhalb der Gebäudekomplexe aussparten, die dann von Bildhauer*innen *bekleidet* werden konnten. Dies führte zu realistischen Figurationen um die Gemeindebauten herum. Einer der interessantesten Ansätze zur Verteidigung des Projekts der Wagner-Schule kam seinerzeit von dem marxistischen Ökonom, Museumsdirektor und Historiker Otto Neurath[53]. Nach seiner Zeit als Präsident des Zentralwirtschaftsamts des Münchner Arbeiterrates, das für die Wirtschaftsreform der kurzlebigen revolutionären Regierung in Bayern im Jahr 1919 verantwortlich gewesen war, zog Neurath nach Wien und wurde dort zu einem prominenten Teilnehmer der Debatten zur Stadtentwicklung. Gemeinsam mit Adolf Loos und Oskar Strnad entwarf er einen Generalarchitekturplan, der zwar nicht realisiert, aber später zur Vorlage für viele der in den 1970er Jahre in Wien erbauten Großwohnanlagen wurde, wie am Beispiel des Wohnparks Alt-Erlaa zu sehen ist. Im Laufe der 1920er Jahre verfasste er einige Artikel über Stadtentwicklung, in denen er auch die Romantik der Avantgarde adressierte (zum Beispiel kritisierte er die „Würfelromantik" des Bauhaus-Pioniers Peter Behrens).[5]

Eine der aufschlussreichsten dieser Neurath'schen Kritiken erschien unter dem Titel „Rationalismus, Arbeiterklasse, Gebäudeform". Darin legt er dar, dass der Avantgardismus von Bauhaus, Neuer Sachlichkeit und Konstruktivismus sich „damit begnüge, ein Spektakel aus dem Rationalismus zu bauen, statt sich auf eine tiefere Auseinandersetzung mit dessen Prinzip einzulassen", und so zu einer Romantik werde, „die sich der Realität entzieht".[6] Der Punkt, auf den es ihm dabei ankommt: Nur weil etwas wie Rationalismus aussieht – zum Beispiel durch das Vorhandensein von stahlgerahmten, kubischen Glasfenstern, die die Produktionsweisen der Tayloristischen Fabrik nachahmen –, bedeutet das nicht, dass es auch der damals viel diskutierten „Rationalität des Proletariats" folgt. So kann die avantgardistische Rhetorik, die den Unterschied zwischen Oberfläche und Struktur für obsolet erklärt, als Begriffsverwirrung verstanden werden, als Taschenspielertrick, mit dem das sich gerade neu formierende Bürgertum die Logik des Kapitals (Taylorismus) zur Logik des Proletariats verklärte: Die rationalistische Oberfläche mystifizierte ganz einfach die rationalistische Struktur.

Was ist diese proletarische Rationalität dann, und wo ist sie Neurath zufolge zu finden? Strukturell gibt es zwei Hauptunterschiede zwischen den Wiener Gemeindebauten und ihrem deutschen Gegenstück, den Siedlungen, die in den Ausstellungen des Werkbunds in den 1920er Jahren vorgestellt wurden. So sehr die deutschen Modernisten sich in ihrem Schaffen auch mit einer Rhetorik des Taylorismus und der vorgefertigten Bauteile schmückten, waren die von ihnen ersonnenen Lösungen doch häufig sehr viel teurer und erreichten nicht das von ihnen adressierte Proletariat, welches sie ästhetisch erziehen wollten. Im Gegensatz dazu wurden in den Gemeindebauten vorgefertigte Elemente nur für Treppen, Türen und Fenster eingesetzt. In den Fassaden und Interieurs kamen arbeitsintensive (statt kapitalintensive) Produktionsweisen zum Einsatz, beispielsweise mit Stuck besetzte tragende Wandkonstruktionen, glasierte Kacheln sowie ornamentales Mauerwerk und Metallarbeiten, die bewusst platziert wurden. Diese Elemente konnten sowohl als materielle als auch symbolische

5 – Zitiert nach Blau, *Architecture*, S. 374. Im Original: Otto Neurath an Franz Roh, Brief vom 14. Juni 1924, Roh Sammlung, GRI.

6 – Otto Neurath, „Rationalismus, Arbeiterklasse und Gebäudeform", *Aufbau*, Mai 1926, S. 52.

Verweise auf das Handwerk verstanden werden, da sie in ein ehrgeiziges Programm zur Beschäftigung von Arbeiter*innen eingebettet waren, dessen erklärtes Ziel es war, die Kapazitäten des Staates zu nutzen, um stabile Löhne zu gewährleisten.

Die deutschen Wohnsiedlungen des Werkbunds dagegen standen für eine hochgradig individualistische Lebensweise. Sie befanden sich häufig außerhalb der Stadtzentren und waren nicht gut an den städtischen Raum angebunden. Damit bereiteten sie dem Exodus in die Einfamilienhäuser der Vorstädte den Weg, der in den Nachkriegsjahren in vielen Industrienationen an Fahrt aufnahm – ein Prozess, der letztendlich darauf hinauslief, dass öffentliche Wohnanlagen wie die New Yorker First Houses zu den vernachlässigten Infrastrukturen wurden, die sie heute sind. Anders als die deutschen Siedlungen waren die Gemeindebauten jedoch explizit so gestaltet, dass sie Kollektivität förderten, statt das städtische Leben in funktionelle, ordentlich voneinander getrennte Zonen des Individuellen aufzuteilen. Es gab Waschküchen, Badehäuser, Büchereien, Theater, Kindergärten, Werkstätten, Kinos und Kliniken, wodurch sie sich drastisch von den Entwürfen des Werkbundes unterschieden, die sich darauf konzentrierten, den privaten Raum zu reformieren. Der Aspekt des Kollektiven wurde räumlich noch dadurch dramatisiert, dass die einstmals privaten Innenräume der Wohnblocks zu halböffentlichen Räumen umgestaltet wurden.

Um zu der Frage zurückzukehren, die durch Hirtes *Die Begegnung* aufgeworfen wird: Durch das Herausarbeiten der Details, die das Rote Wien mit einer Art realistischer Figuration verbindet, wird eine zaghafte Erinnerung an die Stilkonflikte der Zwischenkriegszeit hergestellt, eine allegorische Anspielung auf einen Moment, als die Trennlinien zwischen Form und Politik noch nicht so sauber verliefen. Das Festhalten des Roten Wiens am Realismus des handwerklichen Könnens bedeutet hier nicht so sehr ein reaktionäres Beharren gegen den modernistischen Fetisch der Automatisierung, sondern muss vor allen Dingen als Teil eines größeren Kampfes gegen die Aufspaltung der Produktionsprozesse (durch die Arbeit billiger, prekärer und leichter ersetzbar wurde) verstanden werden. Dadurch, dass *Die Begegnung* nur ein Fragment liefert und im Grunde den Klassenkampf in einem steinernen Ausschnitt komprimiert, inszeniert Hirte die Welt der Gemeindebauten aber als etwas, das unwiederbringlich verloren ist. Gewissermaßen parallel zum melancholischen Melodram von *First Houses* verweist *Die Begegnung* auf eine Welt, deren Bezug zur Gegenwart prekär ist. Und doch wird die Melancholie durch die funktionalen und figurativen Zweideutigkeiten abgewehrt, die sowohl in *Die Begegnung* als auch in *Erdbergstraße* präsent sind. Wo endet der Torso der Nilpferd-Figur und wo beginnt ihr Hals in der späteren Skulptur? Soll der *Brunnen für die Erdbergstraße* Wasser spenden wie ein Springbrunnen, leiten wie ein Abfluss oder sammeln wie ein Becken? Vielleicht deutet die Skulptur an, dass Wasser – wie Macht – es an sich hat, nach dem Trickle-down-Prinzip nach unten zu sickern. Wie und wo diese Umverteilung organisiert wird, bleibt allerdings Teil des Konflikts um die Neugestaltung unserer öffentlichen Infrastrukturen.

Cover

Motif based on *Vector (Marlboro Theme)*, 2015

See 67

1

Untitled (stool), 2010

Combination of three chairs
45×40×45 cm
Courtesy Benjamin Hirte and Layr, Vienna
Lone Haugaard Madsen, Benjamin Hirte,
Grazer Kunstverein, Graz, 2010

The sculpture consists of a found stool frame and a found seat. The seat was manipulated by Hirte to match the shape of a chair design by Arne Jacobsen, but with its backrest partially cut.

2

Solace, 2021

Styrofoam, glass fibre reinforced plastic, lacquer
ø 200×45 cm
Courtesy Benjamin Hirte and Layr, Vienna
Autohaus St. Marx, Group show, organized by
Benjamin Hirte, Neuer Kunstverein Wien, Vienna, 2021

An object that functions as a bench and is suitable for outdoor use. It resembles a component of playground or amusement park architecture and its decorative formal features are combined with shapes that suggest mechanical use.

See 34

3

First Houses, Layr, Vienna, 2020
Installation view

Für Ihre Lieben / For Your Loved Ones, 2020

Various materials, beverage can, model building
street lamp, toy castle, cigarette box, part of a chair,
cardboard box
Variable dimensions
Courtesy Benjamin Hirte and Layr, Vienna

An assemblage of materials loosely resembling maquettes of a cityscape or just litter.

See 77, 117

Intricate Greyhound, 2020

Polystyrene, CNC milled
60×40×40 cm
Courtesy Benjamin Hirte and Layr, Vienna

The styrofoam object was CNC milled after a scan Hirte made of a dog sculpture in the courtyard of the First Houses public housing complex in New York's Lower East Side. The already weathered statue lost some of its shape through the scanning process and appears almost as a ruin here.

See 61, 64

4

Gutter / Rinne, 2017

Aluminum, steel, various material
18×250×25 cm
Courtesy Benjamin Hirte and Layr, Vienna
The Long Zoom, Group show, Christian Andersen,
Copenhagen, 2018

A work originally made to divide the floor levels of the gallery Layr in Vienna. By installing the boxed metal drain over the full length of the staircase, Hirte created an edge that made it harder to cross from one level to the other. The length of the sculpture is therefore exactly the width of that particular gallery space. At the gallery Christian Andersen in Copenhagen the work seems to imitate the drain that was once a significant part of the location's original architecture, as it used to serve as an auto repair shop. Hirte's drain sculpture contains the dust and dirt it collected over the course of the original exhibition, as well as some insignificant objects from Hirte's wallet and other people's pockets. As places to store, contain, and connect, objects such as drains, pools, and basins always seem to reference symbolic infrastructural innards.

5

BBQ on Broome Street, 2020

Lambda print, framed
32×27 cm
Courtesy Benjamin Hirte and Layr, Vienna
First Houses, Layr, Vienna, 2020

The photo was taken in the summer of 2019 on the rooftop of 334 Broome Street, New York City.

6

Untitled, 2012

Display case, MDF, wall paint, glasses, various materials
115×70×40 cm
Courtesy Benjamin Hirte and Layr, Vienna
The Classic Mob Ballet, MAK – Museum of Applied Arts,
Vienna, 2012

A vitrine built by Hirte containing a drain and several objects: a cast of chopsticks designed by Philippe Starck in the MAK collection covered by a plastic bag, a camera lid, a cut-out of a Coca-Cola can, two wine glasses, and a broken Heurigen glass (typically used in the local wineries in and around Vienna).

7

Apotheke / Pharmacy, 2018

Plexiglass, tape, aluminum, steel
25.5 × 23 × 18 cm
Courtesy Benjamin Hirte and Layr, Vienna
Hamilton Beach, JTT Gallery, New York City—as part of Condo, presented by Layr, Vienna, 2018

Five plexiglass plates held together by duct tape to form a transparent box. Attached to the box is the letter A cut from aluminum in the shape of German pharmacy (Apotheke) signs.

See 41

8

Untitled (tags), 2014

Cement treated chipboard
110 × 80 × 190 cm
Collection Belvedere, Vienna
Benjamin Hirte, Layr, Vienna, 2014

The shapes of the *Tags* series derive from the "Euro slot" system, a system for product packaging, hanging, and display. The product is usually attached to a cardboard piece through various openings and then hung for display with the iconically-shaped slot. The board usually carries general information, imagery, and advertisting related to the product.

See 35, 45

9

The Robbers, 2021

Plaster
45 × 10 × 12 cm
Courtesy Benjamin Hirte and Layr, Vienna
Trust, Sydney, Sydney, 2021

Plaster casts of toys that are stacked like a totem pole. Hirte produced this work during a stay in Tokyo.

10

Building a Region / Eine Region bauen, 2016

Powder coated steel
Variable dimensions
Courtesy Benjamin Hirte and Layr, Vienna
Kunstraum Weikendorf, KOERNOE – Art in Public Space Lower Austria, 2016

The installation alludes to the particularity of the area around Weikendorf, a town east of Vienna. This is a region that borders three countries that were formerly part of the Warsaw Pact: Hungary, Czech Republic, Slovakia.

11

Playground Element Seward Park, 2021

Modeling board, wall paint
75 × 50 × 2 cm
Courtesy Benjamin Hirte and Layr, Vienna
Palai, Lecce, 2021

This relief is part of a series made of CNC milled polyurethane board. The cut-out shapes derive from 3D scans of elements in public space and of public infrastructure. Hirte made the scans with his smartphone while taking walks in the Lower East Side of New York over the course of a year.

12

BBQ Station "Donauwelle," Donauinsel, Vienna
Design by Benjamin Kromoser and Martin Ritt

13

Water tower at Stadionbad, a public pool in Vienna's Prater area.

See 41

14

Workshop of Walter Pichler, St. Martin an der Raab

15

Barrel, 2018

Aluminum, straw
ø 11 × 8 cm
Collection of Wien Museum / Museum of the City of Vienna
Hamilton Beach, JTT Gallery, New York City—as part of Condo, presented by Layr, Vienna, 2018

A soda can that has been sanded down, polished, filled with hay, and with four small drains attached to it.

See 41

16

~, 2014

Steel, plastic, resin
21 × 23 × 3.8 cm
Courtesy Benjamin Hirte and Christian Andersen, Copenhagen
Winter, Christian Andersen, Copenhagen, 2014

Part of a series of wall works modeled from plumbing material.

See 38

17

Benjamin Hirte, Layr, Vienna, 2014
Installation view

1.1, 2014

Aluminum, rubber
77×100×100 cm
Private Collection

1.2, *1.3*, 2014

Aluminum, rubber
Each 77×100×100 cm
Courtesy Benjamin Hirte and Layr, Vienna

A series of three identical box-like objects made from folded industrial-sized aluminum sheets. Rubber joints along their edges make it possible to stack them.

18

Bernd & Hilla Becher, Metropolitan Museum of Art, New York City, 2022

19

Rudolf Beran
Male Figure, 1953
Anton-Schmid-Hof, Municipal Housing Complex, Vienna

20

Plumbers Font, 2014

Courtesy Benjamin Hirte

Plumbers Tape is a metal tape used on construction sites to strap objects together and attach them to walls, etc. Its basic form consists of rectangles with punched-out circular holes. Hirte created a font based on this structure.

See 39, 44, 46

21

Gamebreaker, 2013

Bowling ball
ø 20.3 cm
Private Collection
Flat Bed, Group show, curated by Marie Lund, Joe Sheftel Gallery, New York City, 2013

The first one in a series of bowling balls, all with an edge sliced off. The cut was made just deep enough to lay bare the ball's core.

22

Untitled (wig), 2012

Silkscreen on burlap
150×120 cm
Private Collection
A to K, Layr, Vienna, 2012

A motif borrowed from a Mickey Mouse comic featuring Goofy's hand holding a baroque-style peruke. The story —a comedy of errors—takes place during the French Revolution.

23

Jewelry box (with jewels from the Berla archive), 2023

30×35×2.5 cm
Aluminum cast
Courtesy Benjamin Hirte and Layr, Vienna
Anna-Sophie Berger, *The Years*, MAK – Museum of Applied Arts, Geymüllerschlössel, Vienna, 2023

A jewelry box that combines the basic forms of a happy, a sad, and an indifferent Emoji. The placement of objects inside the box alters its facial expression.

24

Untitled, 2012

Marble
ø 40×31 cm
Private Collection
A to K, Layr, Vienna, 2012

The cap of a spray paint can carved in stone.

25

Backbone, 2017

Synthetic leather, felt, foam
45×70×50 cm
Courtesy Benjamin Hirte and Layr, Vienna
Jaws, Layr, Vienna, 2017

A cartoonish pouf in the form of a backbone with an egg yolk on top.

26

The beehive symbol can be found on apartment houses all over Vienna. It denotes housing that was financed after World War II with the help of funds from the Marshall Plan.

See 27

27

We labour but not for ourselves, 2021

Polyurethane model board, wall paint
40 × 35 × 35 cm
Courtesy Benjamin Hirte and Layr, Vienna
Antwerp, Benjamin Hirte, Nancy Lupo, Mackey Garage – MAK Center, Los Angeles, 2021

Inspired by the aforementioned beehive symbol found on apartment houses all over Vienna.

See 26

28

Lots, 2021

Rubber, miniature street lamps, electronics, steel, wire
Two parts, each 120 × 130 × 10 cm
Courtesy Benjamin Hirte and Layr, Vienna
Antwerp, Benjamin Hirte, Nancy Lupo, Mackey Garage – MAK Center, Los Angeles, 2021

Two suspended sheets of black rubber, atop which seven rows of miniature models of street lamps are mounted. The black surface of the rubber, sparsely illuminated by LED lights, appears as a vast parking lot in bird's-eye view—a cinematic landscape both romanticized and problematized as a site of danger and crime.

29, 30

Antwerp, 2021

Video projection
8:20 min.
Courtesy Benjamin Hirte and Layr, Vienna
Antwerp, Benjamin Hirte, Nancy Lupo, Mackey Garage – MAK Center, Los Angeles, 2021

Hirte extensively filmed indoor and outdoor drone footage of a former Siemens office complex. The buildings are used in the interim for language courses and studios until they make space for a new city development plan. Hirte's imagery is of a seemingly deserted building, accompanied by an adaptation of music characteristic of true crime documentaries that make the building seem haunted and eerie.

31

Untitled, 2013

Inflatable Tropical Jump and Slide Combo
650 × 400 × 400 cm
SMILE, Final Projects, Artists and Architects-in-Residence Program at the Mackey Apartments, MAK Center, Los Angeles, 2013

For his final exhibition of the MAK Schindler Scholarship Program, Hirte installed a large tropical-themed bouncy castle in the front garden. It was accompanied indoors by an edition of small booklets with an epic style poem written during his residency.

32

National Public Library, 42nd Street, New York City

See 33

33

Ghost, 2019

Steel, bluing stain, chrome plated chains
ø125 × 250 cm
Courtesy Benjamin Hirte and Layr, Vienna
Life and Limbs, Swiss Institute, New York City, 2019

Ghost is modeled after a chandelier at the New York Public Library, and appears here as a ruin or relic. The piece, as opposed to the original, is defined by lack: small chains are all that is left of a structure adorned with countless lightbulbs. Whether this change is the intentional result of design or precarization is left open.

See 32

34

The Eavesdroppers, 2023

Styrofoam
346 × 286 × 64 cm
Courtesy Benjamin Hirte and Layr, Vienna
Autohaus St. Marx, Group show, organized by Benjamin Hirte, Neuer Kunstverein Wien, Vienna, 2021

The form of the piece derives from the plinth of a public sculpture in Vienna's 3rd district. The original sculpture features a workers' couple moved by the sound of music. These figures are omitted in Hirte's work.

See 68, 69, 102

35

Untitled (tags), 2014

Cement treated chipboard
Various dimensions
Private Collection
Viennacontemporary, with Layr, Vienna, 2014

The shapes of the *Tags* series derive from the "Euro slot" system, a system for product packaging, hanging, and display. The product is usually attached to a cardboard piece through various openings and then hung for display with the iconically-shaped slot. The board usually carries general information, imagery, and advertising related to the product.

See 8, 45

36

Gaußplatz, Vienna

37

Clip, 2015

Aluminum
130×80×1.5 cm
Courtesy Benjamin Hirte and Layr, Vienna
Jürgen Ponto-Stiftung, MMK – Museum für Moderne Kunst, Frankfurt, 2015

The wall piece is an enlarged replica of a soda can tab.

38

Jürgen Ponto-Stiftung, MMK – Museum für Moderne Kunst, Frankfurt, 2015
Installation view

Untitled, 2015

Glass, steel
6 pieces, 320×90 cm
Courtesy Benjamin Hirte and Layr, Vienna

~, 2014

Steel, plastic, resin
21×23×3.8 cm
Courtesy Benjamin Hirte and Layr, Vienna

A series of modular glass pieces form a wall system. The perforations in the glass stem from security architecture openings that enable communication. Attached to it is an older work made of plumbing elements that was part of the show *Winter* at Christian Andersen in 2014.

See 16

Untitled (A – Z), 2015

3D animation, flat screen
2:46 min.
Courtesy Benjamin Hirte and Layr, Vienna

See 39

39

Untitled (A – Z), 2015

3D animation, flat screen
2:46 min.
Courtesy Benjamin Hirte and Layr, Vienna
Jürgen Ponto-Stiftung, MMK – Museum für Moderne Kunst, Frankfurt, 2015

This video animation is a sculptural adaptation of the *Plumbers Font* in 3D. It features a slow rotating cube presenting each letter in order of the alphabet. As there are only four horizontal sides, the cube is constantly changing shape, particularly on the edges where the bas-relief shapes collide.

See 20, 38

40

Shack, 2018

Wood, aluminum, steel, stain
28×20×15.5 cm
Courtesy Benjamin Hirte and Layr, Vienna
Hamilton Beach, JTT Gallery, New York City—as part of Condo, presented by Layr, Vienna, 2018

This maquette of a countryside shack has no entry door but what appears to be a handrail or pipe in place of it.

41

Hamilton Beach, JTT Gallery, New York City—as part of Condo, presented by Layr, Vienna, 2018
Installation view

Factory, 2018

Recyclables, seagrass rope
43×48×30.5 cm
Private Collection

Factory consists of recyclables, partly connected through plumbing pipe elements and covered with seagrass rope. The recyclables stem from the daily use of the artist and include objects such as glass jars, cans, and plastic bottles. They are extensively covered in seagrass rope, which is similar to a method used to cover heating pipes in New York to prevent people from burning themselves. Due to the old heating system, pipes in NYC are burning hot, apartments and shops are often overheated, and heat levels are regulated by opening windows and doors. This system evolved in the US in the aftermath of the Spanish flu, influenced by the Fresh Air Movement in the 1920s, and it included the idea to keep the windows open even in the wintertime. Form and surface of the artwork are somewhat in conflict. Its shape gives the impression of an old factory production system, while on the surface it displays a somewhat ecological and ethnological look. This is a formula not unusual in the recent architecture and design longing for sustainable aesthetics while still relying on very classic modes of production. The size and form of the work is variable; it grows by the addition of more recyclables and rope.

Water tower, 2018

18×12×12 cm
Wood, plastic, aluminum, lacquer
Courtesy Benjamin Hirte and Layr, Vienna

See 13

Apotheke / Pharmacy, 2018

Plexiglass, tape, aluminum, steel
25.5 × 23 × 18 cm
Courtesy Benjamin Hirte and Layr, Vienna

See 7

Barrel, 2018

Aluminum, straw
ø 11 × 8 cm
Collection of Wien Museum / Museum of the City of Vienna

See 15

42

Turnstile Table Nr. 2, 2022

Stainless steel, marble, lacquer
ø 90 × 60 cm
Courtesy Benjamin Hirte and Layr, Vienna
Art Basel, with Layr, Vienna, 2022

The frame of this table design by Hirte is based on the shape of a turnstile—a device in public and semipublic space to regulate access. The stone tabletop is covered with a resin lacquer coat, its marble texture only visible from the side.

43

Untitled, 2015

Polyamide, galvanized steel
ø 95 × 70 cm
Courtesy Benjamin Hirte and Layr, Vienna
Liste Art Fair Basel, with Layr, Vienna, 2015

A table Hirte designed for the booth of Layr at Liste Art Fair. It has a hole in the center that usually serves the purpose of storing an umbrella, but given the circumstances and general design, the purpose of the hole is unclear to the viewer.

44

Untitled (A), 2015

Aluminum honeycomb panel, reinforced rubber sheet, thread screws, UV print
150 × 103 × 2.5 cm
Private Collection
Liste Art Fair Basel, with Layr, Vienna, 2015

A series of works made from rubber sheets atop of prints mounted on honeycomb aluminum panel. The print consists of collaged research material while the rubber shape is the letter A from the *Plumbers Font*.

See 20

45

Untitled (Fact Magazine), 2015

Watercut aluminum honeycomb, reinforced rubber, UV print
170 × 110 × 2.5 cm
Private Collection

A series of works made from rubber sheets atop of prints mounted on honeycomb aluminum panels. The print consists of collaged research material while the rubber shape stems from Hirte's *Tags* series.

See 8, 35

46

C, 2017

Aluminum, steel, plastic, water, fountain pump, lacquer, stain
240 × 160 × 80 cm
Courtesy Benjamin Hirte and Layr, Vienna
Viennacontemporary, with Layr, Vienna, 2017

The sculpture consists of six discrete elements that were originally exhibited individually spread across the Museum Pietro Canonica in Rome. Assembled and in bird's-eye view, they compose the letter C from Hirte's *Plumbers Font*.

See 20

47

Untitled (hinge), 2012

Aluminum, steel
250 × 127 cm
Private Collection
A to K, Layr, Vienna, 2012

Two aluminum sheets connected with a hinge that Hirte made. The work is situated close to an entrance of one of the gallery's rooms. The respective sizes of the sheets relate to the previous and present height of the doorway, which was changed by the gallery at some point.

48

oO, 2014

Steel, aluminum
16 × 10.5 × 5.5 cm
Courtesy Benjamin Hirte and Christian Andersen, Copenhagen
Winter, Christian Andersen, Copenhagen, 2014

Part of a series of wall works modeled from plumbing material.

49

Bulb, 2022

Carrara marble
40×40×80 cm
Private Collection

A two-part marble sculpture that resembles fingers or leaves on a plinth. Hirte added a drain so that water can run through the sculpture.

50

Untitled, 2013

Wick cough sirup, Sinupret drops, plinth
25×165 cm
Private Collection
No Brow, Curated by, Layr, Vienna, 2013

On the plinth sits a bottle of cough syrup with a smaller vessel of medicine for sinus cavities poured into it and left inserted upside down. Together the two medicines target the part of the body where the voice is formed.

51

Architectural detail from Kempelenpark, a former Siemens office complex in Vienna. The complex is used in the interim for official language courses, smaller creative offices, and studios. Furnishings like these were designed as part of the interim use as sites for social gathering and interaction. Hirte had his studio here from 2019 to 2023.

See Back cover

52

Fountain for Erdbergstraße / Brunnen für die Erdbergstraße, 2020

Red sandstone
75×80×65 cm
Collection of Wien Museum / Museum of the City of Vienna
First Houses, Layr, Vienna, 2020

The sculpture is inspired by a public sculpture—a hippo statue in front of a municipal housing complex in the 3rd district of Vienna where Hirte used to live. By retaining only the torso of the hippo as sculptural element and carving out the shape of a sink in the front with outlets on each side, Hirte renders the sculpture somewhat of a device ready to be used.

See 115

53

Otto Neurath (10 December 1882–22 December 1945) was an Austrian-born philosopher of science, sociologist, and political economist. He was also the inventor of the ISOTYPE method of pictorial statistics and an innovator in museum practice. Before he fled his native country in 1934, Neurath was one of the leading figures of the Vienna Circle. Neurath used to sign his letters with a drawing of an elephant.

54

Detail of the Hamilton Fish Pool, a public pool in New York's Lower East Side, in winter.

55

Sink, 2022

Marble
35×30×7 cm, 117.5×36×35 cm (with plinth)
Courtesy Benjamin Hirte and Layr, Vienna
New Space Show, Layr, Vienna, 2022

While the marble object looks like a detail from sacral architecture, it also resembles sanitary infrastructure.

56

Cocc, 2016

Spring steel, rubber, screws
50×40×2.5 cm
Private Collection
Lieber Rücken / Gentle spine, Benjamin Hirte, Signe Rose, Kunstbuero, Vienna, 2016

Hirte modeled this wall work out of spring steel band after a decorative detail of a stair railing—an extruding ornament at the very beginning of the stairwell in a Viennese late nineteenth-century house he used to live in.

57

Untitled, 2022

Aluminum lithography on paper
23×32 cm
Courtesy Benjamin Hirte and Layr, Vienna

A lithography series produced from drawings Hirte made on his smartphone.

58

The Encounter / Die Begegnung, 2022, detail

Red sandstone
49.5×33×29.5 cm
Private Collection

See 60

59

Margarete Hanusch
Familie, 1956, detail
Kurt-Steyrer-Hof, Landstraßer Hauptstraße 92–94, Vienna

See 103

60

The Encounter / Die Begegnung, 2022

Red sandstone
49.5 × 32.9 × 29.5 cm
Private Collection
Art Basel, with Layr, Vienna, 2022

This stone piece is part of a sculptural series in which Hirte documents and uses fragments from public space. The center part depicts a sleeved arm. The form derives from a 3D scan detail of a public sculpture that was integrated into a social housing complex in Vienna's 3rd district. The other parts of the relief are fictitious, suggesting a hybrid of organic and mechanical origin. Hirte often includes utilitarian elements, such as drains and sinks, in his works.

See 58

61

Intricate Greyhound, 2020

Polystyrene, CNC milled
60 × 40 × 40 cm
Courtesy Benjamin Hirte and Layr, Vienna
First Houses, Layr, Vienna, 2020

The styrofoam object was CNC milled after a scan Hirte made of a dog sculpture in the courtyard of the First Houses public housing complex in New York's Lower East Side. The already weathered statue lost some of its shape through the scanning process and appears almost as a ruin here.

See 3, 64

62

Inner courtyard of the First Houses, a social housing complex and landmark in New York's Lower East Side. The animal figures were designed by artists associated with the Works Progress Administration.

63

Animal figure in the inner courtyard of the First Houses, a social housing complex and landmark in New York's Lower East Side.

See 62

64

Animal figure in the inner courtyard of the First Houses, a social housing complex and landmark in New York's Lower East Side.

See 62

65

Dog-shaped vessel, National Museum of Anthropology (Museo Nacional de Antropologia), Mexico City.

66

Playground element at Stadionbad, a public pool in Vienna's Prater area.

67

Vector (Marlboro Theme), 2015

PVC, eyelets
250 × 180 cm
Courtesy Benjamin Hirte and Christian Andersen, Copenhagen
Teams, Christian Andersen, Copenhagen, 2015

For Hirte, the Marlboro logo in its basic form resembles an abstracted house or an arrow.

See Cover

68, 69

The Eavesdroppers, 2023

Jura marble
Two parts, each 346 × 286 × 64 cm
Courtesy Maschinenfabrik LASKA, Linz
Permanent installation at Maschinenfabrik LASKA, Linz, 2023

Hirte conceived two complementing sculptures made from Jura marble—a stone common in the area and along the Danube—for the compound of Maschinenfabrik LASKA in Linz, Austria. They are freely accessible and can be sat on. Although the pieces negotiate the architecture of stairs, their form derives from the plinth of a public sculpture in Vienna's 3rd district. The original sculpture features a workers' couple moved by the sound of music. These figures are omitted in Hirte's work. One sculpture is a faithful reconstruction of the original plinth while its counterpart presents a partly dismantled version of it.

See 34, 102

70

6th Avenue and 33rd Street, New York City

71

True Sculpture, Christian Andersen, Copenhagen, 2023
Installation view

Hirte thinks of "True Sculpture" within the framework of magic realism, which situates surreal elements in a realistic environment and often in an allegedly historical setting. Its speculation and romanticism are invested with a claim of functionality. *Venus, House, Plague,* and *Fountain* —the titles of the stone pieces—refer to canonical (while eclectic) topics of sculpture. Owing to certain features of the single stones, they could be read as elements of a deconstructed body.

See 72–74

72

Plague, 2023

Red sandstone, lacquer
42.5 × 50 × 22 cm
Courtesy Benjamin Hirte and Christian Andersen, Copenhagen
True Sculpture, Christian Andersen, Copenhagen, 2023

See 71

73

House, 2023

Red sandstone, plastic, lacquer
42 × 52 × 22 cm
Courtesy Benjamin Hirte and Christian Andersen, Copenhagen
True Sculpture, Christian Andersen, Copenhagen, 2023

House incorporates a plastic structure. Its features derive from common designs of bait stations and traps for rodents. These usually closed entities, when opened, reveal an elaborate yet enigmatic architecture to lure and kill.

See 71

74

Fountain, 2023

Red sandstone
44.5 × 45 × 45 cm
Courtesy Benjamin Hirte and Christian Andersen, Copenhagen
True Sculpture, Christian Andersen, Copenhagen, 2023

See 71

75

Favoriten, Niloufar Emamifar, Benjamin Hirte, Kevin Space, Vienna, 2023
Installation view

Spinnerin am Kreuz / Spinner at the cross, 2023

Aluminum
190 × 150 × 25 cm
Courtesy Benjamin Hirte and Layr, Vienna

Hirte used the the segmentation of the coat of arms of Vienna's Favoriten district and altered them slightly to create an aluminum sculpture. The depth of the piece and the added drain accentuates the idea of a possible function.

Two Bears, 2023

Plaster, wall paint
18 × 16 × 20 cm
Courtesy Benjamin Hirte and Layr, Vienna

See 76

76

Two Bears, 2023

Plaster, wall paint
18 × 16 × 20 cm
Courtesy Benjamin Hirte and Layr, Vienna
Favoriten, Niloufar Emamifar, Benjamin Hirte, Kevin Space, Vienna, 2023

See 75

77

Untitled, 2023

Aluminum can, model LED street lamp, battery
ø 5 × 23.5 cm
Courtesy Benjamin Hirte and Layr, Vienna
Favoriten, Niloufar Emamifar, Benjamin Hirte, Kevin Space, Vienna, 2023

A piece from a series of soda cans with a glowing model LED street lamp on top. The necessary electronics and battery are added by cutting the can open.

See 3, 117

78

Aloa Chair, 2020

Aluminum
70 × 50 × 65 cm
Courtesy Benjamin Hirte and Layr, Vienna

79

Alberto Marcos Bursztyn
Henry (Lower East Side Moose), 2022, demolished
Art in the Parks Program, Allen Street & Broome Street, New York City

80

Azadi Square, Tehran

81

Enqelab Square, Tehran

82

Public fountain, Orange County

83

Public fountain, Orange County

84

Henry Moore
Hill Arches, 1978
Karlsplatz, Vienna

85

Buckingham Fountain, Grant Park, Chicago

86

Fountains of Bellagio, Bellagio Resort, Las Vegas

87

Tibor Bártfay, Virgil Droppa, Juraj Hlavica, Juraj Hovorka, Karol Lacko
Fountain of Union, 1979–80
Bratislava

88

Lillie and Hugh Roy Cullen Sculpture Garden, Museum of Fine Arts, Houston
Designed by Isamu Noguchi

89

Glassell School of Art, Houston

90

Corner of Grand Street and Essex Street, New York City

91

New York City Subway bench

92

Public bench design, New York City

93

Public bench design, Apple Store, 5th Avenue, New York City

94

Grafitti on the New Museum, New York City

95

Siah Armajani
Irene Hixon Whitney Bridge, 1988
Minneapolis

96

Siah Armajani
Alfred Whitehead Reading Room, 2013
Parasol Unit, London

97

Bruce Nauman
Square Depression, 2007
Skulptur Projekte Münster

98

Oscar Tuazon
Burn the Formwork [Verbrennt die Verschalung], 2017
Skulptur Projekte Münster

99

Isa Genzken
Rose III, 2016
Zuccotti Park, New York City

100

Karl-Marx-Hof, Municipal Housing Complex, Vienna

101

Rabenhof, Municipal Housing Complex, Vienna

102

Siegfried Charoux
Die Lauschenden / The Listeners, 1954
Richard-Strauss-Hof, Vienna

See 34, 68, 69

103

Margarete Hanusch
Familie, 1956
Kurt-Steyrer-Hof, Vienna

See 59

104

Rabenhof, Municipal Housing Complex, Vienna

105

Alfred Hridlicka
Badende, 1965
Vorgartenstraße 232–238, Vienna

106

Rudolf Schmidt
Nilpferd mit Jungem, 1963
Erdbergstraße 12–14, Vienna

107

Josef Schagerl
Bär, 1956
Kurt-Steyrer-Hof, Vienna

108

Gertrude Fronius
Eisbär, 1961
Johann-Böhm-Wohnhausanlage, Vienna

109

Mehdi Ghadyanloo
Freshness, 2008
Tehran

110

Diego Rivera
Man at the Crossroads, 1932–34, destroyed
Rockefeller Center, New York City

111

First Houses, a social housing complex and landmark in New York's Lower East Side.

See 62–64, 112

112

Animal figure in the inner courtyard of the First Houses, a social housing complex and landmark in New York's Lower East Side.

See 62

113

Pardis, a satellite city northeast of Tehran.

114

Street vendor in Pardis, a satellite city northeast of Tehran.

115

Fountain for Erdbergstraße / Brunnen für die Erdbergstraße, 2020

Red sandstone
75 × 80 × 65 cm
Collection of Wien Museum / Museum of the City of Vienna
First Houses, Layr, Vienna, 2020

See 52

116

The Arcade Tool, 2021

Carrara marble
85 × 120 × 20 cm
Courtesy Benjamin Hirte and Layr, Vienna
Lichtenfels Sculpture, Group show, Lichtenfels Castle, 2021

A carrara marble sculpture, shown as part of Lichtenfels Sculpture, an outdoor sculpture exhibition near Vienna. The object has the basic features of a standard shower tray that is used indoors in housing, albeit with the multiplication of the basin and drain. Despite its transfer from private indoor to publicly accessible outdoor space, where it is exposed to the weather without connection to a sewer or shower spray, the basin retains its basic function to collect and divert wastewater.

117

First Houses, Layr, Vienna, 2020
Installation view

See 3, 118–122

118

First Houses, 2020

Video projection
27:00 min.
Courtesy Benjamin Hirte and Layr, Vienna
First Houses, Layr, Vienna, 2020

The eponymous First Houses, one of the first social housing programs in the US from the 1930s, only appears once in the video. Following the classical logic of the slide show, the video strings together various images of New York's infrastructure and buildings, especially from the Lower East Side where Hirte used to live. The slide show format lends a rather documentary quality, whereas the motifs themselves seem surreal. The technology used here is not classic photography but a 3D scan app for the iPhone. In order to scan a form, the user walks around the desired object, ideally in a 360-degree circle. The image sections in the video are views from these 360-degree scans, appearing as individual thin skins, almost like a sculptural negative form that frays at the edges. Hirte's intervention is of course ultimately photographic, but it is the technology of the app that causes the various "errors" or violations of the original scanned objects and locations. It seems relevant here that this foray through the city actually refers to the scanning body of the artist, who moves in circles around the things, which he can then save in turn, like a real archive of things. Thus, it is less the quality or the precision of the technology that is demonstrated in the video than the pedestrian's relationship to these everyday places, walked.

See 117, 119–122

119–122

First Houses (Video stills), 2020

Video projection
27:00 min.
Courtesy Benjamin Hirte and Layr, Vienna
First Houses, Layr, Vienna, 2020

See 117, 118

123

Detail of the Hochstrahlbrunnen, a public fountain at Schwarzenbergplatz, Vienna.

124

Backside of a bust sculpture at Schwarzenbergplatz, Vienna.

Back cover

Kempelenpark, Vienna

Photo Credits

Maximilian Anelli-Monti: 46, 76, 77, 78; b4_flight: 94; Charles Benton: 7, 15, 40, 41; Anna-Sophie Berger / Benjamin Hirte: 23, 49, 68, 69, 75; Tag Christof: 27, 28, 29, 30; Niloufar Emamifar: 85; Mark Escribano: 31; Mehdi Ghadyanloo: 109; Johanna Glösl: 1; Benjamin Hirte: 12, 13, 14, 18, 19, 26, 32, 36, 51, 54, 59, 63, 64, 65, 66, 70, 79, 90, 91, 92, 93, 100, 101, 102, 103, 104, 105, 107, 108, 111, 112, 116, 123, 124, Back cover; Joe Sheftel Gallery, New York City: 21; Ewald Judt: 106; Kunstbuero, Vienna: 56; kunst-dokumentation.com: 2, 3, 34, 42, 52, 58, 60, 61, 115, 117, 118; Layr, Vienna: 45; Paul Levack: 55; Liste Art Fair Basel: 43, 44; Lordkinbote: 82; Malle Madsen: 4, 16, 48, 67, 71, 72, 73, 74; MAK – Museum of Applied Arts, Vienna / Katrin Wißkirchen: 6; Jessica Mauer: 9; Till Megerle: 10; Michele Nastasi: 97; Old Stage Studios, Gualala: 110; Palai, Lecce: 11; Maria de la Paz: 80; Stefano Perego: 87; Georg Petermichl: 8, 17, 22, 24, 35, 47, 50; Klaus Pichler: 25; Public domain: 53, 81, 83, 84, 86, 88, 89, 95, 113, 114; Henning Rogge: 98; Timothy Schenck: 99; Axel Schneider: 37, 38, 39; Harvey Smith: 62; Swiss Institute, New York City: 33; Stephen White: 96

Benjamin Hirte
Modest Homes

Editors
Benjamin Hirte
Layr, Vienna

Concept
Benjamin Hirte
Alexander Nussbaumer

Texts
Katharina Hausladen
Pujan Karambeigi

Conversation
Niloufar Emamifar
Benjamin Hirte

Copyediting
Diana Artus (DE)
Elizabeth H. Stern (EN)

Proofreading
Nina Franz (DE)
Kenneth Loe (EN)

Translations
Gerrit Jackson (DE – EN, Katharina Hausladen)
Nina Franz (EN – DE, Pujan Karambeigi)

Graphic design
FONDAZIONE Europa, fondazione.biz

With the kind support of
Federal Ministry for Arts, Culture, the Civil Service and Sport, Austria
Layr, Vienna

Thanks to
Anna-Sophie Berger
Emanuel Layr

Federal Ministry
Republic of Austria
Arts, Culture,
Civil Service and Sport

Published and distributed by
Mousse Publishing
Contrappunto s.r.l.
Via Pier Candido Decembrio 28,
20137 Milan, Italy

Available through

Mousse Publishing, Milan
moussemagazine.it

DAP | Distributed Art Publishers, New York
artbook.com

Les presses du réel, Dijon
lespressesdureel.com

Antenne Books, London
antennebooks.com

Idea Books, Amsterdam
ideabooks.nl

Motto, Berlin
mottodistribution.com

LibroCo, Florence
libroco.it

First edition
2023

Printed in Austria by Print Alliance HAV Produktions GmbH, Bad Vöslau

ISBN 978-88-6749-601-3

€ 27 / $ 30